JOHN GARDNER

Literary Outlaw

ALSO BY BARRY SILESKY

Ferlinghetti: The Artist in His Time
In the Ruins (poems)
The New Tenants (poems)
Greatest Hits (poems)
One Thing That Can Save Us (short short fiction)

for Jesse: 1987–2001

ℝ
A Shannon Ravenel Book

Published by
Algonquin Books of Chapel Hill
Post Office Box 2225
Chapel Hill, North Carolina 27515-2225

a division of
Workman Publishing
708 Broadway
New York, New York 10003

For permission to print excerpts from these works, grateful acknowledgment
is made to the holders of copyright, publishers, or representatives named on
pages 357–58, which constitute an extension of the copyright page.

Library of Congress Cataloging-in-Publication Data
Silesky, Barry, 1949–
    John Gardner : literary outlaw / Barry Silesky.
        p. cm.
    Includes bibliographical references.
    ISBN 1-56512-218-6
    1. Gardner, John, 1933–1982   2. Novelists, American—20th
century—Biography.   I. Title.
PS3557.A712Z85 2004
813'.54—dc22
    [B]   2003057891

10 9 8 7 6 5 4 3 2 1
First Edition

JOHN GARDNER

Literary Outlaw

by Barry Silesky

A Shannon Ravenel Book

ALGONQUIN BOOKS OF CHAPEL HILL 2004

CONTENTS

Acknowledgments   ix

Preface   xi

Prologue   1

  1   A Great Roar   7

  2   Intimations   19

  3   West of New York   38

  4   A Whisper Behind   69

  5   City on the Edge   98

  6   A Different Farm   118

  7   Rules   145

  8   The Epic Conversation   175

  9   Illinois Tales   194

 10   Old Bennington   216

 11   Moral Fiction   233

 12   A New House   253

 13   Killing the Dragon   272

 14   The Oldest Story   297

 15   The Last Trip   318

Selected Bibliography   329

Index   337

ACKNOWLEDGMENTS

There are always hundreds to thank and too many forgotten. First, best friend and wife, Sharon Solwitz, for the prickly, demanding insight, helping in vital ways to shape the work. Then, Alan Cheuse, who brought me the idea, and Nicholas Delbanco, who equally wanted it to happen. With them, my agent Nat Sobel and editor Shannon Ravenel, for their patience and devotion to literature, as well as copy editor Jude Grant and all those at Algonquin who helped.

Among Gardner's family, countless friends, acquaintances, associates, and others whose help was indispensable, most all of whom felt as I did that the story demanded telling and were willing to trust me with theirs: Liz Rosenberg and Susan Thornton especially; Bill Gardner, Jimmy Gardner, Wanda Gardner, Steve Huff, Marge Cervone, Joan Gardner, Joel Gardner, Lucy Carson, Jim Judkins, Jene Hatchett, Jim Grinnell, Dick Day, Donald Finkel, William Murray, Donald Justice, Vance Bourjaily, Robert Dana, Carl Dennis, Jarvis Thurston, Kazuko Wong, Dewey Ganzel, George Soule, Lennis Dunlap, Carl Peterson, Eric Solomon, Leo Litwak, Maxine Chernoff, David Ray, Bill Burns, Tom Porter, William Gass, Lore Segal, Charles Johnson, John Howell, Myron Kartman, Carroll Riley, Cynthia Riley, Brent Riley, Robert Russell, Lenore Russell, Jerry Osbourne, Barry Sanders, Joe Baber, Pat Gray, Steve Falcolne, Ed Epstein, Alex Paul, Joyce Carol Oates, Robert Pack, Margaret Pigott, Joan Elkin, Blue Argo, Irene Allen, Jan Quakenbush, David Bain, Jay Parini, Ron Hansen, Susan Shreve, Ted Hower, Mike Kelley, Joe Palmer, Jeanette Robertson, Jim Rose, Herb Yellin, Warren Benson, Anne Calcagno, Charlie Boyd, Maria Cardinale, Vince Iglesias, Peter Dworzinski, Jerianne Barnes, Sarah de Sanctis, Larry Janowski, and S. L. Wisenberg.

And, of course, the proverbial more . . .

Poets, for instance, made poems that might—if the poet was lucky and talented and careful—endure for a thousand years. But what was it that a lawyer made, preparing a brief of, say, four hundred closely reasoned, meticulously researched, precisely stated pages? Did the poet put in any more of his heart's blood, his brain's electricity, torment of soul?

At best, the lawyer established a precedent. . . . At best. *Where will I go?* he had asked himself. *What will I do? Nowhere. Nothing.*

—*The Sunlight Dialogues*

W HEN I TYPED that passage on a card and taped it to a wall in my Chicago apartment in the winter of 1973 I was twenty-three and unemployed. A couple of months before, I had quit a job I hated, teaching sixth- and seventh-graders in an inner-city school, and mainly I had been relieved. I collected applications for law schools, in preparation for the career most of my relatives expected me to choose, as I had expected too for most of my life. I had to make a living.

I worked sporadically at application essays, played my guitar (not very well), wrote poetry (badly), and read books I wished I could have written. Short of money, like some who buy clothes or food they'll never need to salve their anxieties, I splurged to buy a hardback first edition of *The Sunlight Dialogues* for the outrageously expensive price of $8.95. It was an unusual bestseller, I'd heard.

From the first page, it had me. My apartment slipped further into shadow, and the more I thought about the suits and cocktails and legal nit-picking that seemed usually to benefit the wrong people, the more the whole business of being a lawyer seemed a grim prospect.

It was a prospect one of the novel's characters had faced, and succumbed to, leaving him restless and unhappy. Even more involving was the struggle between the young, disaffected protagonist and the small-town police chief, whose discussions were driven by ancient Babylonian ideas—I found out later—that Gardner used to establish their conflict. The novel's most striking feature, however, was the language itself, which created that world so convincingly, as I realized it creates ours. In short, I knew I had found something important, even if I didn't quite know what it was. Nothing I could do, I was certain, nothing anyone can do, could be more worthwhile than the work Gardner was doing.

JOHN GARDNER WAS ALREADY a figure in the literary world when *The Sunlight Dialogues* was published in December 1972. He had published three novels before, the first of which didn't do well enough to merit a paperback edition. The second and shorter one, published a year earlier and told from the point of view of *Beowulf*'s monster, Grendel, received widespread praise from critics and achieved a certain popular following, but it was far from a best-seller.

After the new one had spent fourteen weeks on the *New York Times* best-seller list, though, Gardner was a major American novelist, and by the end of the decade his penchant for picking intellectual fights with his peers, as much as his seemingly continual outpouring of serious books, three more of which achieved best-seller status, made him as close to a household name as any serious author could be. Few other novelists had generated as much critical respect or controversy by the end of their lives as Gardner had by the end of his.

Though he hadn't published more than a few critical articles and one short story by the time he was thirty, when he died at age forty-nine, he had published twenty-nine books including nine novels, two collections of short stories, an epic poem, three books of children's stories, two instructional books for writing fiction, a book-length critical essay, six books of medieval criticism, and a major biography. Twenty years later, given publishers' increasingly voracious appetite for the next big thing, most of Gardner's books had gone out of print. The fate still surprises the countless fans he attracted.

Many writers and critics agree that his ideas changed the way the art of fiction has been practiced since. Novelist and commentator Alan Cheuse, for instance, points out that in both his teaching and criticism, Gardner "led the charge" against "metafictionists" who saw fiction as an elaborate game and instead claimed for it an important role in its explorations of essential principles and conditions.

"He was the driving force in bringing fiction back toward

Tolstoyan realism," says writer and translator Jay Parini. "He took it away from the dominant academic, self-referential, post-structuralist mode and directed it toward a more realistic, moral bent."

Novelist Charles Johnson, who was one of his students, says, "Gardner's argument for 'moral fiction' was ten years ahead of its time and is now a position any self-respecting critic would claim. For Gardner, craft itself—making the art object well—is a moral activity, though skillful means, of course, are not enough if the craft serves a vision that is fundamentally incorrect or unwise or simply wrong."

Even now, *The Art of Fiction*, more than any other text, Cheuse reminds us, "helps young writers to position themselves imaginatively with regard to their material. It forces them to think about point of view and the other mechanics of fiction writing. . . . It leads them to questions about the heart of motive, and human psychology."

Just after Gardner's death, Craig Riley wrote in *Best Sellers*, "Very few writers, of any age, are alchemist enough to capture the respect of the intellectual community *and* the imagination of others who . . . prefer [Jacqueline] Susann and [Judith] Krantz. Based on critical acclaim, and sales volume, it would seem that this man accomplished both."

Gardner was often termed a philosophical novelist in the tradition of Mann or Dostoyevsky, whose fiction served, among other things, to dramatize complex ideologies discussed by academic thinkers. It's a tradition not often practiced with any success in our time, but as in other ways Gardner was a memorable exception. If some of his novels are criticized for being weighed down by too much discussion of ideas, his fiction is nonetheless dominated by the exploration of universal conflicts in fully human contexts—and it is that humanness that gives the novels the vigor so many readers came to appreciate.

Not surprisingly, as much as the circumstances his fiction engages are universal, the work is distinctly American. It is about the struggle between civilization and the wilderness; between freedom and anarchy; between the accepted, settled world and the untamed beyond; between, as one critic put it, order and chaos.

Along with all he wrote, his very character was magnetic, attracting nearly everyone he contacted. His generosity toward students, toward almost everyone he met, was nearly legendary and sharpened under the most difficult circumstances.

"He used to talk about stewardship," says Liz Rosenberg, Gardner's second wife. "That's why he wrote *The Art of Fiction* when he thought he was dying."

In December 1977 he was operated on for life-threatening colon cancer. "He was literally hooked up to an intravenous machine and waiting to go into surgery and typing away," she says. "In every way he was dedicated to younger writers and helping them." The book, as Rosenberg puts it, was to be his "Adonais," a sort of elegy-memorial for aspiring young writers whom he loved teaching, work that he increasingly took to be his primary mission.

Writers often talk about the dedication it takes to do the work of making real literature, and Gardner is a startling case in point. During the years they lived together, Rosenberg says, "He wrote six, seven, ten hours a day." The same devotion is also true of the years before, at least since he was a doctoral student at the University of Iowa in his twenties. Most writers—serious authors—say they work all day, Gardner said in an interview once. "But really, they are only at it three or four hours a day. I work all the time."

Still, though Gardner might spend ten hours a day writing, it seemed clear to Rosenberg that he'd been a good father and husband to his family. It was another part of the generosity and deeply held, lifelong compassion for which he was also known. Rosenberg recounts a story told of Gardner's childhood, when he was six, about a fellow classmate who was part Native American and who had come newly to his first-grade class, terrified at the new surroundings: "John came over and put his arms around [the new child] and comforted him. He was incredibly intuitive and empathetic, and an incredible judge of character. Almost everyone liked him."

At the same time, Rosenberg notes that "he could be a warrior" in pursuit of his own principles. The sparks he raised in public media, from the *New York Times* to the *Dick Cavett Show*, were for him necessary by-products of the only thing worth the effort—the making of art. Like everything he did, he could only do it one way: with complete devotion and full speed ahead. Or, as motorcycle racers whom he liked to think of as models might say: flat out.

Gardner grew up on a farm and learned to ride a motorcycle when he was just old enough to sit on it—about the same time he learned to drive a tractor, manage horses and chickens, and milk cows. He learned to use his hands, to fix what broke, to build what he needed. He was never alone. Apart from parents and siblings, his grandparents, cousins, aunts, and uncles lived nearby. Likewise, everywhere he lived as an adult he attracted countless people who were drawn to the energy he loved to keep feeding. Parties went on, the phone always ringing, as he stirred people to produce theater, music, any art. He made all those around him believe they could be part of it. If there is such a thing as charisma, John Gardner embodied it.

At the same time, he drank—gin, vodka, scotch, whatever was around—as he kept talking, leaning against the wall, the sink, slumped in a chair, until everyone else went off to bed, passed out, or disappeared. Then he went to his typewriter and wrote. The story sounds invented, surely exaggerated, except for all the people who testify to the same. Most of his life, he slept only five or six hours at a time.

No one could keep up, and he couldn't wait. Some physical anomaly? Maybe. How he managed to live that way and write so much is a question that goes to the very root of the person he was. The answer might begin with his parents, though they are hardly the beginning, or with an event, so large it touches everything—if there is such a thing. Whatever the answer, it isn't simple.

But I never did send in an application to law school.

PROLOGUE

ON APRIL 4, 1945, the Wednesday after Easter, Allied troops were closing in on Berlin, and the Nazis were falling back. Though the battle for Okinawa, which would result in some fifty thousand American casualties, began just days earlier, the United States had started to win back some of the territory in the Pacific. Final victory still seemed a long way off, but there were finally genuine reasons for optimism.

In western New York, the day fairly glowed, as if to echo the spirit, with robins returning, trees beginning to leaf, and the heady aromas of high spring everywhere. The Gardner farm, in Genesee County for a hundred years, bathed in it, but this was no day to sit around and soak it in. At most there might be some time to listen to the radio or read or just sit before sleep. But the planting had to be done, and to do that, fields had to be readied. The rows that had been plowed up had to be tamped down. There were the cows to milk at dawn and nightfall, all the animals to feed, and the endless repairs to make to keep it all going.

John Gardner Sr. was busy, as he had been throughout the war years. Besides running the farm, he'd also taken on stockroom work at a medical company in nearby Batavia to make extra money. A cheerful man, he was exhausted much of the time now and always seemed to be in need of sleep amid the constant activity. He never complained, though. That afternoon, besides everything else, he had to go to Wyoming County, some twenty-five miles south, to pick up his nephew Bill, who had been at an overnight retreat at the Y camp on Silver Lake.

While he was gone, his eleven-year-old son, John Jr.—everyone called him Buddy—was to take the tractor up the road to his grandparents' Locust Level farm, drop off a flatbed trailer there, and pick up the cultipacker—the fifteen-hundred-pound double-roller that the tractor pulled over the plowed rows to flatten them for planting. The trip to the other farm was only a couple of miles, a ride Buddy had taken many times, with and without his father. It would be a fine and simple chore in such warm blue air.

As he was getting ready to go, his six-and-a-half-year-old brother Gib (as they called Gilbert) came running and asked if he could go along. Then four-year-old sister Sandy wanted to come too. For safety's sake, the family rule was that no children could ride on a tractor that another of the children was driving, but riding on the wide flatbed that traveled so slowly and close to the ground didn't seem to present any possible danger. Priscilla, their mother, said that Gib and Sandy could go, and they climbed on the trailer. Bud started the tractor, and the three of them rode though the picture-book day. At Locust Level, Buddy unhooked the trailer and hitched up the cultipacker. It was a scene Priscilla played over and over in her mind for the rest of her life.

"The thing I had to live with ever after," she said, "was that I didn't ask 'How are you coming back?' That didn't occur to me at all."

With nowhere to sit, Sandy climbed onto Bud's lap. Gib, however, in the way of boys his age, especially boys with older brothers and something to prove, loved being a daredevil. He had once climbed all the way to the top of a windmill and had to be laboriously talked down. Now he jumped on the drawbar that linked the one-and-a-half-ton cultipacker to the tractor. The perch was precarious, but if anything, that heightened the adventure. And so they headed back. The trip home may have been a little bumpy, but that was part of the fun—a kind of homemade amusement-park ride—especially for Gilbert, perched on the drawbar in the open air.

They were almost back, heading down a small knoll on the road in front of their house, when the tractor ran out of gas. The engine quit with a jerk and pitched Gilbert onto the ground in front of the cultipacker. But the cultipacker kept rolling. Sandy screamed, and Bud swung around in time to see the huge roller moving up his brother's body to his stomach. Sandy saw blood pour out of his mouth. Stanley Demski, a neighbor who lived just down the road and on the other side from the Gardners, heard the cries and ran outside. He was slightly retarded, but he certainly recognized that there was trouble. He ran out to the tractor, saw Gib lying beside the cultipacker that Bud had managed to steer off him, and lifted him up, carrying him into the Gardner house, with Bud and Sandy following.

When they came in, Bud was crying, "I've killed Gilbert! I've killed Gilbert!"

"You have *not*," Priscilla shouted back. "Don't say such a thing."

But Sandy was spattered with blood, and Gib was covered with it. Demski drove Priscilla and Gib to the hospital in town. When they got there, a nurse they knew, a close friend of Priscilla's sister, met them. She looked at Gib and listened for a heartbeat. There was none.

Priscilla went home to the children. John Sr. arrived soon after on his motorcycle with his nephew Bill. Sandy was still spattered with blood, and Priscilla's recollection was that Sandy told him what had happened. Bill, however, remembers Priscilla's coming out and screaming, "Don't kill me, don't hit me, I didn't do it."

John went to the hospital then, and they were all told that Gilbert was indeed dead. "I remember [John] sat there so silent and overwhelmed, and Bud was sobbing so," Priscilla said.

She prompted John to comfort their son, and so he tried, assuring Bud that the accident wasn't his fault, but Bud remained distraught. He kept seeing every moment as if it were happening again—blood pouring out of Gib's mouth as the cultipacker ran over him and his father on the ground where he'd thrown himself, later, sobbing hysterically in the dirt. He couldn't put the images away.

Gib's body was laid in an open casket in the living room. Bill remembers coming in one night and sitting by the casket, trying to understand the meaning of this trauma. For more than a year afterward, Priscilla set a place for Gib at every meal, with an empty chair for him.

At times John Sr. tried to come to terms with the tragedy by saying that Gib had always been careless and what happened was the result, even that he somehow had it coming. But Bud would find him crying in the barn. John Sr. took up smoking cigarettes for the first time. He went for long rides on his motorcycle. He sought comfort in other women.

"He became," writes his son in "Redemption," the story about the accident that Priscilla said was as close to truth as anything she knew, ". . . a hunter of women . . . trading off his sorrow for the sorrows of weary, unfulfilled country wives."

Years later, Susan Thornton, about to marry the forty-eight-year-old novelist, said, "From what he told me, his [father's] love affairs had been habitual and constant."

Likewise, John Jr. commented on his mother's habit late in their lives of touching her husband's forearm in company and plucking his sleeve. "It's the gesture of the betrayed wife," he says. "He was always unfaithful to her. . . . It's like, 'Look, I'm still here. Don't forget me.'"

Both parents told their son over and over that it wasn't his fault, that there was nothing he could possibly have done, that Gilbert knew better than to ride in such a dangerous place, that the one-and-a-half-ton weight rolling downhill could never have been stopped in time. "Nobody could stop that," Priscilla remembered saying. "No human power could do it, and God doesn't work that way."

A few years after the accident, when his parents discovered how their son still blamed himself, his father even wrote him a letter, Priscilla recounted, telling him how Gilbert had been with his father on a hay rake the summer before, and without John Sr.'s knowing, had dozed off, fallen from the equipment, "and had just been rolled along by the rake—not hurt in the least. John said to Bud, 'He could have been killed *then*—I could have done it.'"

For the rest of his life, though, John Jr. held himself responsible. He was the oldest, he kept thinking. He was driving. He could have hit the brakes and stopped. But he kept going.

1

A Great Roar

A great roar began, an exhalation of breath that swelled
to a rumbling of voices then to the growling and clap-
ping and stomping of men gone mad on art.

—*Grendel*

JOHN CHAMPLIN GARDNER, SR. was well known
throughout Genesee County as a performer. He recited Shakespeare and poetry and gave speeches at
school assemblies, churches, and wherever else local audiences
might gather. He was heard reciting Shakespeare while milking
his cows and in response to his wife's cues. He had also been a lay
preacher taking on ministerial duties and giving sermons when
the pastor at their Presbyterian church could not. In fact, it had
been his penchant for performing that first drew Priscilla to him
in 1927.

She had been a twenty-four-year-old schoolteacher at the rural Batavia high school; he was one of the tenth-grade students.
Though he wasn't in her class, everyone knew everyone else at
the small school, and even at fifteen years old he stood out. For

one thing, he was a Gardner. Not being from around Genesee County, the name wouldn't have meant anything to Priscilla at first, but no one could live there for any length of time without hearing about the family.

Their history has been traced back to the England of Chaucer, or just after, and to Sir Thomas Gardiner, knight of Collynbyn Hall, West Riding of Yorkshire, in the 1400s. It was two centuries later, in 1628, when George Gardiner (the English spelling was changed a century later by the first John) took ship for the colonies at the age of thirty-nine. Apparently an educated man, his name appears in colonial records as a participant in various civic affairs. His involvement was a precedent that his progeny would continue.

Whatever upset sent him to the New World didn't entirely subside there either—another element that would continue to characterize the Gardners. He divorced his wife and met one Herodias Long Hicks, a woman whose heritage certainly fit the novelist's penchant for storytelling. Like many writers, Gardner was often enough given to painting his life more dramatically than it may have actually been, but in his ancestor's case the story didn't need elaboration.

Herodias Long was only thirteen when she was married the first time, to John Hicks of London. Shortly afterward, the two made their way to Newport. Soon after arriving, however, Hicks left her, going, as she testified later, "to the Dutch"—probably meaning to someone or a community from New Amsterdam— and taking with him the money and resources her mother had left her. Determined not to resign herself to a life of lonely destitution, she found Gardiner, and married him in 1640 by going before a collection of friends and declaring the fact. As irregular in its beginnings as their union was, the two remained together long enough to have seven children.

Nonetheless, Herodias later insisted that George was not a suitable husband. In a petition for divorce that she brought before the colony's general assembly, she claimed that he wouldn't provide for the family. A divorce was granted, and she left in pursuit of John Porter, after whom she walked, with a baby at her breast, all the way from Newport to Boston. Porter was one of the colony's original landowners and got a convenient divorce from his wife to marry Herodias in 1669, agreeing to provide for her children. A man of his word, he gave each a farm of several hundred acres, some of the farms adjoining Gardiner's, and went on to have six more children with Herodias. Thus, she became the first (that we know of) in a family history of determined, single-minded women.

The John Gardner of our time never knew these details. However, his attraction to myth, to the old and archetypal played out in human character, was clearly spawned in fertile ground. From the medieval translations and criticism he wrote at the beginning of his career, to the Babylonian myth he translated just before his death, to his own novels and poems, ancient stories and ideas were primary elements.

The adventurousness of his ancestors didn't stop with Herodias either. A century later, one of her and George Gardiner's great-grandsons became the first John Gardner. That John left Rhode Island for the open lands of New York, stopping first near Albany before going on to settle in the northwest part of the state in 1797. The Big Tree Treaty with the defeated Seneca Indians of the

Iroquois Confederacy had just opened the area to European settlement, and so Genesee County was born. Gardner cousins,
brothers, and other family members followed, and by the mid-
nineteenth century, John Champlin Gardner II and his family
owned two farms in the county. The older farm, more than one
hundred acres and later called Locust Level, had been bought by
John II in 1875, when he moved off his brother Jeffrey's farm in
Elba. When John II's son Fred—the novelist's grandfather—
took over the operation in the 1930s, Locust Level had a herd of
cows, fields of hay, chickens, sheep, grapevines, more than ten
acres of vegetable garden, and hired hands to help manage it all.

It would be wrong to say they were wealthy, but the Gardner
farm was substantial. When the third John married Priscilla in
1930, the family had been community pillars for a century, making their mark in more than farming. In 1849, for instance, John
Champlin Gardner II, who had become the first lawyer in the
family, was elected to the state assembly. Forty years later, his
nephew, Fred, whose father had also been a church deacon, twice
ran for political office and was an active officer of the church.
Fred was also a trustee of the local school district, an important
member and onetime president of the grange (a farmers' organization that met to exchange information about the farming
business, work for farmers' issues in local government, and provide entertainments), and a justice of the peace.

Alice Day, the woman Fred married in 1907 and who became
the novelist's grandmother, may not have shown Herodias's solitary determination, but she was clearly just as driven to make her
mark. She had followed the calling of her grandfather Moses
Taggart, who had come to the county from Massachusetts in

1817, at the age of eighteen. He studied and practiced law and became a member of the New York Constitutional Convention in 1846. There, he would have at least met John Gardner II, and if the two weren't directly involved, their acquaintance seems likely to have been a factor in the meeting of Gardner's nephew, Fred, and Taggart's granddaughter, Alice.

Born in 1873, Alice was one of seven children of Moses's daughter Fannie and her husband, William Harris Day. No doubt encouraged by her grandfather's example, as well as by her father's—William also studied law, then joined his father-in-law's practice—and at a time when girls rarely went beyond high school, if that, Alice graduated from Smith College in 1896 and began working for her father. After three years, she went on to law school in Buffalo and finished the two-year course in a year and a half, taking home top honors. She said later that she'd done so much reading while she was working for her father that the schoolwork was easy. And so she became the county's first female lawyer.

She went into practice with her father, Harris, and in 1904 her brother (also named Harris) joined them. Three years later, she met and married John (a cousin of the assemblyman John II) and Sarah Gardner's son Fred, who had studied to be a lawyer but had given up the profession to run the Locust Level farm. Alice abandoned her law practice in 1908, at the birth of their first son (named Harris after her father). However, after the last of her five was born in 1919, she resumed her career (with her brother now, who after a few years farming, then teaching, also went to law school) and continued until retiring in 1951 at the age of seventy-eight.

All the while novelist John was growing up, his grandmother Alice, with her record of accomplishment, stood as a model for achievement. That legacy, coupled with community involvement, were cornerstones of family responsibility, and in Fred's case community involvement was informed as well by a strong dose of populist sympathy.

As in most rural communities, everyone in the county was Republican; the party's stated principles of self-reliance, laissez-faire economics, and less governmental involvement in public affairs seemed more beneficial to rural, farming interests. Fred, however, favored a decidedly populist version. In 1928, he ran for a seat in the U.S. House of Representatives and announced that he wanted to be considered "a dirt farmer candidate who is not unmindful of the rights of all classes, having in mind always the welfare of the nation as a whole." It was a view betraying a liberal flavor, which didn't play well to the county majority—he lost the election—but the democratic temper in which it was grounded just as surely made up another key element of family tradition.

So the Gardners embodied a deep strain of civic involvement; active sympathy for those less fortunate (just a little out of keeping with the political conservatism around them); and strong-minded, educated women. Amid this mix, whether occasioned by marriages of cousins or other circumstances we can't account for, there was also a dash of madness.

Its first evidence crops up in a local newspaper account of November 1896, which reports that Fred's sister, Cora, a teacher at the West Main Street School in Alexander (near Batavia), suffered a nervous breakdown and was committed to the Willard

Hospital. After a six-month stay, she was released as "cured," but two years later, then again two years after that, she was re-committed, both times for brief stays.

It is perhaps no more than an exotic detail in Gardner lineage, but it's also an element that the author, who loved to display his own penchant for life on the edge, would certainly have enjoyed. And if Cora was the only certified victim of mental illness in the family, she was hardly the only Gardner woman witnessed off the proverbial path.

In a 1928 photo in the local newspaper, candidate Fred Gardner is posed on the Locust Level farmhouse front porch. Standing with him are sons Harris, John, Grant, Howard, and Arthur; their sister, Sarah; and their mother, Alice, who in deference to featuring her husband's candidacy is identified only as "Mrs. Gardner." Twenty-year-old Harris is identified as a farmer, and indeed he did run the farm for the next decade, following family tradition. In 1937, though, he left it for his brother John to run while he attended the New York State College for Teachers in Albany. After teaching and working as a principal for three years at a county school, he decided to take up law, moved to Buffalo for three years to take the necessary courses, and returned to practice with his mother.

Very likely Harris's career shifts were driven in part by the woman he married. The daughter of a tenant farmer, Mildred Stamp had her own family difficulties and was apparently stirred to larger ambitions. Chafing under her father's rule, Millie was eager to get away, and initially, the family story goes, she had her eye set on John. When he failed to display interest, she decided to go for Harris. "Anything to get into the Gardner family, which is where success was, as she saw it," says her son, Bill.

It was not a happy marriage, and the results echoed into the next generation. Millie was one of the energetic, self-willed women Gardner men seemed to find (or who found them), and her ambition upset the "normal" course of family. "They were like oil and water," Bill says. Millie was "a very driving, go-go-go, I'm going to get to the top, it's my world type of person."

Harris, on the other hand, was more sedate. "He was the guy who as a kid would let everybody else go off to the movies or to a picnic when he had to stay home and do chores," Bill says. "He was a stick-in-the-mud, un-fun person to be with."

When Harris began practicing law in Batavia with his mother, Millie worked as a secretary at the Presbyterian church. There she got romantically involved with the minister—and pregnant. Knowledge of her pregnancy became public and led to an unusual public confession by the minister, which Bill remembers hearing played on a tape recorder to the assembled church congregation one Sunday. Not surprisingly, Harris and Millie divorced.

John Sr.'s disinterest in Millie at the beginning may have been the result of simple personality differences, but it was also rooted in a romance that began for him in high school. Like farm boys everywhere, he worked hard at the family business, performing chores that went on from first light or before until dark or later. Schoolwork had to be done in the cracks between. In the Gardner family, however, school and learning were of prime importance. That emphasis no doubt led John to apply himself to studies and attracted him to other activities around school. One of those activities was centered around the new English teacher.

Priscilla Jones had undertaken to lead a drama group, and, as his older brother had, John took to performing in it. Priscilla surely encouraged him, and the chemistry between them led to more than the usual comradery. Students' infatuation with their teachers is nothing new. Though Priscilla surely had more admirers than sophomore John Gardner, she must have found him particularly handsome and well spoken. At the least, his family's intellectual and cultural background likely put a finer finish on him than that which the other rough country farm boys were likely to exhibit. Still, he was just another student, a boy nine years younger, this a seemingly unbridgeable gulf. John persisted in his interest, however, and Priscilla found herself falling for him in return.

She was born in St. Louis in 1903, between her older brother, James, and younger sister, Lucy, who was named after their mother. James, named for an uncle who headed west during the 1849 California gold rush, contracted lockjaw from a cut while in his late teens. Priscilla was still a child. With no tetanus vaccine and no cure, James starved to death, unable to eat.

Priscilla's father, also named John, was a carpenter, and better than most. He was known for putting a roof on the then-tallest building in St. Louis and for building houses complete with child-sized built-in seats next to full-sized adult ones. However, while still in the prime of his life, he was struck with arthritis and was forced to give up the trade. In 1916, the family moved east to Steuben, New York, some one hundred miles east of Batavia. Steuben was only a mile or two from Remsen, the name of a town in Wales, and the Welsh population that came to New York fostered a community there that had drawn Priscilla's ancestors. Many first-generation Welsh had gone to St. Louis from Remsen, so it was natural for the family to retrace those steps. Thus, they settled back into Remsen culture, operating a farm with the help of extended family who lived there.

Priscilla's roots, then, reached back to a country known still for its poetic musicality in speech as well as song, a heritage that likely contributed to her interest in English literature, which in turn she passed on to her son. Years later, son John would remember childhood visits to his mother's family in St. Louis and the songfests in which everyone participated.

He would also remember sleeping in a room with his grandmother Jones when he was a small child. He read stories to her, and she told him stories, which he said evoked the strange and mysterious, like stories his uncle told of their ancestors' lives in caves.

"She made my world mythic," Gardner wrote of his grandmother, speaking of her tales of angels and odd happenings. All of it was told in the shadowy world of childhood, made even stranger by the old, unfamiliar rooms and farm. That mythic texture became, of course, a fundamental element of Gardner's fiction, and he was always quick to note its sources.

After Priscilla finished high school, she went on to Albany's New York State College for Teachers. While she was a student there, her father passed away, and so when she graduated in 1924 she found a job teaching high school in the Alexander school near Batavia. She moved there with her mother and sister and taught English and coached drama. As the English teacher, she was also the adviser to the school paper. Two years later, when John showed up in her drama group, she coached him in speaking contests (before him, Harris had also been active in debate and public speaking) and directed him in plays.

Priscilla was a calmer personality than her fiery, red-haired younger sister, Lucy. Those who knew them both note that Lucy was decidedly more attractive—not that there was ever competition on that score from John, though he did become known for his eye for the ladies. Priscilla also shared the Gardner belief in community service. After she quit teaching, as her children grew, she spent time working with the young members of their Presbyterian church.

In the beginning, however, regardless of the Gardners' distinction, neither Priscilla's mother nor anyone else in the family would have approved of a romance between Priscilla and her much younger student—had they known about it. But they didn't. John and Priscilla did their best to keep them from knowing, and, with the help of Lucy, Priscilla's mother remained (as far as anyone knew) happily unaware.

Lucy had taken up with George Preston, a veteran of World War I, who had suffered through a gas attack that had caused some impairment of his motor skills. This didn't at all inhibit his garrulous temperament or, later, keep him from working as a traveling salesman. To get around their parents, Priscilla and Lucy would double-date with John and George, but they'd tell their parents that John was younger daughter Lucy's date and that the older George was escorting Priscilla.

The ruse apparently worked well enough, at least until John graduated in 1929. Shortly afterward, the romance between him and his English teacher blossomed into a public engagement. On October 11 of the following year, with the consent (if not blessing) of all the parents, Priscilla and John were married (and a few months later Lucy married George). The wedding took place in the Presbyterian church, with all the requisite attendants and newspaper notice. The reception afterward was held at the new 176-acre Devon Stock Farm, adjacent to Locust Level, which John's mother, Alice, her brother, and his sister Sarah's father-in-law, Percy Hinckley, had bought and deeded to the newlyweds.

For the first years, John and Priscilla worked hard and became accustomed to their new lives together. Even though it was the middle of the Great Depression, the Gardner farms were relatively prosperous. In midsummer 1933, on July 21, Priscilla gave birth to their first child—the first of a new generation of Gardners—whom they named, after his father and the two before him, John Champlin.

2

Intimations

What are a poet's lying words to the rich and the secret intimations of a piano chord, a great pipe organ, an orchestra, a voice?

—"The Music Lover"

P RISCILLA QUIT TEACHING to care for the family while John worked the farm—actually two farms now—with his father and the help they hired. There were two dozen or so cows to milk (the number varying with the farm economy and the cows' health), hay to plant and harvest, machinery to repair.

John was a hard worker, resourceful and energetic, but not always meticulous. His cows' milk didn't always make Grade A, for instance, the standard that paid much better but required more expensive equipment and adherence to elaborate requirements to ensure cleanliness for human consumption. He often kept vehicles and machinery running with temporary fixes and, when they stopped, abandoned them about the grounds. He was "the old-time farmer who fixed everything with baling wire and a welder," a neighbor remembers. "He kept the machinery going, though it often wouldn't have needed fixing except it was left out in the weather."

Another friend recalls that he was always welding something. Often enough it was something on one of the motorcycles he had owned since the machine's earliest days. In times of stress he would take long rides through the country, and when the children were older he went to work on the bike to get around a state law that said a motorcycle could only carry as many passengers as there were foot pegs. He simply welded on extra foot pegs so he could carry more people. When he and Priscilla got much older, he traded in his Harley for a larger, smoother-running BMW and attached a sidecar for Priscilla to ride with him.

With two farms and no mortgage, the Gardners may have been a picture of success in the community, but the once-elegant Italianate-style brick farmhouse that the newlyweds moved into was far from posh. Built originally of Medina sandstone quarried from the same lode that had supplied the state capitol in Albany in the previous century, the rectangular two-story building had long been divided in half, the front room at one time given to monthly grange meetings and other community functions. At the time the Gardner family bought the property for the newlyweds for four thousand dollars, the house had been used as a storage shed for grain, apples, and potatoes. Six thousand dollars and a lot of hard work was then spent converting it back into a real house.

The Gardners were farmers, though, not carpenters, and the work they did on the house was strictly utilitarian. The front of the house became a separate apartment again, to be occupied by either tenants or extended family. John and Priscilla lived in the back half with their children. Neither half was very spacious. The first room off the back entrance was the kitchen, and the small room that opened off it was Buddy's. The living room was behind the kitchen, while John Sr. and Priscilla, and then the daughter they called Sandy (actually named Priscilla, after her mother), born in 1940, had rooms upstairs.

John Sr.'s interests didn't run much to books, but he had the family-bred respect for intellectual achievement, and he kept up on current events. Their novelist son remembered Priscilla's quoting lines from Shakespeare while her husband milked the cows and his responding to her cues from memory. Sometimes he recited poetry to the cows as he milked them. He became known in the area for extensive recitations of Shakespeare and other long passages of poetry at various local gatherings and for giving performances with Priscilla at the local school. Says Bill's younger brother Greg of his uncle John, "His talent was in understatement, and not in sonorous delivery. He was essentially a whisperer. . . . He was perhaps the best person I've known at expressing kindness through softness of manner." Though John was known to everyone in the area, Greg goes on, "I'm not sure that he was what you would call a 'local celebrity.' Frankly, he smelled too much of the barn to inspire much hero worship."

Another neighbor agrees that "he wasn't the cleanest farmer. . . . He always smelled of the barn." He was on the school board in Alexander, the neighbor continues, and "more than once he came into meetings smelling of that, and I remember people remarking on it." Nonetheless, Greg says, "He was certainly loved by the community," and another neighbor confirms that, saying he and Priscilla were "absolutely wonderful people. I never heard a discouraging word from either of them."

Both were active in the church and committed to the social principles of Christianity, though John Sr. was known to be skeptical of religious doctrine. Family tradition and his interest in performing, however, were no doubt factors in his becoming a lay minister and later a teacher at the Sunday school. As lay minister, he delivered sermons when the regular pastor wasn't available and helped with the tending of the church and congregation. The sermons he gave, one congregant remembers, "weren't occasions for spouting liturgy or learned quotations, but folksy, down-to-earth stuff."

The family always sat in the front row in church, and extended their prominence in other community involvements as well. John Sr. served on the local school board for a dozen years and was active with the Boy Scouts for fifteen. Then, through the 1950s and 1960s, after their own children grew up and moved away, he and Priscilla provided a home for thirteen foster children. Though they received a stipend to care for their wards, who supplied some of the work essential to any farming enterprise, all who knew the Gardners are quick to assert that generosity and compassion were much more obviously what motivated them.

Like John's father Fred, despite being professed Republicans, as were most in the community, both John Sr.'s and Priscilla's politics were informed by a generous slice of more liberal, populist sentiment. At the end of the Second World War, for instance, they were active in bringing the One World movement to the county. Though the movement was later accused of being a communist front, discredited, and dissolved, it was founded on ideas of internationality that anticipated the United Nations.

One acquaintance also remembers Priscilla speaking in the late 1940s at a public forum about the mistreatment of African Americans and the horrors of lynching. It was a view not voiced at the time in white rural quarters, south or north, and such more traditionally liberal views drew disapproval from some of their neighbors. But the affability and good-humored intelligence that characterized both John and Priscilla seem to have brought them general respect and affection nonetheless.

One of Buddy's high school friends remembers an evening at the Gardner's when Buddy had to go off for a while on an errand. Priscilla, he says, "told me how John had written fifteen or sixteen lines in some very long and involved verse structure, and how good it was. She was just talking, not bragging about her son to another boy his age, just telling me about the wonderful creation of her son. It was a kind of moral support that amazed me. It was simply uncommon."

With extended family always around, Buddy was seldom left to himself. Though his position as eldest, and at first only, child, might feed a sense of preeminence, he wasn't alone for long. When he was four and a half his brother was born. Gilbert was named after an ancestor of Priscilla's (as was her favorite cousin in St. Louis who was near the same age) and he was moved into John's small room.

Priscilla's family had moved to western New York more than ten years before, but the connection to the family left in St. Louis was strong, and she and John Sr. regularly exchanged visits with the St. Louis family for weddings, funerals, and other important family events. And besides the long affection Priscilla shared with her cousin Gilbert Patterson, they had children of the same age.

Like John and Priscilla's Gilbert, her cousin's daughter, Joan, born just a month after Buddy, also had flaming red hair. When the families got together, she and Buddy made a picture-book pair. At nap time as small babies (John told interviewers much later), they would be fit into the same drawer on family visits. Both were exceedingly bright and from their earliest days were close friends. Not surprisingly, given their quick intelligence, they were also feisty competitors. As they grew, their relationship continued to flower.

Though the depression had hit full force in Buddy's first years, the Gardners weren't much affected. In town, Alice continued her thriving law practice with her brother. On the farm the huge vegetable garden at Locust Level fed the family and their help with plenty to spare. The cows continued to give milk and butter and cheese, and though prices had fallen the farm itself was more or less self-sufficient.

Buddy's schooling began at the old one-room school in Batavia, which in 1938 was succeeded by the new consolidated Alexander Central School. The big new yellow-brick school housed second through twelfth grades, in two dozen classrooms on two floors, and Buddy's second-grade class was the first to begin there. As he grew, the sympathy for others that led to his reaching out to the new Native American student when he was six, led to physical confrontations as well. Though Priscilla always saw her son as particularly sensitive, he was as willing to fight with his peers as most any boy. Still, she was surprised when she learned about that side of him.

"One day, while he was in elementary school, I went after him to drive him home," Priscilla recalled, "and some kid told me he was having a fight with another kid. I said, 'No!' I couldn't believe it! It wasn't at all that he was too angelic, but that wasn't his temperament. . . . Then, before he got back to the car, he fought *another* boy—two in one day! The neighbor woman said, 'You know, that docile, quiet little boy of yours isn't so quiet on the playground. Anybody picks on somebody, he lights into him, no matter how much bigger they are.'"

Buddy's expressions of sympathy must have seemed very natural in the Gardner family, where emotions ran close to the surface. Bill Gardner, the same age as his cousin, Bud, lived with his mother and sister in the front half of the Devon Stock Farm house for some time when they were growing up, and he remembers that "one of the differences between the two families was that they [John and Priscilla's] were much more emotional, much more effusive." In fact, John seemed to Bill in many ways the model father. His own father, Harris, was "a hardworking, stiff guy," but his uncle John was "fun-loving, playful, [and] would get down on the floor to play with the kids."

Though Priscilla wasn't much of a cook, at family dinners everyone would hold hands and say grace over the meal. It was generally simple fare—macaroni and cheese and bread pudding were two common dishes that Bill remembers—but the practice of holding hands made for "very emotional contact, in the Gardner household."

The openness and commitment to family had led John Sr. and Priscilla to take in Priscilla's aging mother when Buddy was in elementary school. It was an aspect of this spirit too that led them to open the front half of the house to Harris's family when Harris left the farm. Even though the farm was successful, it couldn't comfortably support Fred and Alice and both John's and Harris's families through the depression. Thus, given Millie's ambition for Harris and herself, if not mainly his own inclination, Harris went to Albany in 1937, to study at the New York State College for Teachers. A decade later when Harris went to law school in Buffalo and Millie worked there as a waitress, Bill and his younger sister Audrey Jean again lived in the front of the house.

Only nine months apart in age, Bill and Buddy thus grew up as close friends, sharing an interest in both intellectual and physical pursuits. For young boys, physical ability is the primary virtue, and both admired another cousin, Duncan, who was John Sr.'s sister Sarah and her husband Percy Hinckley's son. Some two years older than Bill and Buddy, Duncan was stronger and more muscular, and Bill and Buddy habitually competed for his attention. As they got older, though, Bill and Buddy moved in another direction. "We were much more picky people," remembers Bill, "into books instead of muscles and running around outside."

Buddy's interests were broad, but he was always attracted to the sentimental, perhaps a manifestation of the emotional temperament evident in the family. This was not a taste his brother shared. Priscilla remembered that both he and Gilbert had the same first-grade teacher, and both had to memorize the same short, sentimental poem. For Bud, she said, the poem about a toeless goldfish that a little boy watching wishes he could play with but can't," was such a *sad* little story . . . [while] Gilbert . . . thought it was hilariously funny."

Bill remembers that Buddy also loved *Winnie-the-Pooh*, which supports Priscilla's specific recollection of her son's telling her, "I remember when you read me that last chapter—where Winnie-the-Pooh and Christopher Robin are parting—I just cried all night."

Bill and Buddy would often retreat to an attic room upstairs and pore over the romantic novels they found there of Grace Livingston Hill, a popular author of the time. Her plots generally had a protagonist tempted into the terrible ways of the world, but turning in the end to Christian saintliness. Bill and Buddy spent hours reading in the attic room, moved profoundly by the stories.

Gardner himself also recalled beginning to write stories and poems around the age of five and making little books of the stories that he'd give as presents to relatives at Christmas. Particularly, he recalled being drawn to the ledger paper tablets his grandmother Alice used in her work as a lawyer. "There's something nice about a page with a red line down the middle," he said in one interview.

As John got a little older, Bill recalls, he wrote "thrillers"— novels, he called them—which he'd read a chapter at a time to Bill and Duncan and anyone else around to listen—not that the other boys paid rapt attention. Likewise, when Bill went through a phase of religious enthusiasm at age eleven or twelve, after church services and dinner with the family at Locust Level, Buddy would lead his cousins up to the orchard grandfather Fred had planted, and they'd play-act their own church services. Bill would lead the "service" and Buddy would give "sermons." Priscilla recalled, "He never went through a period of wanting to be a minister. He just naturally was one."

He didn't by any means shy from the physical side of farm life, however, and he clearly inherited the family's industriousness. He joined the Cub Scouts in elementary school, and though his scoutmaster many years later recalled that he always remained a little outside the social side of the group, he worked diligently at earning the badges. With single-minded focus, he worked through each project book page by page until it was completed and he achieved the badge that went with it. He continued through Boy Scouts, then as a teenager through Eagle Scouts. One of the leaders of his scout troop commented to his son, who knew Buddy in later years, that he'd never seen anyone pick up the scouting book and go through it so fast. Meantime, John Sr. became active in leading the Boy Scouts, and the family regularly opened their farm to the troop, hosting camp-outs, picnics, and other gatherings. The barbecue pit Bud built in the front yard for an Eagle Scout project remains even now as a souvenir.

With a large family whose members, most in the same geographic area, stayed in constant touch with each other, the Gardners fostered a warm and inclusive environment. Thus, Buddy's childhood seemed pretty well balanced between the intellectual and physical. But three months before his twelfth birthday, that childhood, and his life, changed permanently with Gilbert's death.

In the weeks afterward, relatives and neighbors came to help with the farmwork, and for a time John and Priscilla retreated from the public. John was used to reciting poetry at church, at schools, at grange meetings, the VA hospital, the orphanage—Priscilla often accompanying him with songs and always with applause—but for a month or so the performances stopped. Harris's family went back to Buffalo.

When summer came, Priscilla remembered, "[John] would go to all the carnivals and fairs and take little kids for rides. To him it was a kind of satisfaction he was giving to Gilbert. . . . As long as mothers and fathers would let him, he'd keep giving kids rides on bumper cars and merry-go-rounds, and that was a comfort to him."

Priscilla at one time tried to understand what had happened by saying that Gilbert's death was their sacrifice for the war— kids working on farms to replace men at war being what led to this tragedy. Her reaction to children was the opposite of John's: she didn't like being around them at all. "To me," she said of that time, "other children were an agony."

The only possible relief might be to somehow fill the space with another child of their own. No one could replace Gilbert, of course, but a new child might help soothe and distract from the pain. Because privacy was needed to make such a thing possible, Priscilla wrote to her family in St. Louis, and Buddy was put on the train to stay there with the Pattersons. He finished the school year in the class with his cousin Joan.

At the beginning of adolescence, the two cousins, who had been thrown together since they were babies and had come to feel real affection for each other, grew even closer. Joan's quick intelligence was a match for Buddy's, and neither was shy about speaking out to anyone who might hear. Only a month apart in age, their personalities complemented each other and reinforced their comradery amid the larger family.

Meantime, Priscilla and John Sr. conceived another son. The next year, 1946, when Priscilla was forty-three and John Sr. thirty-four, Jimmy was born. When Bud returned from St. Louis, life went on essentially as it had been, despite the unfillable gap left by Gilbert's death. The chores were constant. There was school and the activities surrounding it. There was Boy Scouts. There was time for other things high school boys did too. Though Buddy was slender and no great athlete, he was strong and fit, and in a class of only fifty-one there were plenty of opportunities. He played basketball his first high school year and in the spring joined the track team as a sprinter. In his sophomore year he took up pole-vaulting, and his determination made an impression.

"I remember one spring day going out to watch him pole-vault after school," a friend at that time recalls. "He had on a white T-shirt and blue gym shorts, and the black gym shoes that everyone used to wear. I can remember him running and leaping up over the bar. It was exceptionally graceful. And he was very competitive. Even as a kid I knew that John was the kind that if he'd decided to be a dancer, he'd have been a hell of a dancer."

As a bright, industrious student, Bud also represented something of a challenge for his teachers. Recalling those days in a later interview, he said, "I hated school for the most part. Boredom is my chief memory of high school and most of grade school."

Like many bright students, he was restless and found his way to mischief, some of which rose from a serious interest he developed in chemistry, which was taught by the principal, Warren Dayton. "He had a wonderful chemistry teacher in high school," Priscilla said much later, "who made him really crazy about it."

One morning, however, Bud's enthusiasm led him and three friends to concoct a manganese (the main ingredient in stink bombs) bomb, which they exploded in one of the chemistry lab sinks. Another time, they slipped a potion they had contrived into the boiler. This last was so successful in spreading a horrendous odor through the ventilating system that the whole school had to be dismissed.

Bud's role as co-perpetrator was revealed, and so he was punished. In fact, he said in an interview, Dayton got so angry at him at one point that he punched Gardner in the mouth. Another time, a friend of Gardner's remembers, Bud and two friends angered the principal so much that he put them up against a wall in front of the whole school. "You three are the brightest students I've ever had under my tutelage," the friend remembers Dayton saying. "You could be a force for leadership in the school, and instead you're a triumvirate of evil!"

The outburst sounds comical now, but certainly Dayton's frustration at truly bright students going awry was genuine. At the same time, though, Gardner remembered Dayton as one of his very best teachers, and the friend who told the story about his outburst is quick to say that the principal was also "a wonderful guy."

In Bud's case, the antiauthority temperament his waywardness evidenced became a permanent part of his character. Whether or not it was rooted in parental indulgence, or a rare intelligence that made him feel beyond common restraints, it seemed to grow more pronounced the older he got. As a former teacher herself, Priscilla realized something would have to be done about her bright, feisty son. Though Alexander Central School was closer to their farm, and the one for their district, Bud clearly wasn't getting enough stimulation there to keep him challenged, so after his junior year, Priscilla arranged to have him transfer to Batavia, where he finished at the larger high school.

During this time, both before and after the accident, Buddy also went regularly to the movies in Attica, a few miles south of Batavia. Some of the images and ideas from the movies stuck with him, ultimately finding their way into stories and novels he would write. He was fascinated by Mickey Mouse, Donald Duck, and all the exaggerated, surreal figures of Walt Disney's cartoons. In later years, he often mentioned those fairy-tale dramas and the characters who had embedded themselves in his childhood vision as sources for his own characters.

He found them so striking, in fact, that he had to see if he could create such powerful figures himself. In Mary Greco's ninth-grade art class at Alexander his odd, deft cartoon figures earned particular praise. Clearly he had a knack for this kind of drawing. And his teacher's praise didn't end in art class. She saw particular talent and encouraged him to send his cartoons to magazines. He followed her encouragement and sent one to *Seventeen* magazine. The cartoon was of an elephant—the common symbol of memory—with only minimal strokes composing the animal. Sitting on a low stool in a suggestively human pose, a foreleg was bent upward like an arm, touching its trunk. The forehead was lined with three creases, as if the champion of remembrance were lost in thought, with the caption below reading, "That face! . . . That face! Where *have* I seen that face?"

The magazine's editors liked it, and in the July 1947 issue, which came out just before his fifteenth birthday, Gardner saw his first publication. With such heady encouragement, he spread beyond paper. Drawing on the wall is a common enough childhood impulse, and most parents emphatically quash it. Bud, however, had earned extraordinary notice for his drawing with the *Seventeen* publication. Priscilla and John Sr., apparently charmed by his talent, and respecting the integrity of his personal domain, watched Buddy's cartoon figures spread. Certainly, whatever work might have been required to remove them was no great project for John, whose fixing and building was an every day occupation. It must have seemed a good idea to encourage Bud's interest. In the next three years, the cartoon drawings grew to cover every wall from floor to ceiling, making a truly eccentric spectacle for visitors.

In the year after Gilbert's accident, Priscilla also engaged Bud in an activity that came to be a part of him for the rest of his life. Its source may well have been in the singing and music of the Welsh culture that had surrounded her as she grew up. Bud himself had always liked singing church hymns for as long as anyone remembered, but now he was pushed to get serious.

It began with French horn classes at school. Then Priscilla decided to take him to the Eastman School of Music in Rochester, about an hour and a half away, where she enrolled him in lessons. Bud demonstrated a real talent, and beginning in October 1948, and continuing through his high school years, each Saturday he boarded a bus to Rochester for a French horn lesson with horn master Arcady Yegudkin.

In the story he wrote years later about Gilbert's accident, the young protagonist finds in the music he plays a way to cope with the guilt he suffers for the accidental death of his brother. Many details of the portrait of the French horn teacher, to whom he gives the same name as his own teacher, are verifiable. Born in

1884, Yegudkin "was a barrel-shaped, solidly muscular man, hard as a boulder for all his age. His hair and moustache were as black as coal except for touches of silver, especially where it grew, with majestic indifference to ordinary taste, from his cavernous nostrils and large, dusty-looking ears." The story goes on to describe his "formal black suits, a huge black overcoat and . . . [the] black fedora" he always wore; the big cigar he was always smoking and waving, and his "erect and imperious" manner, which earned him the name "the General." It was a title the staff picture of him seems to bear out, projecting a manner he encouraged.

In Russia, the records tell us, Yegudkin had been a horn player in the orchestra of the Imperial Mariinsky Theater of St. Petersburg and in the St. Petersburg Symphony Orchestra. However, "at the time of the purge of the Kerenskyites," Gardner's story notes, "the Bolsheviks had loaded Yegudkin and his wife, along with hundreds more, onto railroad flatcars, reportedly to carry them to Siberia. In a desolate place, machine guns opened fire on the people on the flatcars, then soldiers pushed the bodies into a ravine, and the train moved on." Yegudkin was one of the few who survived, "nursed back to health" by "local peasants, . . . and in time [he] escaped to Europe [where he] played horn with all the great orchestras and received such praise—so he claimed, spreading out his clippings—as no other master of French horn had received in all history."

Eastman's records have Yegudkin arriving in New York City in 1920, where he spent a year, then going to Detroit as first horn in the Detroit Symphony. A year later, he returned to play in the New York Symphony and settled finally in Rochester where he taught at Eastman. Whether or not the stories of Yegudkin's hardship were literal, they were an essential aspect of the impression he gave of a distinguished, even noble survivor. It was an image he conveyed powerfully, and Gardner recalled it vividly, tinged in his description with a hint of satire.

Though "the old man was too deaf to play in orchestras anymore," Gardner writes, " 'What's the difference?' [Yegudkin] said. 'Every symphony in America, they got Yegudkins. I have teach them all. Who teach you this? *The General!*' He would smile, chin lifted, triumphant, and salute the ceiling."

In his first year at Eastman, Bud was a B student, but from then on he earned all A's, including in theory classes he began taking his second year. During his junior year in high school, he played in the Batavia Civic Orchestra and, in his senior year, the school band. He also directed an orchestra quintet drawn from the band. Each year he made all-state as a musician in both voice and instrument (though in his class of only fifty-one, competition wasn't particularly intense). Still, the honor did mean a weekend in Buffalo or Albany—wherever the competition was held that year.

In his last year at Eastman, he competed for a scholarship for study at Eastman beyond high school. He had played with many different people by the time of the audition for the scholarship, but there was no question in his mind that he'd most like to have his favorite cousin accompany him. Joan had also become an especially accomplished musician, adept at playing the piano, and as they'd become teenagers their closeness continued more strongly than ever. This would be another chance for him to be with her.

The families arranged for her to come to Batavia to accompany

Bud at his scholarship audition in Rochester. Based on both the teacher's recommendation and student need, he was awarded the scholarship. By the time he graduated from high school, a future in music seemed a real possibility. For the rest of his life he played and retained serious interest in music and in the French horn.

Other interests, however, led him in different directions. Despite the scholarship offer, Bud wanted a wider field. Neither he nor the family wanted him to go too far from home, however. His father's younger brother Arthur had gone away to DePauw University in Greencastle, Indiana, some forty miles west of Indianapolis. And DePauw also had a significant music school, whose association with the liberal arts school DePauw featured —so Bud's interests in both music and liberal arts might both be served there. Seven hundred miles was a fair distance from Batavia, but it was reachable in a long day's drive. Also important, Buddy's academic achievement had earned him the Rector Scholarship, which would pay his tuition and most of his expenses, an opportunity conferred on only a few students each year.

Not least, for him, DePauw was halfway to St. Louis. Bud was crazy about Joan, and whenever they got together they joked about getting married. He had taken another girl he knew from the Batavia Civic Orchestra to the prom, but though he was very polite she had heard all about his attachment to Joan. There was no question in his mind about what was important.

His father, however, didn't at all like the idea of his going far away to DePauw. "You won't like those people at the university," John remembered his saying.

John Sr.'s hope was that his eldest son would stay in Batavia and take over the farm eventually. But in September 1951, Bud packed his bags and drove with his family west and south, across Ohio and into Indiana, to begin his college career in Greencastle. When he got there his parents settled him into his dorm room. A new phase had begun.

"We had gone inside and seen the hall," Priscilla remembered. "Then we were in the car ready to leave, and he came out to the car to say good-bye to us. And then — he just turned and ran as fast as he could go."

3

West of New York

"Care to have an interesting experience?" she'd said.

—Stillness

FOUNDED IN 1837, DePauw had some thirty buildings on a campus of sixty acres at the time Bud arrived. With just seventeen hundred students, it wasn't so overwhelming as to swallow a newcomer fresh from the farm. His uncle Arthur's having graduated from there and its Protestant origins and history would have made his parents feel comfortable. More important to Bud, though, was that one of his friends from home, John Berry—one of Mr. Dayton's "triumvirate of evil"—enrolled at the same time. And hardly least important, of course, Greencastle was halfway to St. Louis, where his cousin Joan lived.

By now, he was completely in love. Joan had grown strikingly attractive with her red hair, and her intelligence and talent matched his. She had also become an exceptional pianist, the music forming another major connection between them. She had traveled to Batavia and gone with him to Rochester to be his accompanist at his scholarship audition at Eastman.

Bud and Berry were housed in Florence Hall, a dorm with thirty or so students, half of them freshmen, with a housemother to oversee them. His roommate, Harold Petersen, was from a small town in Minnesota and shared some of the same rural background. Also like Bud, Petersen had come on scholarship and was interested in literature and writing. But the similarities ended there.

The year before Bud's arrival, the school had officially joined with the school of music, which had been founded in 1884. The university advertised the association between the music and liberal arts schools in its catalog, and the connection would have appealed to Bud as well as to his parents. Bud joined both the orchestra, directed by Herman Berg, another graduate of Eastman, and the marching band. And beginning his first semester, he took twice-weekly lessons in French horn, along with a music theory class. The orchestra, meantime, practiced Tuesday and Thursday afternoons in the chapel of the East College building, the oldest building on the campus, and a half-dozen times each year gave performances in student productions. The band performed at football games, of course, as well as at outdoor concerts at the student union and at some high schools around Indiana and neighboring states during a spring vacation tour Bud's first year. His music education and experience grew steadily.

At one point he took Petersen to the music school to teach him to sing, assuring him that regardless of his skepticism anyone could learn to do it. Petersen had no musical background or skill, however. Looking back, he says, "I think I have some responsibility for making him a writer. He was sure he could teach me to sing." After a few hours of trying to get Petersen to repeat notes Bud played and sang, however, they both gave up. Petersen just couldn't get his voice to do it. Bud's experiment as a music teacher was a flop.

Mr. Dayton's chemistry class had also been a powerful influence during Bud's last year in Batavia, and he had come to DePauw thinking he might major in chemistry. He quickly realized, however, that he wasn't destined to stand out in chemistry or in any of the sciences. In his first-year science class, he only made a C both semesters. The following year he took chemistry, for which he earned a B his first semester. None of the classes, though, were at all as engaging as Mr. Dayton's had been, and Bud began skipping them. A lab fee was collected from each student in the chemistry class, to be returned to those who didn't break anything. Bud complained at home, "I had to pay for breakage, and I wasn't there enough to break anything."

He also took elementary French the first year and only earned a C in that. His interest in literature, however, solidified. The one A he got his first semester was in freshman English, and Petersen says he learned quickly that John "had both the passion and genius for writing—which I did not." Nonetheless, Petersen is quick to say, "John never discouraged me from writing. In fact, when he read my short story for freshman English, he was generous with his praise. He smiled as he read it . . . and he said, 'This is the nuts.' I got a B on the story, but John's enjoyment of it was more important to me than the grade. I do suspect [his reaction] was [from] enjoyment and not literary merit."

In what would be a lifelong practice, Gardner's interest in writing also led him to type late into the nights, composing a novel. He asked Petersen if it bothered him, and Petersen assured him it didn't, though he says now that the staccato beat of the machine was impossible to shut out. In the spring Gardner finished it, but when he looked it over he decided it was no good and threw it out. Petersen, however, fished it out of the wastebasket and read part of it, then gave it back to him about two weeks later. "All I can remember is that it had dragons and princesses and magic spells," Petersen says.

Even at an age when sneering at magic seems an almost universal characteristic, the same enchantment that had Gardner fix on Disney's cartoon characters had asserted itself. The novel itself may have been far from memorable, but to complete such an extensive project was still an impressive accomplishment.

In Bud's sophomore year, he only earned a B in his Victorian literature class. The professor, Raymond Pence, was "something of an icon" at DePauw, says Petersen, "thought to be a great teacher of writing, particularly fiction." Gardner, however, "couldn't stand [him]. . . . He thought him an arrogant fool. But this did not dissuade John from writing. Rather, he took it as a lesson in how not to teach."

That year, he earned A's in all the other English classes he took. One was a two-semester sequence on the English novel, in which he studied some of the classics, including Melville, whose novels became a lifelong passion, and Dickens, likewise. He also took two creative writing courses — one in verse and one in fiction, along with a course on the problems of writing.

Just as important, if not more so, however, would have been

that February's issue of the *Boulder*, the student literary magazine. Bud was one of nine on the editorial staff, along with three editors, of the twenty-page collection. In the February issue, on the first page, appeared "Freshman," which he had written for his freshman English class. About five hundred words, it is less a story than a simple fable in which first a rich man, then a poor man, commit suicide, having lived happy lives as a result of doing whatever they wanted. The only apparent difference between them is their wealth, and at their deaths the rich man is praised while the poor man is dismissed as a "simpleton." The one-dimensional figures that play out the simplistic student theme aren't really characters that extend themselves beyond the one idea, and the writing isn't especially noteworthy, though it is smoother than what freshmen are usually able to achieve and it does occasionally show a hint of real flair. At best, the obvious symbolic tenor might evoke a sort of tongue-in-cheek chuckle, as it does with Gardner's description of the rich man as "gracious and kindly, and endowed with the rare gift of changing sense into dollars. There were of course people who thought him deranged but he only pitied them for their sober lives."

Despite the apparent self-assurance he carried even then, and the busyness with his studies and music, he suffered acutely from homesickness. "I remember distinctly," Priscilla said, "a letter from Bud meant he was sad. And so in a way I was sorry to have the letters come because they meant he was lonesome. Whether he said it or not, we knew that."

During his second year, he again lived with Petersen, this time in Locust Manor, another dorm, and during the first semester, for the only time in his life, he kept a journal. In bold block letters on the cover he titled it "Lies! Lies! Lies!" and wrote below as an epigraph, "If it's worth telling, it's worth stretching." In its opening pages he ruminates about the significance of lies, saying they are essential to spice the monotony of the ordinary and may tell a different kind of valuable truth. But he vows to be "sincere" in the journal, to not misrepresent character, and be "true to my mood" even though details may not always to be accurate. A few days later, however, he decides that the facts are at least as interesting as anything he might make up. "I see that I was wrong in thinking that a good story is better when stretched," he writes, thus adding foundation to the fiction he would come to write himself.

The early entries retrace some of the texture of his life as a sophomore student, giving us a familiar picture of an aspiring intellectual in a boys' dormitory. There are stories of short-sheeting beds and unscrewing doorknobs, all related with the labored archness of tone and attitude common to such writing. In Bud's journal, though, the prose imitates the mock heroic tone of the eighteenth-century novels of Fielding or Richardson. His ability to copy that tone so effectively shows an understanding and command well beyond the usual:

> I was just serenely in bed when the door sneaked open. In crept two black shadows. I could not see, in the darkness, who lived in the black hulks, but I had no fear for there are none but sweet, gentle souls in Locust Manor.
>
> For a long time the shadows crouched at the foot of the bed next to mine—whispering and giggling. Then they became silent. I almost thought them worried. But I made no

move, for I was dog-tired and needed my sleep. At length, one of the shadows moved foreward and patted the bed next to me. Some hurried whispers followed. Then the shadows examined the bed where I slept. I saw the faces then. The Goose and another. They were pained faces. Wretched.

More to the point, however, the journal entries demonstrate the beginnings of ideas he would develop and mature in his writing and teaching. At one point he begins by asserting that he can describe the same thing—in this case a head cold from which he is suffering—in several different ways and then goes on to do so:

> I can say—"26 Sept. 52—Have a hell of a cold," and go to bed. Or, "my red nose houses tonight a slithering half-formed serpent, whose tail whacks at the stalactites in my mind's chamber, while his head swells, as from his own foul venom, till my nostrils (mostly the right one—the left one only now and then) can scarcely contain him." Or, "Curse this ugly world. I have a cold. What joy is there in life? and what reward? A fie and a pox on this unguided, ungodded universe." Or, "I got a runny nose. Now, I know it's none of my affair; my nose is as odd as I am and ought to know its business by this time; but we're in Greencastle instead of here in St. Louis. Better still, take a tip from this year's presidential candidates and don't run at all till I ask you."

A few pages later, he recounts a formal tea at which he was a guest, with the careful detail of scene and quotation of the novelist he would become.

He also writes of loving Fielding's *Tom Jones,* whose digressions he finds engaging and important, despite teachers' and noted critics' reservations that he says he has encountered. And he vows to utilize those techniques in his own writing. Then he rages against *Moll Flanders,* calling it "328 pages of unparalleled, incomparable, unrivaled, unbelievable, uninhibited rot." Developing his aesthetic, he goes on:

> Blame the silly representation of character upon the times, and take what's left. Blame the wandering, bouncing, impossible plot on Defoe's own full life, and take what's left. Blame the soaked handkerchiefs and red eyes on the "demand of the market" for sentimentalism, and take what's left. Blame the style on the era; philosophy in the eighteenth century; blame the constant hypocritical apology for sin on the censors, and then, take what's left in the book and cherish it—for it is called a great book. But what's left?"

To demonstrate, he copies a passage from the novel that he's seen praised and goes on to burlesque the style in a paragraph of his own. "In appraising—praising—the book, wise men site this passage," he writes:

> As soon as she was gone and I had shut the door, I threw off my hood and bursting out into tears, "My dear," says I, "do you not know me?" He turned pale and stood speechless, like one thunderstruck, and not able to conquer the surprise, said no more but this, "Let me sit down"; and sitting down by the table, and leaning his head on his hand, fixed

his eyes on he ground as one stupid. I cried so vehemently, on the other hand, that it was a good while ere I could speak any more; but after I had given some vent to my passion by tears, I repeated the same words, "My dear, do you not know me?" At which he answered, Yes, and said no more for a good while.

After castigating Defoe's plot, on the next page he parodies the passage:

(Remember, Moll is 65, her spouse is 60—but well preserved. Moll is a withered wreck. (Note good use of sentimentalism!).

"My dear," croaks I, "do you not know me?" He turned pale and started retching, like one thunderstruck in the belly, and not able to conquer his odorous vomiting, said no more but this, "Let me sit down!" and sitting down by a table, he laid his elbow upon his plate of beans and potatoes, and hanging his chin off his hand, fixed his eyes on his nose. As one stupid. I cried so vehemently on the other hand, that it was a good while ere I could speak anymore; but after I had given some vent to my amorous passion (for 65 is not as old as you think) I stopped crying and let him go, saying, "My dear, do you not know me?" At which he puked some more and answered, "Glurgle," and said no more for a good while.

At the end he comments on his work: "Oh, mother! Don't I write pretty prose!?"

The flexibility and grace of the style are worth noting. Thomas

Gavin, who edited the journal, points out that the copying would have informed the aspiring writer in ways of which he may not have been conscious, helping to embed Defoe's distinctive sentence rhythms for revision and use later.

Gavin further argues that Gardner's engagement with Fielding is evident in both *Grendel* and *The Sunlight Dialogues*. The former's utilization of epic structure, he suggests, echoes the mock epic tone and organization of *Tom Jones*. And the dialogues between the Sunlight Man and Chief Clumly in the latter, which address larger philosophical ideas and interrupt the novel's story, are reminiscent of Fielding's narrative intrusions.

The journal also rants against Thackeray for his criticism of Swift, whom Gardner loves. He begins outlining *Gulliver's Travels* in detail and declares that he should himself write an extensive history of English satire in the tradition of *A Modest Proposal*. Then he goes on to assert his own need to "read and read and read," which in his later teaching he will regularly insist is essential for all writers.

There are as well cartoons and drawings sprinkled throughout, echoing his work as a cartoonist; a poem by Robert Frost, whom he says he admires; and references to auditions for this year's Monon, the annual musical written and staged by students, instigated more than twenty years before.

Each year's script was selected in open competition, and with his background Gardner was a logical competitor. The music for the play he submitted that fall of 1952, *The Serpent and the Dove*, was written by another friend, but despite having worked on it "all year," he wrote in the journal, the play didn't win, and Gardner's disappointment is clear. "You'd be mad too," he wrote.

"Ya see, the guy who won, won last year. A good writer. But his book was only half finished, and his music just started. What music he had was so bad that the young judges got Beth, my partner, to re-write it for him."

The following year he entered again, with a story and song lyrics for a musical he called *The Caucus Race*. The title came from Lewis Carroll, the music composed this time by another friend who was a piano player and who had composed and orchestrated a major fraternity show. This time, Gardner's show won. Set in the Adirondack Mountains of upstate New York, familiar territory not far from Batavia, the play centered on a rural family confronted by a milk strike, problems of modernization, a love triangle, and smuggling. Altogether that made too many threads to compose a successful whole, a writer in the school paper said in harsh criticism. Still, because eighty cents for a ticket wasn't very expensive, even at 1953 prices, and there weren't a lot of competing activities in Greencastle, the Friday and Saturday run in February 1954 filled the auditorium.

But Gardner didn't see it. By that second year, though he was interested in his English classes and wrote a winning script for the Monon, he was skipping other classes that didn't hold his attention, which certainly contributed to lower grades in his science classes and probably in French as well. At least one reason for his lack of engagement was his relationship with Joan. He had brought his motorcycle from Batavia that year, and as one of his journal entries suggests, he had ridden all the way to St. Louis to see her on some weekends. On others, she had come to Greencastle. Bud's roommates and good friends well knew of his devotion and were not surprised when the two decided that this commuting wouldn't do. In the summer of 1953, at the end of their sophomore year, Bud and Joan decided they would marry.

"My father went into a blistering rage," Gardner said when he talked about it twenty-five years later. "He refused point-blank to come to the wedding. Mom and Aunt Lucy had hard work to turn him around."

Not only were they cousins, Bud and Joan were not yet twenty. Moreover (though this wouldn't have been a source of concern for his father), they had some real differences in temperament. In *Stillness*, the novella from which the story with that name that Gardner wrote in 1979 is fashioned, he describes the relationship. Though the story is fiction (and infuriated Joan), like most of his work it is based on biographical facts, which others' testimony confirms. Thus, as his DePauw journal promises to be "sincere" —by which he means true to the characters and texture if not every detail—*Stillness* likewise seems to be essentially accurate in its overview.

"She was brilliant and lively, wonderfully funny, she kept things hopping" is the mother's view of the Joan character. Though the characterization is of his mother's attitude, and the characters are necessarily at some remove from the people on whom they are patterned, Joan's wit and liveliness were re-marked on by many. However, she also had a streak of what some called genuine meanness, readily using her wit to make fun of people in clever, biting ways that often enough caused slightly guilty laughs in those who heard and certainly made some uncomfortable. Her father was also more successful fi-nancially than John Sr., so she had grown up in more prosper-ous circumstances and was also more interested in the material benefits of success—pretty clothes and the luxuries that money brought.

Bud, on the other hand, saw himself (as he believed most others did) as darker and more dour in temperament. He thought material concerns superficial, and he affected a somewhat disheveled appearance wherever he went. He owned only one suit, which he rarely wore, and he would come to visit Joan in St. Louis without clean clothes, bringing only a toothbrush, his French horn, and a book or two.

Mainly, however, writes novelist Joyce Carol Oates, echoing others who knew them, "Joan was John's equal in every way, including audacity. She had a fey, funny, wildly inventive manner. John, more brooding on the surface, sucking at his pipe, was not only husband/lover, but a kind of soul-mate; there was something fairytale-like about them, as if . . . their lives were fated to entwine, regardless of consequences."

Thus, Bud transferred to Washington University in St. Louis for his last two years, and on June 6, 1953, he and Joan were married. Joan's father and brother-in-law remodeled the upstairs of her parents' house in Florissant, a suburb of St. Louis to make a private apartment for the newlyweds. Bud built a study in the garage for himself—"so small my elbows touched each wall," he wrote, though Joan says it was hardly that small—and got a part-time job at a bank to help bring in some money while he went to school. He worked after classes first as a bank teller, then as a check printer. Joan continued working at the ballet school where she had been employed since high school, but then she too enrolled at Washington University, working toward a degree in music education with a minor in English.

On the whole, their lives together seemed happy, but both had volatile tempers and had been in various ways indulged by their parents. Their respective intellectual acuteness and temperamental differences contributed to flare-ups from their earliest years. Still, they also made up just as passionately, and the energy they brought together was a magnet for those around them.

For his part, John was serious about his music, and during his senior year at Washington he was hired to play French horn for the St. Louis Philharmonic Orchestra. It quickly became too much, however, with his class work and the writing he wanted to do, and after a few weeks he resigned. In a letter he wrote years later, he explained the decision this way: "One night in Milwaukee—a night I will never forget—when we were all standing in the rain waiting for the St. Louis chartered bus, the string players all trying to keep their cigarettes lit in the rain. . . . I realized suddenly, that rainy night, that everything I'd been taught to play I would never get to play; I would just play notes, and it was taking time from my writing (which I took less seriously)."

We can't know if his decision was that dramatically clear and focused—Joan says such circumstances could not have been. He was, after all, a fiction writer, never above elaboration for the sake of a good story, but nonetheless he did quit the symphony and thus his foray into the world of professional musicianship, devoting himself instead to his English studies at Washington. And he was an exceptional student.

From his first semester, he attracted the attention of Jarvis Thurston, the most accomplished teacher of creative writing at Washington and the faculty adviser to the student literary magazine *Reflections*. Thurston had been a student of Paul Engle's, the founder and director of the graduate writing workshop at the University of Iowa who had led it to national prominence. Thurston had also been a classmate of Flannery O'Connor's, another of Engle's workshop students.

Thurston met poet Mona Van Duyn in Iowa, and the two became a couple. After earning their degrees, they got jobs teaching at the University of Louisville and founded the literary magazine *Perspective,* which became a journal of major importance for new writers. It published the first poem ever of W. S. Merwin and the second story of William Gass.

Meanwhile, Gardner shone in both the writing and literature classes he took with Thurston, and in his senior year he became a coeditor of *Reflections.* "He made the class easier for me," Thurston recalls of a creative writing class, "because he functioned as a kind of teacher, and so cut down the amount of work I had to do in criticizing students. John's critical abilities were extraordinary at that time. And he was gentle to these students."

In a modern poetry class as well, Gardner impressed Thurston with his ability. Though he'd only earned a C in elementary French at DePauw and B's at Washington, he'd learned enough to make good use of his skills in translation.

Recalls Thurston, "I had in the margins of Eliot's [French] poems translations which I'd done for teaching purposes. I don't know French very well—and John borrowed my book once, either because he didn't have the copy or he wanted to read more—and he returned the book with complete translations of the French poems. I recognized immediately that they were very good."

It was in Thurston's creative writing class during senior year that Gardner wrote a short story that he published in the 1955 issue of *Reflections*. Set in a small town in western New York, it centers on a lonely, enormously fat man who operates a highway diner. The man's one employee is a young woman in love with a boy with whom she gets pregnant. The boy abandons her, however, leaving the narrator contriving to somehow help her. He gave the story the name of the nearby mountain the narrator imagines driving away to—"Nickel Mountain."

It would be nearly twenty years and countless revisions before the novel *Nickel Mountain* would be published. By then, Losh Soames, the unhappy, fat narrator of the original would be Henry Soames, and the novel would be much more complex. Even so, many essentials, including even particular lines and phrases, remain from that first, undergraduate version. The fat Soames, for instance, remains the central figure, his size and manner inspired partly by Gardner's preoccupation with Disney cartoon characters. That is, the enormous fatness makes him a sort of caricature—like a cartoon character—with features exaggerated almost beyond belief, though always in a carefully drawn, realistic context. Such cartoon caricatures thus became a recurrent element, as Gardner pointed out in later interviews, in several of his novels.

As with many writers and celebrities, Gardner's later recountings of origins and significance of his work must be viewed with a hint of skepticism. However, he said in at least one interview that it was when he began working on *Nickel Mountain* that he first considered himself a "serious novelist." Indeed, he worked on the novel steadily in coming years. In a later description of that time, he wrote about rushing through his work at the bank and slipping into a back room where he wrote his fiction, then doing more at home when his class work let him. He gave the stories to "Nellie Patterson [Joan's mother, who] lovingly and laboriously typed [them and sent them off] . . . mostly to *The Saturday Evening Post,* which was not amused."

In his two years at Washington, Gardner went to readings by poets William Carlos Williams, Robinson Jeffers, Randall Jarrell, and Wallace Stevens, and in a class with critic Albert Levy he first read Proust, whose famously detailed portrait of his past seems to have helped inform Gardner's own developing aesthetic. In a letter he wrote to his son, Joel, years later, the Proustian influence is apparent: "I think art imitates the ways of God, a novel that recaptures the past, making long lost people and places seem alive again, making time seem as illusory as we know it is when we think how events from fifteen years ago seem to have happened only yesterday, as only ultimately the whole history of the planet happened only yesterday. A novel which makes all time what it is in our dreams, simultaneous, imitates the real nature of existence."

In Thurston's literature class, Gardner also formed what became a lifelong friendship with Burton Weber, who went on to be his coeditor of *Reflections* and who at graduation was awarded a Woodrow Wilson fellowship to the University of Toronto. Some fifteen years later, when Gardner was editing a scholarly series for Southern Illinois University Press, he published two of Weber's books.

Gardner as well took a year of Greek philosophy and a semester of contemporary philosophy, classes that fed what became another lifelong interest. He never went on to study or write philosophy formally, but ideas, from Wittgenstein and Sartre particularly, are clearly present in novels and stories he came to write.

He focused increasingly on his literature and writing courses, but the problem of making a living was a lurking concern. Given his focus, it was a problem largely beside the point for him, but nonetheless, and no doubt with his in laws' encouragement, he took a two-year sequence of classes, including a summer school class, to prepare for certification as a secondary-school teacher. He might have been encouraged by Joan as well, as she went on to become certified as a high school music teacher and got a job teaching nearby. Not surprisingly, though, he only made B's in his education classes, despite their reputation as being less rigorous than standard liberal arts classes. In the end, he never became a student teacher, which would have finished the preparation. He simply had no interest in being a high school teacher.

His academic achievement did, however, lead him to graduate in June 1955 with Phi Beta Kappa honors for superior scholarship. Like his friend Burton Weber, he was awarded a Woodrow Wilson fellowship. But Gardner wasn't interested in a career as a scholar either.

Thurston had told him about his experiences at the Iowa Writers' Workshop and encouraged him to go. Besides whatever benefits might accrue by meeting like-minded, aspiring writers, Iowa was also one of the only places where a student could earn a Ph.D. by writing a novel as a dissertation. The idea appealed to Gardner and he applied. When he was accepted, he used his fellowship to move with Joan to Iowa City and enter the graduate school of the University of Iowa.

In fall 1955, Joan and John, as he was called by friends there, found a house in Iowa City. Joan got a job teaching music to high school students, and John enrolled in graduate school.

The Iowa Writers' Workshop, the first such program in the United States, had begun to be recognized among writers and literary aficionados for the talented teachers and students that its director, Paul Engle, had drawn after World War II. Besides O'Connor, in the years just before Gardner arrived, poets Robert Lowell, John Berryman, W. D. Snodgrass, Robert Bly, Robert Dana, and Donald Justice had all been enrolled there. Novelist R. V. Cassill was the primary teacher of fiction, but, among others, novelists Philip Roth, Richard Stern, George P. Elliott, Vance Bourjaily, and William Cotter Murray also spent time there as students and teachers.

When Gardner arrived, poets Philip Levine, William Dickey, and Constance Urdang were among the students at the workshop, and despite his primary interest in fiction, Gardner formed closer friendships with the poets—especially Dickey and Urdang (whom Joan particularly liked), then with Don Finkel, who met Urdang a year later and ultimately married her. Though John came to know them well, he never enrolled in the graduate workshop toward a degree, and he was always quick to deny association with the program, saying he had attended only one workshop class for two or three weeks, then left for good. All three years he was there, however, he *was* enrolled in workshop classes and attended often enough, apparently, to receive credit with A grades.

His denial of academic help is a common enough theme among American writers who like to paint themselves as self-invented, sui generis talents—an aspect of the artist myth that is often enough at the heart of the attraction to writing in the first place. The idea of self-invention became an integral element of the image Gardner sought to foster, but his attitude is also evidence of his ambition to be more than a novelist—even a well-published, successful one. The academic training he diligently pursued is testimony to this.

Instead of the workshop, he enrolled in the graduate school, on track for a Ph.D. During his first semester, he took Italian and Old English, a class on the Romantic period and a seminar on Renaissance literature, and workshops in both fiction and poetry. It was a heavy load. "There was the sense," says fellow student Dick Day, "that he worked really hard and didn't get enough sleep." Day remembers him as "a skinny guy with lots of nervous energy. He was a chain smoker, and he looked like he survived on coffee and cigarettes."

In later interviews, Gardner himself admitted, "I was a drudge." Smoking up to five packs of cigarettes a day, he ate little, getting as thin as he'd ever been, surviving, according to his account, on coffee with heaps of sugar as the only food.

He took Old English that first semester from John McGalliard, and the experience permanently shaped his literary direction. McGalliard, one of the most popular teachers of his time, had come to Iowa right after World War II when he'd been in charge of carrier pigeons. Since he'd been trained as a linguist, it must have seemed to the army the most appropriate assignment. At Iowa, however, he taught Anglo-Saxon and medieval literature, and for a time shared a desk with Thurston, who had been a research assistant at the time McGalliard first came.

After his class in Old English, Gardner took McGalliard's *Beowulf* class the next semester. As exceptional a student as he could be, in these classes Gardner only earned B's. Still, many times in later years he said the McGalliard and Thurston were the two best teachers he ever had, and McGalliard remembered Gardner as one of the very best students he had run across in his long career. "He clearly belongs in the highest two percent of grad students as classified by capacity," he wrote in a recommendation letter. "His mind is alert, quick, efficient, and endowed with notable originality."

In his second year, apparently stirred by the interest McGalliard had inspired in medieval literature and language, Gardner studied Chaucer's *Canterbury Tales*. He only earned a C in that course, but the experience fed an enthusiasm that remained at the center of his career as both teacher and novelist.

The writing workshop classes were held in old corrugated sheet-metal army barracks on the bank of the Iowa River, while the English classes went on in a traditional building on the hill above. If nothing else, this emphasized the separation between the two—which was fine with the writers. Much different sorts than the usual graduate students, the writing students had come with various degrees of accomplishment and from vastly different backgrounds, both culturally and geographically. The only thing uniting most was the interest in writing, and Engle had managed to engineer almost complete autonomy for the program.

There wasn't too much mixing between the fiction writers and the poets, though they did have a ritual of weekly softball games and would get together at the popular Kenney's bar and at other occasional events. There was likewise little mixing between workshop and other graduate students, and Gardner was no exception. If anything, his separateness was even more absolute.

Says novelist William Murray, another student at the time, "He was really a loner." Murray was in a romantic literature class with Gardner, taught by Jeffrey Hartman, who went on to teach at Yale and to a substantial career as a critic. In Hartman's class, Murray goes on, Gardner "would sit right by the door, and the minute Hartman would finish his lecture, he just took off. We had no conversation. He never stayed around after class, as students usually do to talk with each other."

Still, Gardner and Joan regularly hosted parties, and at one they gave the second fall they met poet Donald Finkel, who had given up graduate work at the University of Illinois, where he'd also been an editor of the influential literary magazine *Accent*. John had recognized his name immediately, telling him when they met at that first party that Thurston had taught one of Finkel's poems in his poetry class at Washington.

Finkel distinctly remembers the first meeting with Gardner: "He immediately struck me as very intelligent, very vibrant, full of ideas and responses to anything about literature." At the same time, Finkel says, "What you noticed most . . . was an intensity about him. And an intelligence. I took a backseat to listen to conversations he simply took over. He had a lot to say. And he was so damn sure of himself and his own belief in things." From the beginning, Finkel goes on, "He had no patience for small talk. His only conversation was about literature and art. He was incredibly knowledgeable. And he had judgments about everything. . . . He impressed with brilliance but also with arrogance."

It is the kind of comment made by many who knew Gardner through the years. That arrogance translated as well into an impatience with, if not disdain for, authority, evidenced in his time at Iowa. Workshop students also served as teaching assistants for English Department courses, leading discussion sections after viewing the professor's weekly lecture on television. Though Gardner wasn't an official workshop student, he managed to get the TA job anyway. In one class, he simply turned off the television, saying the lecture was pointless and inaccurate. When the professor found out about it, he called in Gardner and reprimanded him severely.

"It was the first of many times," Finkel says, remembering the incident, that Gardner "clashed with the upper registers. I sympathized with him, but it was just an introductory class, and he was just a teaching assistant."

Later, Gardner says in *Stillness,* he was assigned to teach a sophomore-level poetry class. For that, he discarded the course plan TAs were instructed to follow and made up his own. When the news got to those in charge, the class was taken away from him.

In their second year in Iowa, John and Joan bought a house toward the end of town where R. V. Cassill had built. Their owning such a house was another of the things that made the Gardners stand out. Poet Donald Justice, a former workshop student who was one of the workshop teachers at the time, remembers Gardner as "young, eager, ambitious—a presence. People expected big things from him. And he was very well liked. Something that set him apart was that he seemed to be farther along than most of the students. He had a house and a wife, for one thing. There were other grad students who were married and had the beginnings of a family, but I can't think of another who had a house."

At one point, Gardner decided he and Joan needed more space and so decided he would add a room to the house. He found a master carpenter to head up the work and recruited several student friends to help.

Joan wasn't content to be an ordinary high school teacher either. Their second summer there, she single-handedly organized a tour in the area for her high school band and took them around to performances she arranged. Her friend Connie Urdang remarked later that the feat was nothing less than fantastic. All the while, she was composing music for her students too.

However, the role she wound up assuming in their marriage contributed to problems. On the one hand, her teaching earned most of the money, and in a time when women were not generally wage earners the fact nagged at John, as he tells us in *Stillness*. Meantime, suggestions from her that he might tend better to elements of grooming, and to traditional male responsibilities of car and home maintenance and money management, would spark fights.

John saw himself as the artist who must succeed by his writing and who was beyond the mundane occupations of domestic life. His novella speaks of the gloom that often beset him, exacerbated to some extent by his position relative to Joan, as he skipped classes to write his fiction and regularly worked on it deep into the night. Though Joan too had artistic ambition, it was clearly subordinated to his, and his attitude, and that division of responsibility, became more and more an issue over time.

In the workshop classes, short-story writers and poets met regularly, but those writing novels were left mainly to themselves, only periodically meeting the writers they were working with. Thus, after his first year, Gardner never went to writing classes. He'd simply turn in chapters of his novel for comment as he finished them and go on writing. Teachers' comments were minimal, if any, and in the end he was simply given A's.

In later interviews he was fond of explaining that his style was much different from what was being done and encouraged at Iowa, and depending on the meaning of "much different" this may have been true. Regardless, if he wasn't entirely isolated, he did work largely alone, as he related in a 1971 interview:

> I didn't learn anything from the faculty, but all the best young writers in the country were there and we taught each other. . . . I was writing something that was different from what other people in the workshop were writing. . . . And so I sort of wrote privately and took medieval courses.
>
> . . . And that was very nice, I didn't want any comments because some writers really want to learn how to write correctly. What that really means is that they write exactly like everybody else.

Novelist Marguerite Young was one who did make an impression on him. Appearing in a long cape, Young attracted a coterie drawn to her apparent exoticism. She had come from the Left Bank in Paris, long known as a center for artists and writers. Murray, like others he remembers, was completely taken with her. "She was so 'Left Bank,'" he says. "I simply fell 'head over heels.'"

Her work, itself "embellished and fanciful" (as one of her students, novelist Curtis Harnack, describes it), was a far cry from the realism Gardner himself went on to promote. In a 1967 assessment in the *Southern Review* of *Miss McIntosh, My Darling,* the long novel she had spent years constructing, Gardner likewise commented on her "highly conscious, highly artificial style," which leads to a novel that "lacks the emotive power of compression." Still, perhaps as much testimony to his own generosity and feelings for Young as to anything else, he ultimately judged her difficult, elaborate work noteworthy and distinguished: "[H]er craftsmanship, even genius, is impressive."

More to the point for her students, including Gardner, was her presence itself. She was one of the first serious writers with whom he connected, and as is the case with many writer-teachers one of Young's primary gifts seems to have been the writerly validation she gave to her students, which fueled their work.

At the end of his second year, Gardner completed his master's-degree thesis, which was a collection of four short stories. He sent them out to the *Saturday Review* and some other well-known magazines, but none were accepted for publication. Of these, he only kept "Nickel Mountain," which he continued reworking into the novel by that name, published many years later.

In his third year, in addition to a *Canterbury Tales* class he took courses on Milton, British literature and poetry, and American drama. He also worked as a teaching assistant, reading and grading papers for Clark Griffith, another of the professors who served on his Ph.D. dissertation committee. Griffith also remembers Gardner vividly as a brilliant and energetic student, who kept to himself.

Dick Day, also a doctoral candidate, was managing editor of the *Western Review,* the literary journal there, and remembers going to the editorial office in the Quonset hut next to the workshop classes one day in Gardner's last year. He found the door locked, and Gardner "sitting, looking disconsolate, on the cement pad outside the door." Day asked what he was working on, and Gardner told him three novels. Day remembers being a little startled at the ambition. Writing students are often given to exaggeration, but Gardner was doing just as he said: *Nickel Mountain* was no longer just a short story; he'd begun working on "Squirrels" (a project he'd ultimately abandon); and, most important, he was engaged with "The Old Men," which would be his dissertation.

Set in his home country of upstate New York, "The Old Men" was 678 typed pages, far longer than most dissertations. In that way it prefigures his tendency in later novels to go on at length. More important, the novel introduced themes and elements he would develop in his mature work. As in *Nickel Mountain,* its characters are the rooted, rural inhabitants of upstate New York. Similarly foreshadowing many later works, the novel's world is haunted by an actual ghost, whose presence in this case serves as a reference point, indirectly overseeing characters and action.

The ghost in "The Old Men" is that of Lawrence Leigh, the nineteenth-century preacher who revived the town when it was failing. Says Dr. Utt, a professor character in the novel: "These young people, and the baked old men you see rocking on their porches, *believe* in Leigh's ghost. The thing's a force, a bullwhip for evil in a world where none of us knows for sure what's evil and what's not. . . . I've seen strapping eighteen-year-olds run like sheep till they fell down sobbing, beating the shale, because they'd seen Leigh's face."

More significant, however, is the overall theme, in which the central characters struggle to find a place that will sustain them amid the imminent collapse of traditional values. Finding such a place entails faith—in something—and the search for it is what drives the characters. It is a problem that in different ways came to be the dominant preoccupation of all Gardner's novels, where characters are engaged against looming chaos.

The old men of the title stand largely as observers and commentators in the conflict played out between the sexually charged teenager, Ginger, who embodies the threat to tradition, and the men drawn to her. First is her widower father, unsettled by her physical changes, which "made him feel unclean [though] he knew they were part of the tribulation of parenthood, mortality. Nevertheless, they meant that his girl was a full-blown woman now, or wanted to be. Living in a college town, beset by God knew what vile temptations, she was lucky to have kept her innocence at sixteen."

Ultimately, he dies of heart failure in a fit over her behavior, whereupon she makes loves with her boyfriend in the bedroom above the body. It sounds almost like a joke; and though the conflict between father and maturing daughter is standard, her character gives it resonance as she becomes a centerpiece about which the question of how to live, and what values to embrace, is played out. The question, as will be the case in most of Gardner's novels, is whether to affirm present life and values or to choose another, undetermined, potentially anarchic direction.

As that boyfriend is soon replaced, and Ginger negotiates

among two other men whose interest she draws, she is a force that damages everyone she touches. Driven by guilt at the pain she precipitates, by the end of the novel she is a sort of lost and wandering princess, akin to a character in the ancient tales Gardner loved: "Like the princess in the tale, she'd gone from the shepherd hut out into the forest. Had wandered from place to place—had gone to wolves and bears and to Rosen, the mad prince, her brother, and to Dr. Utt, myopic old priest who saw no visions but believed in them as surely as in food and good conversation, and each place she went she was taken in, blindly, on faith, as Utt took in the stories of Leigh."

The conflicts between order and chaos, between the old and new, between affirmation and denial, at the center of all Gardner's works, are clearly present in the dissertation-novel he wrote at age twenty-five. Not surprisingly, his later assessment of "The Old Men," which remained unpublished, was harsh. In a 1979 interview, at the height of national prominence, he called it "a bad book . . . full of flaws and weak writing." It may be true that it is more distinguished for its ambition than for its accomplishment, which is far from the stylistic rigor he went on to achieve. But it's hardly "full" of "weak writing."

The novel does have more characters and situations than are finally managed successfully, and some passages are weighted with what might be called student verbiage, with overly dramatic language and a cliché or two, as exemplified by a speech of Ginger's toward the end of the novel: "You watch people because it's people that are important, that bring you to life, and you do things, and what you do is all confused with mountains and trees and waterfalls and animals and people you've known before, and whether what you did was sane you only find out afterward, if you find out at all. You have to keep watching, both people and things, because to do something good you have to be pushed — but to see bad things, too, and good and bad things are all mixed together."

Perhaps the speech doesn't seem all that excessive from the young, not especially educated character. In any event, neither Griffith nor Gardner's other Iowa readers had much to criticize as Gardner turned in chapters. "The gothic elements of the novel were sometimes overwrought," Griffith remembers, "but I thought it was damn good for a grad student."

In fact, sentence by sentence much of it is strikingly well written. Certainly, as Griffith noted, it is far better than most student writing.

Ralph Freedman, the director of the dissertation, whom Gardner acknowledges for his "help and encouragement," remembers less about the novel than about Gardner's strong personality "as he was clarifying his identity as a writer." Freedman encouraged him in his ambition to both write the novel and to study medieval literature, and he recalls being pleased to see him finally combine both. In the end, "The Old Men" was accepted for his Ph.D. dissertation.

That last year, then, Gardner took the difficult preliminary examination for his Ph.D. Day took his exam at the same time and remembers talking to Gardner as they waited, and asking him if he felt ready. "I don't think you're ever ready for this," Gardner responded.

Indeed, despite his enthusiasm for Anglo-Saxon and medieval literature, he failed that portion of the exam. For one thing, he'd never learned Anglo-Saxon or Old English. Thus, he wasn't able to get his Ph.D. that spring. However, he did manage to learn enough to pass the second try, and in August 1958, the next year, at the age of only twenty-five, he received his Ph.D.

Like other graduates, he had looked for a job the year before; also like other graduates, he didn't find one right away, despite, in his case, glowing recommendations. Along with McGalliard's praise, Freedman wrote that "Mr. Gardner is a rarely gifted, highly talented person." He went on to praise his "intelligence, and perceptive judgement" and, above all, "his great artistic gifts, which extend from imaginative writing to music."

John didn't want to move too far from country he knew, which limited him to some extent. During the year, however, he had learned of a temporary position at Oberlin College in Ohio, where a professor would be on leave for a year. Like Greencastle, Oberlin was an academic island in rural, farming country—familiar territory—between Iowa and Batavia. Though he hadn't finished his Ph.D. in the winter of 1957, he fully expected to be done in the coming months, and that spring he was offered the position at a salary of just over five thousand dollars for the year, so that summer he and Joan packed up and moved to Oberlin.

4

A Whisper Behind

His mind stood irresolute, precisely like the hunter who
has heard the whisper of a lion behind him.

— *The Resurrection*

L ONG KNOWN for its liberal arts concentration and
socially liberal environment, as well as for its music
conservatory, Oberlin was America's first coeduca-
tional college. Founded in 1833, it also served as a way station for
the Underground Railroad and a center of abolitionism before
and during the Civil War. Its liberal heritage, though, wouldn't
have been the primary attraction for either Gardner. Part of its
appeal was in its rural midwestern location, not too unlike either
John's or Joan's home country, with just under twenty-five hundred students in a town of some six thousand—facts that made
for a familiar landscape. More important, it was a job.

While the house in Iowa City was being sold, John and Joan
moved into the Daub House, as it was known, a brick house
built in the 1870s on a long block, right next door to the student
union. The name belonged to the retired librarian who owned it

and who was now living with her aged mother in the front part of the house. The Gardners moved into the back quarters along with Chester, their cat, and furnished it "graduate student style," according to one friend, with unmatched used furniture, brick-and-board bookshelves, and a TV.

As college teaching schedules go, particularly for the junior professors, it wasn't an easy job. A teaching college, as opposed to a research-centered university, at Oberlin everyone in the English Department taught four yearlong classes and each class met four days per week. Senior professors taught all the advanced literature courses, so junior faculty were left to teach the much more demanding and time-consuming basic composition and introductory classes. As a group, the junior professors didn't much like it. "It was a very unhappy department," remembers George Soule, another of the five professors hired at the same time. "People who had been there a long time taught all the good courses, [and] people who had been there twenty years were still cringing under the thumbs of people who'd been there thirty years."

Like the other new professors, Gardner taught three sections of the basic expository composition class required of beginning students. There were sixteen students in each class and a paper due each week, so the course involved a lot of grading and preparation. The fourth class the junior professors taught was a general literature survey, which dealt with poetry, fiction, drama, and ancient epic.

Everyone was required to teach *The Iliad* in that class, and most didn't like it. But Soule and Gardner felt differently, which was one of the things that drew them together, despite their different backgrounds. Though he had also grown up in a small community (in North Dakota), Soule had gone to Carleton College, then Yale, and finally to Cambridge in England. His education at top-ranked colleges made for a much different experience than Gardner's. "He had lived a grubbier sort of existence," Soule says about John's background. Besides the differences in their colleges, "he was younger and married, full of responsibilities." At the same time, Soule is quick to say, "That didn't get between us."

Carl Peterson, another of the professors hired that year, recalls being particularly struck by an image of the two at a party, coming together despite their differences. They were "sitting on the floor having this intense conversation," he says. "Here was John, the New York farm boy, and George, who'd grown up in North Dakota, and I was thinking, 'Here's a real conversation.'"

Gardner and Soule both taught classes that met at 8 A.M. and took to meeting for breakfast at a nearby café at 7:15, where they would talk and discuss the day's work. "We were doing many of the same things at the same time," says Soule. "I had never read *The Iliad* before teaching it, so I was keeping one or two assignments ahead of the class, and I think John was the same way. We would discuss *The Iliad* every day and found ourselves agreeing on most things and loving *The Iliad,* whereas most of the other professors hated it."

Gardner, in fact, was engaged by the classic to such an extent that he went on to write a complete study guide for students. After he left, the department chair particularly noted the guide among Gardner's accomplishments. His engagement with *The Iliad* stirred an interest in classical mythology that went on to feed his own work and teaching in no small way.

As dedicated as John was to his own writing and scholarship, he was no less concerned with his teaching. Soule, for one, sought his advice about grading student papers, as Oberlin students seemed to him likely more similar to what Gardner would have known at DePauw and Washington and Iowa than what Soule had been used to at Cambridge and Yale. Soule still remembers Gardner's admonition about student papers:

He said, "The thing you should do is flunk them all the first time. Then they'll know who's boss. Then you can start raising them up." He said that's what he did at Iowa. I said, "That's what I'll do." But I couldn't. I gave a few D+'s, but John kept on flunking people.

There was one kid who'd got a prize for the best editorial written by a student in the state of Ohio, and this man got an F on his first theme and an F on his second theme and F on his third theme, and F on his fourth theme. Then on his fifth theme, he got an F+. Which struck me as absolutely the most sadistic grade I'd ever heard.

[Gardner] put up with no nonsense. He was charming, but feisty.

As a colleague, though, says Soule, "I found him very open and friendly at that age."

Despite the apparent cruelty demonstrated by the F's and F+, by all accounts, Gardner was a singularly gifted teacher. Noticeably younger than the other professors, he was regularly mistaken for a student, and so his popularity seems in part to have been due to that closeness in age. "He looked younger than his students," says Dewey Granzel, another of the professors hired at the same time. Peterson's wife, Thalia, also remembers that "he was a very handsome, boyish man." Meantime, his informal style attracted students who heard about him. "He was a very popular teacher," says Granzel. "He would have to beat students off with sticks, pretty much. But they were very enthusiastic toward him. His style was very personal and 'up-close.' I don't want to imply that he was a kind of great flame that everyone could recognize and warm their hands with—he wasn't quite that secure—but those students that he influenced, I think he influenced very deeply."

Peterson likewise remembers Gardner's popularity. In a conversation that fall about a class he was teaching, Peterson says, "John happened to mention that kids were sitting in the aisle. It was a class of twenty-five, and there were sixty or seventy kids. I was startled.... I realized that, hey, John's doing things in a very distinctive, very quiet way."

Adding to his popularity, Granzel recalls, "He saw a lot of students at home—[for] dinner and socially." Though Iowa had perhaps provided an example, "it was unusual at that time to cross the 'student/teacher line.'"

As those who knew him at Iowa noted, Gardner's drive seemed unbounded. "He was a rare person," says Bernard Rosenthal, who later became chairman of Oberlin's English Department. "He just had an amazing amount of energy."

Gardner's seemingly unlimited energy kept him working at myriad tasks, drawing people in a constant stream. Certainly part of his appeal was the assurance he conveyed, though others saw it as arrogance. "He was very sure of himself, far in advance of his years," Soule says. "Not that he was jaded; but he knew what he was doing, and he was doing it, and he was so vigorous about it. He was so clearly in possession of himself, the way students aren't. To see someone just a few years older than you be so good and so intense, in an admirable way, and say things about literature that they found meaningful . . ." Above all, Soule says, he was "absolutely, passionately committed to literature. He worked. He was intensely active. He'd sit down and say something like, 'No good translation has been done of, let's say, *Beowulf.*' And he'd sit down and do it."

Gardner's youth and style, his very popularity, also made him unpopular with more traditional-minded professors, among whom he stirred jealousy. Says Soule, "They disliked John very much. Because if Professor X and John had the same course at the same time, Professor X would have a registration of about five and John would have forty. That doesn't go over very well."

Gardner's distinctiveness extended to the course readings as well. After covering the required epics in the introductory class, teachers were free to teach any modern novel, short stories, drama, whatever they wanted. Peterson remembers Gardner's classroom style: "He was going on about teaching *Anna Karenina* in his introductory class. To teach a novel in translation was surprising at the time. . . . I just had the feeling it was John Gardner talking with a great deal of seriousness and moral intensity, as much or even more than intellectual intensity. It was the way in which he was engaging with Tolstoy, the text and the students."

On the whole, says Granzel, "Gardner was clearly better than anyone else. . . . He said good things, he knew what he was talking about, he was very literate, intelligent, a fine reader of literature."

Still, despite his commitment to teaching and his welcoming informality, he found ways to shelter himself from the students who kept seeking him out. For above all, he was determined to write his fiction. "As great a teacher as he seemed to have been," Granzel says, "he never let his teaching get in the way of his desire to write. If I were asked then whether he was more writer or teacher, I'd say writer. Because it seemed like most of what he was doing in the classroom was really adjunct to his writing. And of course our writing students, and our reading students too, were excited by that kind of commitment."

Clifford Clark, a former president of Oberlin, reiterates Gardner's commitment: "He was not only an obviously gifted writer, but he took writing seriously, and insisted that it could be taught, and that young people could write and publish."

Most of his writing went on at home, late into the night, after Joan and the rest of the world were asleep, as there was neither time nor space at school. Granzel does remember Gardner once sitting cross-legged on his desk and writing, but because the new professors were given two adjacent offices to share, with only a partition separating them, there wasn't much privacy.

Oberlin's primary mission was to teach undergraduates, so none of the professors were hired as specialists in any field, nor were they expected to do much else apart from teach. Academics know, however, that professional advancement depends on publication, and Gardner was from the first driven to write the literary criticism that would gain him time for his fiction. Spurred by interests raised in McGalliard's class, he got the idea of composing a translation-modernization of the work of the anonymous medieval poet who composed *Sir Gawain and the Green*

Knight, along with some other poems for which he felt no good, modern version existed. The identity of the early fifteenth-century *Gawain* poet was unknown, and even though he was a contemporary of Chaucer's the language of the poems attributed to him was strange and distant from the English of Chaucer's London. To present the work in all its interest, in updated language, was an enormous challenge. Engaged, Gardner went to work.

Joan, meantime, got a job working as an assistant to the editor of the Oberlin alumni magazine, which also required a good deal of writing. Her work was certainly more than passable, and her red hair, blue eyes, and quick wit made an equally striking impression. "She was very sexy in her way," Thalia recalls. "She was odd . . . oblique, ironic," says Soule. "But not nasty ironic at all. 'Playful' is a better word." Peterson adds, "She had no hesitation to speak her mind, which was part of the fun of it."

Though her quick intelligence was apparent to all, she disguised it in a way that seemed odd to many, and would seem even more so by today's standards. "She spoke in a sort of small, high-pitched voice," Thalia goes on, "so that I never got the feeling that I was speaking to the woman of intelligence that was there. Though we both knew it was there. She was a very smart woman, but she played the role of the sexy, dumb redhead. There was the Joan I knew; then there was the woman who played this role—and she played it all the time. I remember wondering, 'Why's she doing this?' " In fact, she says of John and Joan, "Both of them seemed a little unreal—an oddity and not your 'normal' academic couple. They stood out, they really did."

Speaking of the ideas for what became *Grendel* some years later, she says, "Here was a man with all these plans, who'd written a dissertation which was a novel, who was dreaming up a book about a monster, and this good-looking redhead wife. They were originals."

As far as friends there could see, they complemented each other well and seemed not to have any real conflicts. The energy and spark that drew everyone to them, however, also fed the feisty competitiveness that had been part of their affair from the beginning. Over the years, it became more pronounced and at times, even at Oberlin, dramatically physical. Still, in these years anyway, if their passions led to occasional fireworks, the results burned out quickly enough and didn't seem to have repercussions. In any event, they certainly didn't get in the way of the writing Gardner was determined to accomplish. He didn't talk about it much, or show it to anyone, but, still, he promoted his literary interests readily in conversations with colleagues.

In later years, he professed some bitterness about his year at Oberlin. He told at least one interviewer, and his second wife, that he'd been fired for organizing a faculty strike. But though both he and Joan made an unusual presence in the Oberlin community, despite his antiauthority bent, no one remembers him ever being disruptive at faculty meetings. Others who knew him suggest that he would have been very happy to stay longer, if he could. The other four who were hired along with him had been given two-year contracts. Gardner was a late choice and hired for only one year as a temporary replacement.

"I remember his consternation one time that he wasn't on tenure track," says Granzel. "I think he would very much have liked to stay."

The department chair's recommendation also praised his

teaching, saying, "He is the kind of person we would reappoint if we had a place for him." Unfortunately, there was no wiggle room in the bureaucracy. The one-year contract simply wasn't negotiable. "When the year was over," says Granzel, "he was done." Because of the jealousy his popularity had stirred, Granzel adds, "I don't think any of the senior professors were sad to see him go off to Chico State."

Forced to look for another job, John found one, in the heart of almond country, in the strange new world of California. Chico State University, as it was then called, is ninety miles north of Sacramento and two miles from the foothills of the Sierra Nevada. Though the population of Chico was about ten thousand at the time, roughly the same as Batavia and Greencastle and Iowa City and Oberlin, not much else seemed familiar. The main industry was farming, but it was a different kind entirely, as were the climate and culture. The new environment had little effect on Gardner's day-to-day teaching and writing, however.

Established in 1887 when wealthy landowner and pioneer John Bidwell donated eight acres of cherry orchard, Chico State Teachers College expanded into a liberal arts state college in 1935, though the emphasis remained on preparing teachers. Thus, like Oberlin, it wasn't designed to attract faculty for research but instead to serve the practical ends of teaching. There were only about thirty-five hundred students when Gardner came, so it was comfortably small. In fact, it didn't even have a separate English department; English was part of the Language Arts Department, which included foreign languages as well.

Gardner was again hired as an instructor, but this position

held more promise than the one at Oberlin had: instructors at Chico could be, and regularly were, promoted to professorships. The two dozen or so who taught the English classes—all men— formed a close-knit community, with offices and classes in the same building. They had lunch with each other most days, and the workload also fostered comradery. As at Oberlin, they each taught four classes per semester.

Lennis Dunlap, who had come from Vanderbilt, the Sorbonne, and Oxford, had been hired the year before and became one of Gardner's closest friends. "He was a very handsome young man," he says of Gardner in those days. "He looked almost frail and thin. But he wasn't at all. He was very strong and very muscular."

The main thing that struck Dunlap, as it had Gardner's Oberlin colleagues, was his "enormous energy.... He was in high gear all the time." Dunlap would go over to the house the Gardners rented and see John at work. "He used to unwrap a loaf of Wonder bread, or Rainbo, or something like that and set it out on the counter, cover each slice with peanut butter, open a big box of candy bars, make twenty gallons of coffee, and write continuously nonstop. Or read or study or whatever he was doing—but hour after hour after hour."

Though he'd been hired to teach whatever in literature needed teaching, Gardner's interest was mainly in creative writing— and the department was open to expanding.

At the time they came on board, says Dunlap, "The department was entirely dead. Nothing was happening. But a few of us decided to stir things up. And the Creative Writing Program took off with John. He was the force behind it."

That first fall, one of Gardner's students was Raymond Carver, who had moved down the previous year from rural Washington. For him, that first introductory fiction writing class with Gardner was memorable, as he wrote later in a memoir: "On the first day of class, he marched us outside and had us sit on the lawn. He went around, asking us to name the authors we liked to read." After hearing the names, "he announced that he didn't think any of us had what it took to become real writers—as far as he could see none of us had the necessary *fire*. But he said he was going to do what he could for us, though it was obvious he didn't expect much to come of it."

That sort of teacherly discouragement is, of course, designed to fuel whatever fire might be there—to set up those students who have the drive to prove the teacher wrong. For those who were discouraged by such a pronouncement, Gardner realized, it was just as well. He himself had yet to see any fiction he'd sent out published. Having received nothing but rejections for everything, he understood the determination, regardless of talent, that it took to persevere. However, when the twenty-year-old Carver demonstrated his own ambition and talent, Gardner gave him the keys to his office so that he could use it to write, away from the demands of his wife and small children, during weekends when Gardner wasn't there.

Carver remembered the boxes on the shelves there, with Gardner's unpublished manuscripts, each labeled with grease pencil, and he recalled feeling honored to be in the atmosphere of a "real writer." At the same time, he remembered seeing John and Joan on Sundays in their black dress clothes, driving to and from church. As in the class itself, Gardner looked entirely conventional. "In those days, he looked and dressed like a Presby-terian minister, or an FBI man," Carver wrote. "He always wore a black suit, a white shirt, and a tie. And he had a crewcut."

Though Dunlap is quick to point out, however, that "in those days, we all looked like Presbyterian ministers."

But, Carver continued, "he was unconventional in other ways."

At a time when smoking wasn't allowed, for instance, Gardner was a chain smoker in class. When another professor complained about the residue left in the room, Gardner remarked to the class of the man's small-mindedness and went on smoking.

He only required one ten- to fifteen-page story from each stu-dent in the semester, but he demanded that students go over and over their work, following detailed instructions for revisions that he marked on their pages and explained in private conferences. "He used to go over my early manuscripts, word for word, line by line," Carver wrote.

He also brought literary magazines to class and distributed them, so students could see where serious literary writing began. Carver himself then got involved in another project Gardner initiated with Dunlap. They decided that Chico should have a magazine to publish student poetry and fiction, to encourage budding writers, give them experience editing, and help build the Creative Writing Program. Carver thus became one of the founding editors of *Selections*, the magazine of student writing. When he transferred to Humboldt State the next year, Carver had his first published story, "The Furious Seasons," in the sec-ond issue (winter of 1960 to 1961) of *Selections*.

To further promote creative writing at Chico, Gardner also

took advantage of developing television technology. He found he could use television for a series of closed-circuit broadcasts he conceived, in which he lectured and instructed on creative writing.

He and Dunlap and a few others also began a live lecture series—originally taking turns themselves, lecturing to whatever audience they could attract. Gardner planned and supervised the Modern Novel lecture series, though one of the lectures he gave was on Robert Frost, whom he'd first noted favorably in his DePauw journal. And out of a conversation between Gardner and Dunlap over a beer near the campus, they decided to expand even further.

Driven to develop the writing he thought important and to introduce his own new generation of writers, Gardner wanted to begin a professional literary magazine like *Perspective* or *Accent* or the *Western Review*. Initially, they planned to call it "Mount Shasta Selections," after the mountain in California. Gardner designed the cover and recruited Janet Turner, a printmaker from the Art Department, to be art editor. At the same time, he got another art teacher, Ken Morrow, whom he thought a particularly talented artist, to contribute illustrations. Some didn't agree that Morrow had any particular talent, but Gardner became friends with him, and as he came to do with other friends over the years, he enthusiastically promoted his talent at every opportunity.

Ultimately, he decided on a simpler title, *MSS*—the standard abbreviation for the word *manuscripts* and, perhaps not coincidentally, the acronym for the originally proposed title—and began contacting writers he wanted to include. He knew that for the magazine to get attention, he'd need to attract some established names to accompany the new ones no one recognized, and he asked his old friends from Iowa, Don Finkel and Connie Urdang, to be poetry editors. He told them to write to all the friends and colleagues they knew whose work they thought the best, especially those who had been publishing. He advised them to tell the prospective contributors not to send things from the "bottom of the drawer" but only their best new work.

Finkel requested manuscripts from poets W. S. Merwin and William Stafford, who were virtually unknown at the time. Gardner also wrote to George P. Elliot, the well-established novelist and fiction writer he had met. Elliot obliged by sending a story to Gardner for the magazine. Gardner, however, felt the story had some problems and wrote back with suggestions about what to do. Elliot worked at the story and revised it, then sent it back. But Gardner still wasn't satisfied. At this point, Elliot was put off by what seemed to him astonishing arrogance, and he wrote a sarcastic note to Finkel, including the correspondence between the two, noting, this is what "your friend" has done. It was one of the first examples of the very specific, active role Gardner assumed in his editing. Treating it just as he did his teaching, he never hesitated to give instruction, regardless of the recipient. It was hardly the first, or last, time he offended a more established writer with his insistence.

Gardner wrote to John Hawkes, who had published his first novel in 1949 but who was relatively unknown outside avant-garde circles, and he began a correspondence with William Gass, a young writer he knew about from one of the editors of *Accent*. Its editors had debated over a very long story from Gass, who had also published stories in *Perspective* as well as in a previous issue of *Accent*. Finally, they decided that "The Pedersen Kid" was just too long. One of the editors, Stanley Elkin, had argued that *Accent* should take it, but the vote had gone against him. When Elkin heard about *MSS*, he immediately wrote to Gass, telling him about Gardner's new magazine. When Gass sent "The Pedersen Kid" to Chico, Gardner was impressed and accepted it immediately.

For Gardner, though, there was a right way and a wrong way to do everything in fiction, and though he was enthusiastic about Gass's story he thought some aspects of it should be revised. For one, Gass had given sections of the long story their own titles, as if they were chapters. Gardner felt they weren't appropriate titles and suggested changes.

"His suggestions weren't bad," Gass remembers now, with a note of bemusement, but he contrasts Gardner's "proactive" editing with his own "antiactive" approach. Once he sent out his work, Gass says, he considered it done and opposed making any changes. Thus, Gass insisted that his titles stay, and so they did. (Still, in the version that appears in his 1969 collection, *In the Heart of the Heart of the Country,* the sections are not given subtitles). Gardner's instructional proclivity, then, which many saw as dogmatic rigidity, was in evidence from the beginning, but despite aesthetic differences the correspondence between Gass and Gardner led to a collegial friendship that lasted for the rest of Gardner's career.

Gardner didn't, however, suggest any changes from another young writer whose work he solicited. Joyce Carol Oates was just beginning to see her stories published when she sent Gardner

"The Death of Mrs. Sheer"—one of her "early 'dark comedies,'" she terms it. Though she is certain it "could not have been published in most magazines at that time," Gardner thought it exactly right and included it. Then he took her novella *The Sweet Enemy* for a later issue. The magazine, however, was financed out of Dunlap's and Gardner's pockets, which were not very deep, and that issue was never published, so Gardner advised Oates to send *The Sweet Enemy* to the *Southern Review,* which did publish it. Oates was particularly grateful, and the friendship between the two continued for the rest of John's life. "This was wonderfully generous of John," she says. "He'd become, however indirectly, a true friend."

It was a role Gardner would continue to play in service of fiction he believed important. It was all part of what mattered most, which was the writing that he was determined to accomplish. He continued working to fashion "Nickel Mountain" into a novel; when he got stuck, he worked on "Squirrels" or another story. One, about a pair of elderly sisters living together in the familiar environs of Batavia, he titled "A Little Night Music." After almost ten years of trying, it became the first of Gardner's fiction to be published in an established literary journal when the *Northwest Review,* which had built a respectable national reputation in its three years of existence at the University of Oregon, accepted it for its spring 1961 issue. The story joined poems by the well-respected E. L. Mayo, who had published three collections; an interview with James Michener; and poems, stories, essays, and book reviews by other established writers.

Gardner's story itself is conventional in style and structure, and though the ending discovery contrasts harshly with the carefully ordered, staid-seeming small town, it doesn't really come as a surprise. What distinguishes the work, however, is the fine polish of technique that Gardner had mastered. When, for instance, the policeman narrator, who operates a music store, comes to the house of the elderly sisters, one of whom is the focus of his thievery investigation, the description creates the scene with details that significantly establish the situation beyond physical facts:

> She [the sister of the thief] was sixty, maybe seventy, and the top of her head came level with my chest. She was like a little carved religious statue you could hold in your two hands. She stood with her head tilted, not smiling, not frowning, waiting as if she lived inside a glacier, outside time, by different laws, as if whether or not I came in couldn't change anything at all—not her, not her house . . . she would give you the feeling that she was holding back, talking, reading through the piano music, but at the same time standing back a ways, watching.

Esther, who is the thief and who is discovered having committed suicide at the end, is depicted in archetypal terms—set in a religious context and part of another world "outside time."

John's excitement at having his story published led him to spread the word, not least to Batavia, where the story was set, and his mother bought many copies to give to all her friends. So his fiction career took another major step. In addition to writing, teaching, giving occasional lectures, hosting his weekly closed-circuit TV show, and overseeing the production of the new magazine—a prodigious collection of tasks—he was also seriously interested in medieval literature and the creative possibilities involved in modernizing a language whose precise meanings no one could be sure of. He somehow managed to continue to find time to work on the medieval translation that he'd begun at Oberlin. Dunlap began to help him with the modernization of *Sir Gawain and the Green Knight,* but he was amazed to find that despite Gardner's Ph.D. and proclaimed specialization in medieval literature, he had no knowledge of Middle English nor Anglo-Saxon—minimum requirements for serious work in those areas.

"He was an absolute blank," Dunlap says of Gardner's knowledge of those languages. However, with the intensity of focus that was his trademark, Gardner set to work teaching himself. Dunlap says, "When he decided that he wanted to do something, to learn something, he did it."

Once the translation-modernization of *Sir Gawain and the Green Knight* was done (a poem, Gardner points out in his commentary, that stands as a sort of coda to the other four long *Gawain* poems), he began on the rest, along with the critical commentary to accompany them.

As if all this weren't enough, the interests he shared with Dunlap led to yet another major project that grew out of their teaching and conversations about fiction. Like many teachers, each had his own favorite short stories to use as models for students. Though many of these were standards familiar to most teachers of literature, none of the available anthologies set them in the kind of context that they felt was important for student understanding.

Says Dunlap, "It started over a beer. We just decided that we didn't like the anthologies that we were using and thought we could do a better job." They went to work nights, at each other's houses, to construct the text they imagined. Essentially, they worked side by side, at the same time. "I would be working on one thing," Dunlap recalls, "and John would be working on another, and we'd trade. He'd read mine and rewrite, and I'd read his and rewrite."

Most of the stories they chose were well-known standards, which they divided into "sketches," "fables," "yarns," "tales," "short fiction," and "longer fiction" short of novel length. Along with examples of each type, they wrote analyses and study questions for most of them in a text that took them just under a year of nights to assemble.

The discussions they undertook in the preface and introduction emphasize the close reading principles of the New Criticism, which was dominant at the time, whereby literary works are considered apart from social-historical context. More significant in terms of Gardner's development, however, is that both the individual readings selected for the anthology and, more important, the groupings he chose to illustrate the various hallmarks of great fiction show some of the ideas he was developing that would become the center of his aesthetic.

The anthology contained translations of stories by Tolstoy and Dostoyevsky—(at a time when translations weren't commonly used). Faulkner, another Gardner enthusiasm, was also included, with his "Spotted Horses," as was Melville's "Benito Cereno."

The introduction contains a discussion about the primary qualities Gardner felt were essential to the success of any story:

"intellectual honesty," "emotional honesty," and "aesthetic validity." The first two result from an author's rigid adherence to the real-life, causal consequences of whatever terms are posited. In other words, given a plot's circumstance or event, a characteristic, or a setting, what follows must be absolutely logical. The failure of any story element in that regard undercuts the reader's belief in the fictional world. Such is the problem, for instance, with all O. Henry–style trick endings in which "the reader is led to concern himself with a problem which at the last moment is revealed to be unimportant to the author."

The failure to be "honest" in this way is a failure to be "moral." The discussion carefully distinguishes "moral" from "moralistic"—the latter describing a story that takes some sort of ethical stand or suggests any didactic ethical idea. The idea that literature, and all art, has moral impact, was stirred for Gardner by his engagement with Tolstoy. In his late, philosophical work *What Is Art?*, Tolstoy argues that art has moral effects that rise from religious principles to which an author does or does not adhere and that thus occasion "good" or "bad" art. For Tolstoy, the essence of all art is sincerity, which is essential if the work is to "infect" the audience, causing readers to share the artist's emotions. "Good" art is that which promotes the highest religious values.

Gardner's own ideas were never so rigidly bound to Christian tenets, but the idea that good fiction is "moral," in the way he came to define the term, became the center of his aesthetic as he worked out the idea. Ultimately, the didacticism with which he insisted on the term became a major source of controversy after he became nationally famous.

It took a little less than a year of hard work to compose, and in 1961 *The Forms of Fiction* was sold to Random House. The 657-page book, published the next year, was reprinted a half-dozen times over the next five years. The success led Gardner and Dunlap to embark on a companion book—an anthology of verse, set in the same kind of New Criticism, with analysis and discussion questions. They sold the idea for "Poetry: Form and Substance" to Odyssey Press and went to work on it (though ultimately it was never published).

Along with literary projects, Gardner was also active in the local theater. It was an interest he'd long had, of course, inherited from his parents. He and Joan had worked in community theater performances in Iowa, though they hadn't at Oberlin. But here, at Chico, John wrote an original play for the theater that was produced at the college, and he acted in several performances. Dunlap remembers his doing a notable job playing Jerry, the lead in Edward Albee's *Zoo Story,* which had opened off-Broadway in New York in January 1960. Decidedly unconventional, the play's success first in London, then New York and beyond, fed the new wave of off-Broadway, experimental theater that would spread everywhere in the coming decade. The Chico production "was sort of barn theater," Dunlap says, "but it was very good."

The cast and production for most of the plays constituted in part a group who had come from Manhattan, led by a Japanese guru, who among other things advocated a macrobiotic diet. Dunlap remembers that their community included a well-known soap-opera star, an economist, a jazz pianist who also taught Dunlap's son, and other artists. They were "super bright and eccentric people," he says. After studying maps and consulting their guru, the group concluded that Manhattan was a prime target for Soviet missiles. Chico, they had determined, was the safest place on the continent.

The Manhattan group was one of John's first encounters with the radical side of the California culture and its Eastern-flavored philosophies, largely introduced and boosted by the urban-centered Beat poets, who had sprung up in San Francisco and New York only a few years earlier. Though Gardner shared the antiauthoritarian views at the heart of that urge, it was a movement from which he, as a rural eastern midwesterner, always felt decidedly apart.

Both John and Joan were also involved with the college symphony. John drew some of their program illustrations, and Joan was active in the symphony guild, working on publicity and support. At the same time, she resumed her formal studies, pursuing an M.A. in music composition with a minor in English. She was also pregnant, and on their first New Year's Eve in California, December 31, 1959, their son, Joel, was born.

John was around to help out at home, which allowed Joan to earn her master's, for which she wrote an original piece of music, and to continue her work with the symphony. Still, the traditional tasks of motherhood fell largely to her.

As 1960 dawned, the Gardners seemed to have fallen into a happy routine, with a solid family base, and friends remember them as a lively, intelligent couple who seemed to get along well then. But there was always an air of crisis hovering around them that regularly broke in to shatter the happy picture. It was as if John were some kind of magnet that drew physical disaster and crisis, not only to himself but to anyone around—not from any act of will, but as part of his very nature.

On January 3, 1962, a daughter was born, whom they named Lucy, after relatives of both. On one of the days when Joan was getting the new baby ready for a doctor's appointment, John was lying on their double bed, tossing Joel into the air and catching him, his son laughing, and both loving the play. On her way out with Lucy, Joan asked John to stop, but he didn't, and after one of the tosses a few minutes later the child crashed to the concrete floor. He hit his head hard enough to lapse into unconsciousness.

John was panicked. He thought Joel had stopped breathing. He ran with him to the old Chevy, then sped the three or so miles to the hospital. Leaving the car running, he grabbed Joel and raced into the emergency room. There he saw that Joel was breathing—and conscious—and when the doctor checked him he found the child fine, except that the fall had dislocated a collarbone. The doctor reset it; then John remembered the car. He ran back out to move it, but on the way he slipped and fell hard in the gravel parking lot, scraping his arms. He pulled himself up, retrieved Joel, and drove home.

The next day, Dunlap recalls, "Joan took the baby to a pediatrician, and John couldn't get out of bed. He called a friend and had her take him to Enloe [hospital]. There they discovered that he'd broken both of his arms when he'd fallen the night before."

When Dunlap came a day later to see how he was doing after such a terrible accident, he found John with both arms in casts and slings, sitting at the typewriter and working. It was one of the more dramatic of the physical upheavals that seemed to plague him, gathering, if anything, more strength in their disruptions as time went on. Yet he always managed to survive. Looked at one way, it was as if such crises were fallout from the fury of energy he embodied. From another view, he simply seemed at odds with the physical world around him, a disconnection he came to think of as a sort of punishment for the crimes of which he was sure he was guilty.

Meantime, he was never satisfied to work on just one project — or two or three, for that matter. While he labored at his teaching, at editing the new magazine, constructing the new anthology, translating medieval poems, and his own fiction, along with the theater and symphony, when the holidays came, he found time to make presents by hand for his children and those of his friends.

Informed by his own engagement with myth and ancient tales, he first wrote a children's fable about a dragon, which he illustrated himself. Called "Dragon, Dragon," it tells a story about that traditional medieval figure. This was a distinctly contemporary dragon, however, with the conflicted consciousness of a contemporary adult. He made his story into a little book with cardboard covers he designed and presented it as a Christmas present in 1961 to the Dunlaps' son. It would be years before this and the other children's stories that he went on to write would become more than private gifts and ultimately be published. But the project had begun.

Busier than ever, then, Gardner's tremendous energy and commitment to writing and teaching were known to everyone around. Even the school's president, Glenn Kendall, called on him in the summer of 1960. For publicity and fund-raising purposes, a formal written history of the college, he thought, might help engage the sympathies of donors, as well as those of the general public and relevant politicians. It seemed the right kind of practical use for the talents of someone like Gardner.

Gardner undertook the project, which he told Kendall he would finish in August. Other projects he was working on were more important to him, however, and the college history languished, so he pushed the date back to October. Even so, with his completed accomplishments, and the work in progress, he applied that fall, along with an instructor from the Philosophy Department, for accelerated promotion to assistant professor.

In the spring, however, both promotions were denied. Gardner was inflamed, and with the philosophy instructor, Warren Olson, he launched a protest. For his part, Olson had drawn attention with a speech on behalf of the Civil Rights movement, which was gaining momentum throughout the country. In a talk to the local NAACP chapter, he had supported sit-ins in the South, as justified by civil disobedience. The speech had precipitated letters of protest and an editorial opposing his views in the local paper. Not to mention Kendall's unhappiness.

An ad hoc committee was appointed to investigate "whether policies and procedures had been faithfully carried out in the consideration for promotion of Dr. Warren Olson and Dr. John Gardner." Kendall was concerned that granting Olson's promotion might give the impression that Kendall and the college approved of Olson's controversial views. Both, Kendall said, must remain neutral. He wasn't about to reverse the decision.

Gardner insisted on meeting with Kendall, who finally gave him two reasons for the denial. First, he said, he and "others" hadn't seen enough evidence of Gardner's work to justify promotion at that time. Furthermore, he simply didn't believe in such promotion for someone so young; it was unfair to others. "That a horse gets off to a fast start out of the gate doesn't necessarily mean he's going to finish the race," he said. And though they didn't specifically figure in the decision, he said, there were other considerations also. Not least was the school history that Gardner had begun and not finished—even in May—and the production of *MSS* (still called "Mount Shasta Selections" at the time) that Gardner had undertaken but hadn't yet produced. Kendall went on to say that he couldn't understand the "fad" writing Gardner was teaching in his classes and putting in the student magazine anyway, finally concluding that "if writing [is] beyond understanding, it [is] bad writing."

When Gardner asked him if he thought Faulkner, who had recently been awarded the Nobel Prize and who used techniques sometimes difficult to grasp, was a "fad" writer, Kendall told him that in his opinion, Faulkner was "insane."

Finally, there was the matter of the closed-circuit television lectures. Gardner had appeared in the broadcasts without a sport coat and smoking cigarettes. Though there were no specific prohibitions, as there were about smoking in class, it projected an image that was clearly at odds with what Kendall thought appropriate.

In its report at the end of May, the committee decided that "there has indeed been a violation of the policies for promotion in the cases of Dr. Olson and Dr. Gardner." But that didn't mean that there would be reconsideration. Kendall refuted charges of unfairness, writing in a memo to the faculty that "a number of people who had responsibility in this matter held the judgment that they had not seen enough evidence of the quality of his work to recommend accelerated promotion."

In response, two months later Gardner pointed out that "I was unanimously recommended by my division in a letter which listed in some detail my accomplishments at Chico State College," and that "[as] there was no attempt, except within the division [of English professors] which apparently does not, in the President's opinion, 'have responsibility in this matter,' to evaluate . . . [his] manuscripts, the literary magazine, or his students's work . . . I believe that the decision against promoting me was the President's decision solely."

Nonetheless, the decision stood. And so, for Gardner, the proverbial writing was on more than just the wall.

He went on to finish the written history of Chico State, which purportedly was highly critical of both past and present administrators, though no copy survives. Whether or not it actually existed, however (Dunlap insists he did see it), anyone who knew Gardner believes he certainly could have written such a thing and that it would demonstrate the antiauthority temperament that kept getting him into trouble.

His disdain for the established order and his habitual procrastination of everything but his own writing was also reflected in his unwillingness to help the system he was part of. Even his grades, for instance, were always late, causing inconvenience and delays. At the time, grades were recorded on computer punch cards, but the computers were such that the grades for any student couldn't be processed until all the grades had been turned in. Gardner's tardiness became such a constant that the joke went around campus that when his grades finally did get in, all the machinery broke down.

With a family of four now, there was pressure to make more money—not that Gardner was likely to acknowledge such pressure if he felt it. Stilll, it was clear that he couldn't stay at Chico State. He sent out inquiries and heard of a job from an old friend of his and Joan's whom they'd known at Washington University. The friend, Ruby Cohn, had been a graduate student a çouple of years ahead of John. Her specialty was Samuel Beckett, and she had got a job teaching at what was then San Francisco State College. Now her department head was looking for a specialist in medieval literature. John had impressed Cohn at Washington, as he had most of the students and professors he'd met before and since, and Cohn also liked Joan for her wit and sharpness. She suggested that John would be an excellent addition to the department at San Francisco and encouraged him to apply. He did and was hired as assistant professor, with an annual salary of some eight thousand dollars.

Joan took several trips to San Francisco and stayed with Cohn while looking for a place to live. Another friend she met who also taught there, Jacqueline Hoefer, together with her husband Peter, mentioned that the apartment next to them on Henry Street was being redone. Joan looked at it and decided it would be a fine place to start. In June 1962, they packed up and supervised the movers who were taking their things to San Francisco. Leaving their car with a friend, they took the train to St. Louis and went on to Batavia for a summer visit. In the fall, they would be in San Francisco.

5

City on the Edge

> It didn't seem natural, and he'd tried to see it from their
> side, because if there was any way on earth to explain it,
> the secret had to be in those people's feelings.
> —*Nickel Mountain*

S AN FRANCISCO'S MISSION DISTRICT was predominately Hispanic and poor and crowded—a long way
from St. Louis and suburban Florissant, the closest
either John or Joan had come to urban life—but the rent on
Henry Street was cheap and the apartment was livable.

John's brown hair had gone mostly gray by this time, and he
smoked cigarettes furiously, but he was slender and "had the
clear eyes of a younger man," according to a friend who knew
him then. Like the colleges at Oberlin and Chico, San Francisco
State was primarily a teaching college, and one of the largest of
any in the country. Once again, John had to teach four courses
each semester, but now he was an assistant professor on tenure
track, a significant career advance.

When he arrived, he brought the same storm of exuberance

that went with him everywhere. "He had the most incredible work ethic I'd ever seen," says Eric Solomon, a close friend at the time, who himself became a noted critic of Stephen Crane. "He not only did much of the baby-sitting, he was working and writing all the time. . . . It seemed incredible to me that he could do all these things."

Joan immediately began working on her Ph.D., taking graduate courses in music. The following year she got a teaching job in San Leandro, a suburb south of the city. In 1964, she moved to a school in Sausalito, north of the city.

Solomon and his wife, Irene, had children the same age as Joel and Lucy, and the families became particularly close. In addition to sharing dinners, they went out on many weekends to visit the attractions around San Francisco, spending hours at Golden Gate Park, Oceanside Park, and Stinson Beach. "We never socialized without the kids, which gave us a lot of time to talk," Solomon remembers. "We'd go on some venture . . . and the kids would play, and we'd talk."

Solomon had begun teaching there in 1964, when he'd come with a draft of his book on Crane. He and John quickly found other things in common besides their jobs and families. "We were both mavericks, working in a nonpublishing department," Solomon says. They also had similar attitudes toward their writing, though generally they didn't read each other's. "We both had the idea that what we wrote was between us and the page and the editor," Solomon says. But, he goes on, "I knew how smart John was, so I asked him to read [my manuscript] and give his comments. And this was typical, I think, of how John worked—he gave it back to me the next day. I said, 'Have you read it?' He said, 'Well, I've read enough of it. I know exactly what's wrong with it. Here's what you have to do—' And he was absolutely right."

This quick and insightful critical analysis was something Gardner became known for as he read manuscripts in progress.

Meantime, with two preschool children, life in San Francisco was more hectic than ever. As several friends commented, there was a constant disarray about John and Joan, spurred by the frenetic pace. Likely, it was fostered as well by the gin that John was now drinking. Says Solomon, "The house felt definitely unruly. If you'd go there for dinner, which we did quite often, you'd be lucky to sit down and eat before eleven at night. And since you got there at six, you'd be very drunk."

The people John and Joan drew around them were powerfully attracted to the energy of both, for just as John is remembered for his magnetism and intensity, so Joan's wit and intelligence are equally recalled. "Joan had probably the finest sense of humor I've ever encountered," Solomon says. "She would tell a story—usually about her and her difficulties trying to do the normal kinds of things one does to live in American society—shopping, whatever—she just had a hard time getting things like this together. But she was very funny about it."

Poet Carl Dennis, then a graduate student across the Bay at Berkeley, also speaks of the vitality and spirit surrounding them both. He met them first at one of the many parties they hosted, where he and John discovered other commonalities besides their interests in literature. For one, Dennis had grown up in St. Louis and, like John, had been a student of Jarvis Thurston's at Washington University. Then he'd also gone on to teach at Oberlin, just a little after John had left. "They were a center of attention and activity," says Dennis. "[John] was always a brilliant conversationalist, and full of theories."

The first time they met, Dennis had a long conversation with John about the philosopher Søren Kierkegaard and Herman Melville. He recalls being struck by John's fascination with Ahab, whose "crazy and awesome refusal to accept the limits of the human condition," as John wrote in a later essay, "his wish to be a demi-god, to confront in an epic encounter all the evil of the world, throws into relief all the compromises that ordinary life requires of us."

John's attraction to the character is easy to understand, for like Melville's hero, Gardner struggled with the demands of the everyday. Joan's frustration with his refusal to take charge of household responsibilities fed conflicts between them that were becoming more visible. Though Solomon remembers them getting along fairly well at the time, says Dennis, "Their relationship was stormy, even then."

During their second year in San Francisco, they moved to a ground-floor apartment in a house owned by friends of theirs. The ground floor had been remodeled and rented to the Gardners, while their friends lived upstairs. Neither John nor Joan, though, were handy with maintenance or organized with finances. The rent was always late, and things in the apartment were damaged and fell into disrepair. Relations with the friends upstairs soon became hostile, and it was clear to John and Joan that they would have to move.

Finally, one Sunday, Joan went for a drive, looking for a house to buy. She found a narrow Victorian house that two men had bought as an investment. The price was affordable, and it was a way out of the difficult situation she and John were in at the time. She found the real-estate agent sitting at a card table on the ground floor of the house, and after looking around told him that she'd take the house.

The agent patiently explained that no, that's not the way it works. First, she must offer a price, the seller would make a counteroffer, and then the two sides would get together and agree on a final figure. Joan asked what she should offer, agreed to the price the agent suggested, and the Gardners moved into the small two-story Victorian. Shortly after they moved in, though, the weather got colder, and when Joan sent John to turn up the thermostat he couldn't find it. She complained bitterly about his household incompetence and got up to find it herself. But she couldn't find it either. In fact, the house had no furnace. Its absence was a reason the house had been so inexpensive.

They got out of the deal and found another house just a block off Mission Street, the main street of the district. Like many in the city, it was also a century-old Victorian two-story house. This one had four fireplaces (all working), hardwood floors, and a backyard for the kids, with a small outbuilding and a couple of trees. John had a study in front with a bay window opening out, and now there was enough room to invite people over and entertain the way they liked.

Poet David Ray went to a dinner there with John Logan, another poet who was teaching at San Francisco State. "It struck me as elegant," Ray remembers. But he also recalls the explosiveness between the Gardners. Amid several glasses of wine, "John had started to tell us how great epoxy was," he recounts.

With characteristic enthusiasm, he was going on about its re-markable ability to fix any break without leaving a trace. But Joan "started mocking him and it heated up very quickly."

John grew visibly more furious as she went on, Ray says, and he finally went into the kitchen and came back with a hammer. Without another word, he smashed into fragments a vase that he had repaired with epoxy. To make his point about the wonders of the glue, he challenged anyone to find a trace of the original break. Says Ray, "He still had the hammer in his hand as he turned around to look at us. He was in a rage. He looked as if he could go on smashing more. Logan was flabbergasted. He was very upset about it. I don't think I would have jumped up and insisted on leaving, but [Logan] did." And so they left the Gardners to the debris.

The incendiary atmosphere rose from conflicts John and Joan played out regularly. Many who witnessed the explosions, though, are quick to add that they seemed to make up just as readily, with affection that was equally intense.

In their late twenties and especially energetic, tendencies in their own personalities were fueled as well by social and techno-logical changes of the time, which seemed to touch everyone of their generation. In 1960, the first oral contraceptive was ap-proved, giving women a degree of sexual freedom they'd never had; in 1961, Timothy Leary came to New York to experiment with the effects of hallucinogenic drugs on artists, administering doses of psilocybin to Jack Kerouac and Allen Ginsberg; in 1963, the first topless bathing suit was displayed. That same year Martin Luther King had further fixed attention on civil rights issues, leading a march on Washington in August. Then, in the following year, Mario Savio led the Berkeley Free Speech movement, across the Bay from the Gardners, in demonstrations against the university ban of off-campus political organizers.

John and Joan lived well apart from the political and cultural turmoil even though its center was much closer to them in San Francisco than in the Midwest. But it would have been impossible to be completely untouched by the upheavals. Though his rural background left him essentially conservative politically and socially, John had always taken an interest in the larger community and sought engagement with it. "He was driven by a search for stability," says Dennis, ". . . always searching for order in a chaotic world. . . . He described himself as a radical conservative—always iconoclastic—and against the masses. In that way he was nonsocial." On the other hand, "Joan was more socially driven, so more receptive to the ideas of the sixties, at least on the surface."

Their differences—his greater emphasis on tradition and her greater interest in social experiment—might also have contributed to problems between them, compounded by the more open and permissive social atmosphere that was developing. Married before they were twenty, neither had ever been romantically involved with anyone else. Since this was a time when social conventions were changing radically, the circumstances were decidedly volatile.

At least one friend commented that there seemed to be a double standard on Joan's part, as she invariably tried to quash any flirtatiousness in John, while engaging in it herself. But even according to John's accounts later, her flirtations were largely a reaction to his and a tool she used with men who could open doors to professional opportunities. Whatever the reasons, there was infidelity on both sides.

In a letter to Susan Thornton years later, John wrote about that time, "I became the world's most jealous and angry man." As a result, he wrote, Joan "became a husband beater."

They wound up seeking help from a marriage counselor, and the counselor suggested that John hit her back. "Twenty hits from her were worth one from me," he wrote. "I was a monster. Never meant to be, honest, but it's true, I learned to like it."

Thus, the guilt he'd harbored since Gilbert's accident deepened. And the only way he knew to combat the pressure of remorse was to make something that might compensate, however imperfectly, for the awful root of the trouble. So he wrote, and to further escape, he drank.

He knew that it would be his critical writing that would lead to a more significant academic position somewhere and give him the freedom to write the novels he wanted to write. But he didn't view academic writing wholly as drudge work. He was still keenly interested in medieval literature as well as in fiction. Ruby Cohn readily spoke of his "brilliance" as a medievalist, and Eric Solomon adds, "He had the kind of probing, restless mind that was so good to work with."

Most of his teaching was in the medieval literature courses he'd been hired for, but his restless energy was never satisfied with working on one project at a time. After finishing the translation of *Sir Gawain and the Green Knight,* he went at the four other poems of the *Gawain* poet: *The Pearl, Purity,* and *Patience,* all part of the same manuscript, and *Sir Erkenwald,* which critics think was likely written by the same author. Most significantly for Gardner, *Purity* and *Patience* had never been translated at all, offering an opportunity for his creative side to render the technical and symbolic elements of a dead language.

While he worked, he talked with poet Bill Dickey, a friend from Iowa who was also teaching at San Francisco and whose presence had probably helped attract Gardner there. In the book he finally published, Gardner also credits Don Finkel, though Finkel is quick to say that while they talked about the work and ideas generally (mainly when he and Connie Urdang saw the Gardners during John and Joan's visits to Joan's parents in Florissant), John never showed Finkel the poems or solicited specific comment. "John was just arrogant," Finkel says, not as criticism, but as description of Gardner's trust in his own judgments. "He always thought he knew [all he needed to know]."

It took nearly three years for Gardner to finish the work, complete with commentaries on the poems, the poet, and verse practice of the time, and when he did he wasn't finished with medieval poetry. He went right to work on *The Alliterative Morte Arthure*, another project that offered the same opportunity for creative translation. Sections of the long, anonymous poem from the mid-fourteenth century had been translated, but only once had the whole been done, a prose version, back in 1912. Like the *Gawain* poems, the work offered a ripe, open field.

At the same time, he embarked on an even more extensive project—an analysis of the poetry of Geoffrey Chaucer, combined with a biography. There had been lots written about Chaucer and his poems, and many biographies, but as with any serious subject there was always room for more. The six hundred years since their first appearance had left both Chaucer and his poems obscured in such distance that there was plenty of opportunity for contemporary translation and interpretation.

Gardner's faith in his own insights would have made him sure he had worthwhile ideas to contribute, and he may well have felt some obligation to address the largest, most central subject of his specialty. Even more, he had always been interested in making serious literature available to a public beyond academic specialists. To fashion a text covering such an expansive subject that was academically sound while being accessible to a more general audience was a daunting task, but in the three years he was at San Francisco he wrote nearly a thousand pages combining Chaucer's life and times with analysis of the poetry.

None of it was published during his years at San Francisco State, nor was his translation of *The Alliterative Morte Arthure*. In 1965, however, the University of Chicago Press decided to publish *The Complete Works of the Gawain-Poet*, containing his translation of the five poems, commentary, and attendant notes. In 1966, when he was thirty-three, the book came out—the first book of which he was the sole author.

Friends and colleagues at the time knew him mainly as a medievalist with wide interests. None remembers him talking at all about writing fiction. He did, though, find time in 1963 to write an essay on Melville's "Bartleby," a story addressing a central notion at the heart of his passion. Its theme had always been one of Gardner's interests—the clash between the individual and the demands of the social order.

"The conflict between the rule of the individual preference and the necessary laws of social action take various forms," he says in " 'Bartleby': Art and Social Commitment." While "the individual feels certain preferences, which taken together, establish his personal identity; society makes simultaneously necessary and unreasonable demands which modify individual identity." In Melville's story, he explains, lowly law copyist Bartleby, who has come to live in the office, refuses to conform to the demands of his boss (the embodiment of order), but as a result he is the more clear-sighted. "Estranged from the ordinary view of life (he does not even read the papers)," Gardner writes, "Bartleby perceives reality."

Most important, in Bartleby's estrangement and ultimate disintegration, Gardner finds the transcendental nobility that only art creates. The art rises from imaginative response to restrictive social demands, a response that in turn changes the social order. Thus, in his death, Bartleby "is now transmogrified to eternal life in art."

The story ultimately comprises an argument for the primary importance of imagination, and as in his commentary for *Forms of Fiction* Gardner insists on the essentially "moral" nature of such art, which authentically "transmutes" experience. "Melville suggests in various ways that the conflict between Bartleby and the world (and the conflict within the narrator's mind) is one between imagination and judgment, or reason," he says. "Judgment supports society: ethical law is the law of reason; imagination, on the other hand, supports higher values, those central to poetry and religion: moral law is the law of imagination. Ethical law, always prohibitive, guarantees equal rights to all members of the group, but moral law, always affirmative, points to the absolute, without respect to the needs of the group."

In the end, he concludes about Bartleby's plight, "justice must come either as a Christian afterlife or as a transmutation of purely conceptual experience—that is, as art." Ultimately, the assertion is religious. For as Bartleby's arrival, at the beginning, is called an "advent," and "There is nothing 'ordinarily human about him,'" at the end, he stands alone in the office "like the last pillar of a ruined temple."

In January 1964, the essay was published in the *Philosophical Quarterly*. It was Gardner's first purely academic publication and thus important for his career ambitions. It would also have been especially satisfying for him to place it in such a journal, given his enthusiasm for philosophy. Most important, though, he continued to work on the ideas he developed in it, especially the idea of "moral" art, as conceived by Tolstoy. He went on in the next year to expand some of the ideas in the essay and in *Forms of Fiction* into a much longer manuscript, which he gave the simple working title, "Moral Fiction."

For the time being, however, the manuscript only lay in his office, for his involvement with epics had led him to another idea. This was for a book about the way the classic epics related. His reading and teaching had led him to view the epics as a sort of extended conversation in which each is a response to the previous work. *The Odyssey*, that is, can be seen as a response to *The Iliad*, which it followed, and so with succeeding epic classics. "The Epic Conversation" he would call the book. At the same time, he began a translation of the Latin epic poet, Apollonius Rhodius, whose *Argonautica* contains the original story of Jason and Medea.

His dedication to teaching and writing notwithstanding, the San Francisco rain provided occasion for John to pursue another passion. Since Joan used the car to drive to work, he took the bus to San Francisco State. As Dunlap remembers the story, "John had a transfer on street transportation, his bus was slow, it was raining, and he sheltered in the doorway of a pawn shop. He was looking in the windows of the pawn shop, and there was a banjo. He was fascinated by the banjo, went in to look at it, wrote a hot check, and bought it. Then, instead of taking the bus on to school, he went back to their apartment, called in sick, and holed up for three or four days, cut all his classes, and at the end of that period he was an accomplished banjo player."

Precisely how accomplished he became may be open to question, but he did learn the instrument well enough to bring it out and play for friends there and in coming years. Still, the medieval criticism, the essays, the children's stories, the banjo, the work on Chaucer—all were secondary to his determination to write his own fiction. Between his critical projects, he had continued working on *Nickel Mountain*, and in 1963 he fashioned an episode from the novel into a separate story. Called "The Edge of the Woods," it was accepted by the *Quarterly Review of Literature*, and publication there of his second work of fiction was a step up in prestige from the *Northwest Review*. Just as important, it bolstered his idea of making *Nickel Mountain* a novel of related stories, each of which could stand on its own.

During his last year at Chico he had also begun another novel. The seeds of this one went back to his year at Oberlin, where he had taught *Anna Karenina* and had read much of Tolstoy's other work. Tolstoy has been criticized for the increasing preachiness of his later work, and like many other readers Gardner was particularly troubled by *The Resurrection*, the last of Tolstoy's novels. "I thought it was an awful, wicked book," he said, "and I meant to answer it point by point."

The "wickedness" is in the rigid determinism imposed on the characters, though "wicked" is hardly the description that comes to mind for a novel bound so rigidly in conventional Christian morality. But the label evidences Gardner's seriousness about aesthetic ideas. The center of Tolstoy's novel is the moral dilemma of Prince Nekhlyudlov, who meets a lower-class girl with whom he had a brief affair years before, an alliance that resulted ultimately from his lack of any moral system to curb his appetites. That is, without a moral center of his own, he could only go by others' examples, and his "animal nature," to determine his behavior. Later, he learns of the girl's descent into increasing desperation and her involvement in a murder. She isn't guilty, but when Nekhlyudlov is called as a juror in the case, his misunderstanding leads to her banishment in Siberia. Feeling responsible, the prince determines to give up all his material advantages and go to Siberia to marry her, hoping to compensate for his guilt and "resurrect" his own life and spirit.

Gardner agreed completely with Tolstoy that good art has positive moral effects, but though the main character's fate follows reasonably from situation and action in a realistic world, he still thought the novel failed completely. On the one hand, he shared Tolstoy's opposition to action based entirely on predetermined moral principles. However, the absence of any theoretical principles to guide behavior, which is what Tolstoy was trying to demonstrate, was, he thought, just as bad. The same rigidity results, making the characters unreal. Tolstoy had violated a central principle of good fiction—by using his characters to dramatize an already determined meaning rather than to explore a situation and discover the layers of ambiguity and intent underlying it. The result in Nekhlyudlov was a character who served as no more than the voice of an idea, and in the end the novel is reduced to extended lectures about these ideas.

In his own novel, Gardner wanted to demonstrate the dangers of such an enterprise; what happens, that is, when "people . . . love ideas to the exclusion of people, so that people become ideas."

When he wrote the first draft at Chico, he had called it "When the Jingling Stops," after one of its central metaphors. At one point, a group of blind children play a softball game, the "jingling" sound of bells planted in the ball letting them know where it is. When the ball stops and lies soundless, the blind players can only grope for it in darkness. The situation thus suggests the way we are lost when we rely exclusively on a theory. His protagonist Chandler, an academic philosopher, shares Tolstoy's skepticism at unwavering adherence to theory, but he can't get beyond abstract ideas and so encounter experience directly. Thus, when he dies at the end, his hope of "resurrection" can't be realized. Ultimately, Gardner titled his own novel *The Resurrection*.

In interviews about it, Gardner was asked about being a "philosophical novelist," as his protagonist is a professor of philosophy and raises issues from the discipline. Indeed, the novel engages ideas of philosophy to which Gardner had always been drawn. In this case, Chandler's position, Gardner explained, had been derived from Collingwood. Still, he made clear that though he may be called a philosophical novelist, "What I write is by no means straight philosophy. I make up stories. Meaning creeps in of necessity, to keep things clear. . . . What I write is philosophical only in a limited way. . . . I'm concerned—and finally more concerned—with . . . character . . . and people. It's that that makes me not really a philosopher, but a novelist."

Another of *The Resurrection*'s key elements is a grotesque character who serves as a philosophical counterpoint to the protagonist. Originally stimulated, as he said in later interviews, by Walt Disney cartoons, such grotesques are a recurrent element in his fiction. (In this one, it is the enormously fat John Horne.) During summer 1964, he had seen a striking example of Disney's work when the family had gone to New York to see, like thousands of others, the World's Fair.

Partly because of his own interest, and Joan's background, they had visited the Illinois Pavilion right next door to Missouri's. As part of it, Illinois native son Walt Disney was featured with an exhibit honoring the state's even more famous hero, Abraham Lincoln. An animated robot Lincoln entertained visitors, and Gardner was struck by the construction, which a decade later he remembered thinking was somehow horrific in its overall view. Visitors were ushered into a dim, neoclassical auditorium, where the lights came up to reveal a funeral urn, sculpted draperies, and the figure of Lincoln, clearly dead, seated and enormous. It looked like a mortuary, he said later, a cartoon world that was somber and threatening.

"Like a group of Auschwitz Jews," he wrote, "the audience is moved into a large and plush auditorium, where the doors close automatically, almost silently, and you wait in blackness and unearthly hush for the sound of escaping gas."

It was the same ominous, lurking unreality that grew to feed caricature figures in many of his novels.

When he finished *The Resurrection* in September 1964, he sent it along with the five stories that made up *Nickel Mountain* to his agent, Mavis McIntosh, who in turn sent it to New American Library. There, the book languished amid the slush pile of manuscripts from unknown, unpublished writers. Sometime after Christmas, it came to the attention of editor Edward Burlingame, who wrote back in February, expressing interest in *The Resurrection*. If Gardner would do some revision, he wrote, he wanted to look at it again. At the same time, he rejected the *Nickel Mountain* stories. Gardner went to work on the revision, and by the end of the month he had finished it and sent it off. Then he went back to work on *Nickel Mountain,* and in response to Burlingame's criticism of that manuscript he did some rewriting and wrote four new stories for the sequence, moving it more in the direction of a novel—that is, the new stories aimed to develop the same characters in continuing circumstances.

In June 1966, then, *The Resurrection* appeared in a hardback edition of twenty-five hundred copies. It was a small printing, but even so it was reviewed in almost a dozen established periodicals. The reviewer for *Choice,* widely read by librarians, praised its "generally vivid portraiture" in a prepublication review, though he did go on to say the novel was "awkward in style" and "inclines to the grotesque." Still, the brief review concluded that "it bears the stamp of genuine originality."

However, in *Saturday Review*, widely read by a more general audience, Granville Hicks's assessment was harsh. "Gardner has attempted more than he can handle," he wrote, and "seems to hope, as first novelists sometimes do, that the reader will understand what he is trying to do better than he does." In the end, Hicks said, "I find the book pretty muddled."

Sales didn't justify a paperback edition, so by that measure the novel wasn't successful. But the attention of important reviews helped make Gardner noticeable, and that same month, *The Complete Works of the Gawain-Poet,* which had been published by the University of Chicago Press the previous summer, was also reviewed, and favorably, in both academic journals and some literary and general periodicals. *Choice* noted the rendering of the previously untranslated *Patience* and *Purity,* and termed Gardner's versions "good re-creations that will appeal to eager undergraduates and their teachers" in a "handsomely printed book." Meantime, a review in the *New York Times Book Review* termed Gardner's work in translating the poems "a real service." Though the review faults the book for unclear focus on its audience—that is, Gardner seemed to vacillate between writing for academic specialists and a more general audience—in the end it credits Gardner for a "notable accomplishment."

Indeed, the urge to reach a larger audience seemed to conflict with the more rigorous tone and thorough examination of most academic writing, and the attempt to find a middle ground, an approach that would satisfy both audiences, was a problem that would stalk Gardner's work in coming years. Still, the two books and the attention they garnered provided evidence that his ambition was beginning to bear fruit.

As expected, Gardner's published work led to tenure, so at the relatively young age of thirty-three he was securely established. As beautiful a city as San Francisco was, however—and Joan really liked it there—he wasn't content. The growing political and social turmoil that had first touched him in Chico and that was becoming increasingly prominent throughout California was unsettling. He wanted a more familiar place to live and a job that would require less teaching so that he would have more time to write. Now, with his new publications making him an attractive candidate, he was in position to make a move.

In January 1965, he had written to Southern Illinois University in Carbondale, a small town a little more than a hundred miles southeast of St. Louis, to apply for an advertised professorship in medieval literature. The new chairman of the English Department, Robert Faner, was moving to greatly expand the department, partly to accommodate the rash of baby-boom students who were reaching college age. Located in familiar geography, the job in Carbondale seemed a good opportunity.

In his letter, Gardner listed his publications; professed his enjoyment of teaching his specialties of Old and Middle English, Chaucer, and the Gawain poet; and said he was looking for a lighter teaching load than he had at San Francisco State so that he could finish the biography of Chaucer he was writing. As Southern Illinois University had its own press, which supported publishing as well as teaching, Gardner's writing stood him well. Faner wrote back to say that the position at SIU called for teaching only two classes per semester and that an assistant professorship might be possible. In the spring, the job was offered.

Even though Carbondale was much closer to her childhood home, Joan did not at all want to leave San Francisco. Its beauty and cultural life were rich, she had made good friends, she had a fine job, and there were regular opportunities to play and work on her music. John was determined, however. The professional opportunity was just too good to pass up, and the idea of returning to rural, midwestern farming country was attractive. Their different desires exacerbated conflicts between them, and years later he told Susan Thornton that he had been "on the verge of insisting on divorce." In the end, however, he decided to stay with Joan and persuaded her to come with him.

She sent out an application to teach music at SIU, then in June went by herself to Carbondale to find a house for them to rent. With two children and the house in San Francisco to sell, moving had become more complicated. But John's contract was signed, and they made plans. Their house needed a paint job before it was ready to sell, but John found one of his graduate students who was willing to move in and do the work of preparing it for sale in exchange for rent. Thus, in July 1965, a Mayflower van pulled up, packed the furniture, including Joan's two pianos, and the Gardners moved back to the Midwest, to the rural countryside outside Carbondale.

6

A Different Farm

I loved my wife—loved her only second to adventures
and ideas!

— *The Wreckage of Agathon*

OR JOHN, THE MOVE to Carbondale was a great step.
The rural landscape around Carbondale was something he knew and loved, and here it was part of
a professional world where he felt he could truly flourish. He
would make significantly more money—fourteen hundred dollars more than the eighty-six hundred dollars he made in his final year at San Francisco—in a place where it cost much less to
live. He would have more to say about what he taught; he would
have more advanced, committed students (graduates as well as
undergraduates); and he would have half as many classes.

Gardner was one of the six SIU English Department professors hired for that fall. The department was expanding, along
with the whole university, to serve the enormous wave of post–
World War II children now reaching college age. His office was
in an old building with five other new professors, and he shared

it with Eddie Epstein, a heavy, dark-haired New Yorker who had been hired to teach linguistics and modern literature.

At the time, Gardner's hair was trimmed to his ears, and he had taken up smoking the pipe that would become his trademark. Epstein remembers the first time he saw him in their office, looking out the window into the street, "spewing out spark and smoke like a volcano." It was an image that Gardner loved to foster—the fiery outlaw eccentric (part dragon?)—and it grew stronger in the coming decade. It seemed also to reflect the growing political and social turmoil, which for him mixed always with the classic traditional. As the sixties turned into the seventies, his hair turned blond-white, and he grew it to shoulder length so that, as one friend said of him in the early seventies, "He looked for all the world like a radical bomber."

On the surface, neither Epstein's urban background nor his temperament gave him much in common with Gardener. A connoisseur of fine wine and gourmet food, Epstein's tastes were far from John's more common, rural-bred appetites. Says Jerry Handler, another professor who knew both, unlike Gardner, "Eddie was a guy who when everyone was drinking at a party, he'd be sitting in a corner reading a book." But he also loved opera, a taste that intersected with John's in its combination of classical music and dramatic theater. Those who knew the New Yorker also testify to his intellectual brilliance, which certainly attracted Gardner. Before coming to SIU, Epstein had worked for Noonday Press in New York, one of the most important independent publishers of contemporary literature in the fifties and sixties.

In the beginning, they didn't talk to each other about their work. But for the next three years they shared the same office, and the two became good friends as Gardner found Epstein a lively sounding board and tester of ideas. He had the same wide intellectual interest that Gardner did, and as they got to know each other they came to deeply respect each other's thinking.

That first fall, Gardner proposed new classes in both fiction and poetry writing. He had been hired as a medievalist, though, and was himself assigned to teach a graduate seminar in medieval literature and a general survey course. That was his preference and for the next six years, he happily resisted teaching any creative writing classes. Determined to write his own fiction, he realized that teaching literature required much less time.

"When you're over, you're over," he told John Howell (another colleague who became a good friend) about literature classes. Creative writing classes, on the other hand, required continual hands-on work in conferences to go over students' stories and their rewrites in line-by-line and word-by-word detail. He always liked the connections with students who looked up to him, but the attention brought with it substantial claims on his time. Thus, for several years he taught a *Beowulf* class at his house on Monday nights, and other literature classes on campus, none of which required the detailed attention creative writing classes did.

As at Oberlin and Chico, he was a striking and inspirational teacher for many. Pat Gray, who enrolled in his class at SIU in the fall of 1967, remembers the first time she saw him:

> He was sitting on the desk, cross-legged, yoga style. His white German shepherd, Guinevere, was there. I didn't know who he was, I'd never heard of him. His hair was

gray, but not very, and he looked very young. He had a sweater that was torn at the neck, and one of the elbows was out, and of course he was smoking a pipe. I thought he was one of the students. And I thought, he better get the hell off there because Gardner'll be in here any minute and kick his butt. He was talking to another student, and suddenly the conversation segued from talking to the student to talking to the class as a whole, and that's when it dawned on me that this was in fact John Gardner.

He said, "We need this kind of start. Do you know much about the Middle Ages?" We said no, and he said, "Why don't I talk to you about the 'tripartite soul'?" And that was his first lecture.

His youthfulness and informality, along with his penchant for bending, if not breaking, the rules, are keys to the affinity students felt with him. "Sometime around the middle of the class," Gray remembers, "he said, 'Somebody told me it [is] midterm. Is it midterm?' We said yes, close to it. And he said, 'Well, I guess we should do something about it. Think up a question and answer it, and that'll be your midterm.'"

But it was more than his comparative youth and antiauthoritarian informality that made Gardner such a popular teacher. "You have to love your students," one remembers his saying, and that genuine affection was something most who knew him agree he conveyed. Along with the very personal connection he made with students, the quality of his insights, delivered with an earnestness that assured everyone that they could learn what he was teaching, was equally key.

"He was a spellbinding speaker and made terrific connections," says Stephen Falcolne, another student. "He would start talking about medieval plays, and say how they were like Beckett, then go on to demonstrate the connections."

His effectiveness as a teacher didn't go unnoticed by those above him either. In the winter of 1966, Robert Faner noted in Gardner's file that he was to be commended, not only as a superb teacher of students, but also, in his example, as "a teacher of teachers."

The acuteness of mind that impressed students and colleagues was evident as well in his work as an editor. In addition to his teaching and writing that first year, Gardner took on the editorship of medieval criticism for *Papers on Language and Literature,* an academic journal that had been brought to headquarter at SIU. The job wasn't just another credit to add to his curriculum vitae; it was an opportunity to promote and influence work he thought truly vital.

One paper on Chaucer submitted to the journal had come from a University of Southern California graduate student, and Gardner's written response, as characteristic of all his work, was maniacally detailed. Barry Sanders, whose professor had sent the paper for him, was both flattered and a little shocked when Gardner sent him back an answer of no less than twenty pages. "It looked like someone had bled all over it," Sanders says about the flood of comments in red ink. Ultimately, Gardner told Sanders that if he would make the revisions recommended, his paper would make a wonderful three-page note, which Gardner would publish. Sanders dutifully went to work, and the article was published.

Gardner had also advised Sanders to apply to teach at SIU

once he completed his Ph.D. Sanders had a friend who was teaching there who encouraged the idea, so he eagerly pursued this possibility. Gardner's invitation to Sanders wasn't merely perfunctory. The joining of like-minded artists and thinkers was something he always went out of his way to encourage. Thus, in fall 1966, Sanders and Gardner began a collaboration that only continued for a year or two but made medieval literature live for their students. "We taught together, went into the room together," Sanders says. "He'd play banjo or guitar, sing ballads out loud, and we'd talk about the ballads and romances."

Gardner's affection for traditional ballads solidified another important friendship in his early days in Carbondale. It was a friendship that became longer lasting for both him and Joan. At a dinner party for some of the new English professors that first fall at Thomas Kinsella's, the well-known Irish poet who had come to teach as a visiting professor, Gardner met Carroll (Cal) Riley and his wife, Brent. Riley was an anthropologist at work on a book about early civilizations; Brent was writing children's books. But it wasn't that they were all writing books that connected them. A little later, they were all invited to another party, and there Brent discovered their shared enthusiasm. "John was the only person who loved and cared as much as I about traditional Scottish and Irish ballads," she says. At that second party, they both stayed up with others until dawn, singing and cementing the friendship. This combination of interests went on to feed his teaching of the medieval ballads.

Over the years, his engagement with history joined him with Cal too, and in 1973 they combined to team-teach a course. Fitting right into the impulse John always brought with him, the collaboration grew in no small way from Gardner's desire to unify different aspects of a discipline, and different disciplines, to form an overview. His "epic conversation" idea had originated in that impulse to weave together different strands of thinking, and though the project remained to be realized the urge to synthesize was always strong. The course he and Cal devised thus combined *The Odyssey, The Argonautica,* and the ancient Babylonian *Gilgamesh* epic. "We sort of winged it," Cal says of that class. "We originally planned that I'd give the archaeological and historical background, and he the literary aspects. But we kept upstaging each other all through the course."

The course was a natural for Gardner, combining his major intellectual concerns. His interest in cultural roots, at the foundation of all his writing and teaching, joined his engagement with classical epics that delved into ancient heroes and archetypes.

Meantime, the enthusiasm and flair for teaching that Gardner brought to his classes spilled well beyond the classroom. It was as if he were the center of a vortex wherever he went, constantly venting enthusiasms and generating them among those around him, while convincing students, colleagues, and friends alike that they were on the verge of great accomplishment. His insight and intensity made believers, it seemed, of all those who came near. And though his unorthodoxy sometimes rankled many who were older and more established, it endeared him devotedly to students and younger people.

The center from which it all originated was the farm on Boskeydell Road. Having sold their house in San Francisco at the end of the summer in 1966, John and Joan bought a twenty-acre farm five miles south of Carbondale. It had a good barn, a shed, and an old two-story frame house with pillars in front. The house was run down, but it had fresh white paint and room for the children and guests. They got the whole thing for just thirty-eight thousand dollars. Set in some three hundred acres of unused land with mostly woods and fallow fields, the farm helped John realize a life he had missed since leaving Batavia, as it became the locus of the persona he was forming—the rural, intellectual outsider at the center of serious art.

Like the farm where he had grown up, the place was never particularly neat or orderly, and there was always much that needed upkeep and repair. But things worked well enough. And although the old house was enlarged steadily through the years the disorder never got in the way of living comfortably. He bought horses for the whole family, helping to fill out his vision of country life. Others whom he met boarded their horses there, and the farm welcomed everyone with whom the Gardners connected. Always social and open, John and Joan made the place continually inviting, and the countless gatherings they hosted became legendary in the area.

Jerry Osbourne, who worked as a news director for one of the radio stations, boarded horses there and stored hay in the barn; he came out two or more times a week. He wasn't part of the school, but he was interested in writing fiction, had heard of John, and so was eager to take advantage of the contact when he met him at an event on campus.

Joining others who came out, he remembers playing "John's version of polo, using brooms and soccer balls." "It was pretty much of a party house," he admits. Indeed, parties lubricated with liquor and music typically began around nine in the evening and went on all night, sometimes until the next morning. The liquor went with everything, and not in any moderate quantity. "He loved vodka," says Osbourne. Others said gin was his favorite, but Osbourne maintains, "It didn't make any difference, as long as it was white."

Gardner and Riley took to mixing martinis, spiking them with scotch, and serving them to anyone interested. When Gardner's novels generated substantial income in the early seventies, he had a swimming pool built in back of the house, and John Howell remembers one colleague who had been drinking heavily with Gardner climbing up to the carpeted roof of the adjacent pool room they had built. John egged him on, eventually climbing up himself and pushing him off. He barely got past the concrete walk and into the pool below. Howell also remembers another night when John and Joan left Howell's house fighting, near three in the morning. Gardner was drunk but insisted on driving, and Joan directed him right into the ditch. They made their way back to Howell's and woke him up to take them home. Likewise, Sanders remembers driving around with Gardner on Halloween, trick-or-treating in Gardner's pickup truck, knocking on doors and asking for martinis instead of candy.

Says Pat Gray, "He was an Olympic gin drinker. I've seen him drink fifths, martinis all the time. . . . He was always backed up against the sink, and there was always a crowd around him. I asked him once why he was always in the kitchen, and he said, 'That's where the ice is.'"

In fact, Brent Riley recalls, both John and Joan "were great drinkers. . . . I've seen him drinking and talking about very weighty subjects and finding himself sliding down the wall, and still talking as he reached the floor."

Still, the liquor and wildness never seemed to interfere with his work. His younger brother Jim remembers his coming to Batavia for a visit in the early 1970s and the two of them sitting up and drinking and laughing and carrying on far into the night, until Jim had to crawl off to sleep. Early in the morning he was awakened by the sound of a typewriter. John was hard at work at the dining room table.

Osbourne concurs. After drinking all night with everyone else, he says, "We'd all be going to hit the sack someplace, and he'd be going somewhere to write."

In 1967, Gardner took on the job of writing a CliffsNotes booklet for Malory's *Le Morte d'Arthur*. As Pat Gray remembers the story, he kept putting it off. Then at ten o'clock one night, he made himself a pitcher of martinis and worked until four. By then the pitcher was empty, so he made himself another and finished up the job at nine thirty or ten in the morning, when he took it to the post office and mailed it.

Sanders too remarks how the liquor, though always present, never seemed to interfere with the work. He remembers coming to Boskeydell to go over his writing with John, who'd always "be sitting there with his pipe filled with Dunhill, and his glass filled with gin." Sanders, now a professor of medieval literature, says, "If I know how to write at all it's because of Gardner. He'd go over my writing virtually every night—every line, every word of what I was writing."

In 1968, one party went on for two full days, complete with a light show, two bands that took turns setting up on top of the barn, kegs of beer, and a pig roast. By the late sixties, traditional borders between professors and students had blurred, and the two mixed freely at the parties, students mainly smoking marijuana while the professors drank martinis.

The less formal student-teacher relationships suited John. He regularly exchanged letters with Alex Paul, his former student whom he had engaged to ready the San Francisco house for sale. John asked Paul what he planned to do after he graduated, and Paul wrote that he wanted to continue his studies and write. Gardner suggested that he come out to Carbondale to study with him. He could stay at Boskeydell rent free, in exchange for babysitting the children and training the horses.

Not that Paul was a horseman. Originally from Hackensack, New Jersey, he had grown up far from any stable. Nor had he had much call to do any baby-sitting. Still, he told Gardner he'd be glad to take him up on the offer. Paul, then, came to Carbondale and installed himself in the unused chicken coop, halfway between the house and the barn.

Some fifteen by fifteen feet, the coop was plenty roomy for chickens and became perfectly adequate for Paul, as he cleaned it out and made it a livable space. He wasn't always part of household activities, but he was present during much that went on during the two years he stayed there and was part of the lively, freewheeling atmosphere John liked. Several times, he and John would go off on horses, sometimes all night, and talk. John was far from an expert horseman himself, but he loved riding and all the physical aspects of country life, which were so separate from the intellectual world that occupied most of his time. Excursions with Paul provided a welcome break from the endless calls of his everyday life and kept him abreast of the burgeoning youth culture affecting everything around them. His interest in people and subcultures apart from his usual domain had always been part of him, of course. According to Paul, he and John's neighbor, English sculptor Nicholas Vergette, were key figures at Boskeydell in bridging the separation of students and professors. But beginning at Oberlin, John had always fostered such bridges.

Partly as a result, both Gardners had readily become friends with new people around them each place they moved, though John didn't much keep up with friends he had made after he left. And of all the people who touched his life in Carbondale, Vergette became especially close.

He had come to SIU from Cambridge, England, in 1960 as a visiting professor in the Art Department. When offered a permanent job, he decided to stay, and he and his wife, Helen, bought a farm just two miles down the road from the one the Gardners bought in 1966. Its old frame house had been built in 1890 as a summer home for a wealthy Chicagoan, and the Englishman Vergette loved the idea that he could have his own tract of country here.

Nearly six feet tall, with dark hair, strong and well proportioned, Vergette fit the expression "man's man," says friend Jerry Handler. He was "a very handsome, sexy guy [with] sharp, chiseled features and a fantastically charming smile. . . . A guy, I think, of deep moral conscience."

Soon after John and Joan met the Vergettes, the school made a short instructional film (*Vergette Makes a Pot*, still in release), which shows the slender, dark-haired Vergette in his early forties. He looks almost like an athlete as he shapes the pot he is making, fitting Handler's description as his tongue wags out with concentrated intensity.

Besides living in the same rural neighborhood several miles from colleagues at the university, the two families had much else in common. The Vergettes' son, Marcus, was only two years younger than Joel, and the two became as close as their fathers. Both John and Nick also liked to ride horses, though Vergette was much more experienced. Vergette too liked to drink, and talk, if not quite as much as John. Handler remembers him, actually, as relatively quiet, even "taciturn, except when he was drinking. Then he would get more florid in his speech, intense in his expressions."

Helen and Joan also grew close, and says Handler, she "was the real verbose one. . . . Helen could talk you under the ground."

In August 1968, the two families vacationed together in Guanajuato, Mexico, and during the 1971–72 school year, while the Gardners were on sabbatical in London, the Vergettes also spent part of the summer there. Perhaps most important, however, both men were deeply and fundamentally engaged in the making of art. A sculptor who worked mainly with ceramics, Vergette was "a very creative guy, with very strong views on art," says Handler.

John had always promoted his friends enthusiastically, and as he gained more influence himself he was quick to exert it on behalf of those around him whom he readily proclaimed geniuses. Visitors to the Gardners' were greeted by a four-foot cast of a dragon, the size of a large dog, that had been designed by Vergette and was perched in the tree in the front yard. As John's influence grew at SIU, he was key in arranging for the installation of some of Vergette's large, monumental sculptures on the campus.

Osbourne's comment notwithstanding, the world of Boskeydell was hardly a continual party. But the growing dominance of the youth culture and the loosening social mores that culture spawned, coupled with the very social and antiauthoritarian atmosphere John and Joan fostered, encouraged a sort of "anything goes" feeling in the rural environment. Like so many friends who had known them earlier and in other places, Epstein says, "Both John and Joan were lively, bright, interesting people, and [the farm] was a center of social activity. His atmosphere was exciting."

In the Carbondale countryside, there was both room and time to get involved again in some things John had let lapse. One of these was music, and as with all the arts he pursued his engagement was no idle hobby. In 1968, he met music professor Joe Baber, who was also the violist in a quartet formed with other professors in the music school there. After a concert by the quartet, Gardner went backstage of the improvised auditorium and told him enthusiastically how much he'd enjoyed the show. He proposed that they collaborate on an opera. Baber was skeptical, but Gardner persisted, and a few days later Baber went out to the farm where Gardner elaborated on his proposal. "It didn't sound any less crazy" then, Baber later wrote in a memoir, "though the weight of [Gardner's] personality and way of life were persuasive. . . . I saw his stable of horses and found out how knowledgeable he was, while his incongruities had me swinging between awe and suspicion."

They stayed up late into the night talking and drinking, and though Baber wasn't persuaded then, the friendship blossomed nevertheless. Gardner maintained that most operas failed mainly because the libretto did; that is, the stories were just not well written. He wanted to change that by writing a libretto that would have the force of great literature and live up to the best music. As the night went on, he continued to try to persuade Baber to work with him. While they discussed ideas and hypothetical plots, Baber remembers, "The outrageousness of his humor was part of the image he left me with." Even more, in his continuing insistence on the importance of the art, "the seriousness of John's moral purpose was clear."

The next morning, Baber was shocked to find Gardner at his door with a draft of a libretto he had written the previous night after Baber had gone home late. "The first draft of *Frankenstein* amazed me," Baber wrote. "The subject left me incredulous at first, but my resistance to what seemed like sensationalism waned as I sensed the power of what he had done. The first act was almost complete, the third sketched in, and the other two outlined."

With a good deal still left to finish, Baber agreed to collaborate, and a relationship began that continued for the rest of Gardner's life. The pace of their work was sporadic as Baber left SIU after the next year and went on to teach at the University of Kentucky in Lexington. Much of the work—exchanging drafts and commenting on each others'—was done by mail. The results were not especially successful in conventional terms—none of the operas attracted anything like the attention of Gardner's literary work—but conventional success was secondary to the extension of serious art, which was always Gardner's primary motive. And their collaboration did eventually lead to production of three operas they wrote. They worked at it for eight or nine years, but before satisfactorily finishing it. Says Baber, "It's almost unproducible. It has a cast of twenty-three, an on-stage chorus, and [an] on-stage orchestra. I made a joke once that it had everything in it but ice skating, and John said, 'Well, I think I can work that in.'"

The humor was intentional, but John's engagement with the idea was serious, as it was with all artistic productions. In fall 1975, he came to Lexington to put what both thought would be the finishing touches on *Frankenstein* for production, but from John's point of view their work had only started. Remembers Baber, "We thought we could rewrite it and do a final version as it was being produced . . . [that] we could adapt it. We were holding out, 'knowing nothing of the world,' as John would say."

Though their plans for *Frankenstein* didn't work out at the time, the attempt led immediately to another project that did. In the midst of work on *Frankenstein*, says Baber, [John] would say, 'What's next?' He was jumping right into the next thing. I was really exhausted. I said, 'I don't care what we do, but at least we're going to do something where we don't have to tell the story so hard, where everyone in the audience knows the story. Where everyone in the audience knows she's going to guess Rumpelstiltskin's name, for instance.' I just used that as an example, just out of the air, and he jumped on it instantly. He said, 'Wait a minute, it's never been done. . . . Let's see, what have we got here? We've got the gold, we've got the greed, we've got the bragging.' He immediately got the themes in his mind. He was just lightning."

Fired by the idea, Gardner went to work, and less than a year later, a much more practical, producible opera was completed.

Rumpelstiltskin "was the exact opposite of *Frankenstein*," says Baber. It was "totally practical," shaped according to the resources available to them in Lexington. "We made the orchestra almost exactly like Mozart's orchestra," he says. "We contacted the director here who'd done *Marriage of Figaro* [the previous year] and she said, 'Write a scene and show me.'"

Baber was amazed at Gardner's response. "I expected a month to go by," he says. "Or . . . never [to] hear about it again. You talk, you get all enthusiastic, you go home, and nothing ever happens. But with John . . . three days and the thing arrives. Special Delivery. It was like Saturday morning, and [my wife and I] went back to bed and read this libretto, and we're laughing ourselves silly. It was so wonderful. We showed it to this director and she went crazy. She said, 'We gotta do this thing.'"

It took a year to finish, but *Rumpelstiltskin* opened at the new opera house in Lexington in 1977 and went on to play at the opera house in Philadelphia as the collaboration continued. Gardner, meanwhile, wrote a libretto for another opera, whose idea had come from a visit Baber had made to Omaha, where he'd been asked if he and John had anything that would fit a small company hoping to perform in the public schools. "Something about an hour long that they could do at assemblies and such," Baber recalls.

At first Gardner said it was too much to do. But he was intrigued by the challenge of composing such a short piece, and only a few days after the first conversation with Baber, John sent him the first draft of *Samson and the Witch*. The Omaha group that had asked for it dissolved before it was finished, however, and it wasn't done until Baber finished it himself a decade after John's death.

John and Joan's musical proclivities were an integral part of the atmosphere at Boskeydell. Joan's piano music, medieval ballads, and opera notwithstanding, Lucy recalls that most of the music was folk songs, with John's playing both guitar and banjo. But there was jazz too. John Howell, Cal Riley, and Ed Epstein had all been musicians in younger days, and so with his typical enthusiasm Gardner persuaded them to come together and form a band. In fact, Howell had performed as a jazz drummer with bands in Chicago, in western Canada, and elsewhere. So Gardner borrowed drums from a friend's son who was in a rock group and set them up in the Rileys' dining room. At first, Epstein played piano, though he quickly tired of the idea and quit. But the others, with John's encouragement, kept working. They never performed widely, but they did finally arrange at least one concert at the Presbyterian church where the Gardners were members and friendly with the pastor.

Gardner's long interest in dramatic theater was also rekindled at Carbondale. He hadn't pursued it in San Francisco, but Carbondale was much smaller and less competitive and thus more open to such projects. Here he found the chance to take it up again, combining it with his own literary interests. One of his projects was the translation of the five medieval plays of the so-called Wakefield Master, which were part of a group of thirty-two related plays dramatizing episodes of the Bible. Dating from the fourteenth century, like the *Gawain* poems, they were of unknown authorship and in a dead language. The uncertainties offered the kind of broad opportunity for interpretation in translation and staging that appealed to Gardner.

In the spring of 1968, one of his students came to see him after having visited Wakefield (in Yorkshire, England). Gardner was translating the plays into modern English, and as Stephen Falcolne recalls, "He just said, 'Let's do these plays. You're going to translate one—they're easy.' So I said okay. And I did one. He'd just get everyone going like that."

Pat Gray, who'd taught high school for five years before coming back to graduate school, had studied at the University of Texas experimental theater lab and was trying to envision how those same plays might be staged in modern circumstances. "I did about thirty pages of dramatic action and mood and tone setting," she says. "But I never could do the drawing very well. So I called him up and said, 'I've got this almost prepared, but I can't get down on paper what it looks like.'"

He had her come to his office, where she laid out her plans with books and pencils and paper for props, and they talked about it.

Then he said, "I've got these plays, they're all modernized, we should put them on. You should direct them, you know how to do this. Come over to my house and we'll talk about it." I said, "I'm already signed up for two novel courses," and he said, "Oh, that's all right, you'll get it read, it's okay."

So I went to his house and met Joan. And we drank many drinks before the meal, and during the meal, and after the meal. And we smoked during the meal, talked during the meal, and by one or two o'clock, of course I said I would do it. It was one of the best conversations I ever had in my life.

With Gray directing, she and Gardner enlisted students, colleagues, family, whoever was interested, and undertook to stage all five plays. They arranged to stage them at the Presbyterian church, and to play Jesus, they got the slender bearded minister, Duane Lanchester, whose appearance they thought was perfect for the role.

John's way was always to involve everyone around in artistic collaboration, ignite them with his enthusiasm, but leave each to follow his or her interest in working out details. Still, he remained as closely involved as he could, never stepping back to be a distant director. For one of the plays, an acquaintance of Gardner's was cast as Noah, but after a week he was consistently late to rehearsals and hadn't learned his lines. In the second week, Gray discussed the problem with Gardner, and he agreed that she'd have to replace him. Emotions in Gardner families had always run close to the surface, however, and his involvement with the personal side of those around him was never at a distance. In this case, though he agreed with the decision to replace his friend, he felt closely involved in the problem. When Gray called the friend with the decision, John listened in on the phone conversation. "I tried to be kind," Gray says, "but [the friend] said, 'You just don't understand, I've had so many things going on,' and he started to tell me some of the things. I said, 'You obviously don't have time to be in a play anyway, so I'm just going to ask you to step down.' The man started crying, and when he did, John started to cry and wring his hands. He didn't want me to not do it, he just was sad. And I was too. Then I hung up and John said, 'That was wonderful.'"

Gardner became Noah then, and Joan played Noah's wife; and he played one of the shepherds in the *Second Shepherd's Play*, another of the cycle. The ancient Christian pageant was set firmly in current times, with physical elements that were decidedly contemporary. Jesus, for instance, was dressed in khakis, with sweat running down his back and underarms. At one point, Gray had Mary Magdalene slide down his body, in an unmistakably sexual gesture, and Gray remembers saying, "'I think I'll have her do something else.' But John said, 'Don't have her do anything else. That slide is all I can stand.'"

They rehearsed the five plays three times a week for about five weeks. Meantime, Nick Vergette made five original mosaics, using rock he found in the area in an original technique he developed and which John filmed. When they finally staged the production, they had original music composed by another graduate student who played piano. He started the play with a low boogie-woogie and built to a traditional religious theme. Overhead projectors displayed a medieval village on the back wall, complete with rivers going through it and fish in the sky.

As far as anyone knew, it was the first time the five mystery plays had ever been staged anywhere in the country, and the church auditorium was filled for every performance. There weren't a lot of competing entertainments in the area, and the show was a memorable hit, at least among the university-related audience who had any interest in theater. Certainly, there had never been anything like it in Carbondale.

The Wakefield play was of course only part of the ongoing

maelstrom emanating from Gardner and Boskeydell. Joe Baber repeats the comment of Lennis Dunlap and so many others who knew him, saying, "The guy was just going all the time. Day and night. My wife and I would get tired and go home and he'd just keep going. It was like he never slept."

Not surprisingly, all the drinking and social energy underlined the ongoing problems between John and Joan, which were intensified by her inability to find a solid working situation for herself in Carbondale. When they had first come, Robert Faner had made some effort to help her find a job, but her graduate degree in music and teaching experience in San Leandro rendered her overqualified for most jobs in the area. With prime responsibility for managing their school-aged children, she was stuck in rural Illinois, and the displacement she felt in what for her was a long step away from the civilization of San Francisco was acute.

Their first year there, she did find work as a teaching assistant at the University Lab School, where she taught high school and elementary students; the next three years, she taught three days each week in nearby Alto Pass. But she never did find consistent work teaching, nor anything else that seemed to fit her disposition and experience.

There may have been elements of self-fulfilling prophecy in her search, as her view of the area as a lost backwoods was confirmed and deepened over time. But the fact was, though she participated in the 1968 production of the Wakefield Cycle plays, continued to do some composition, and played the classical piano music at which she had become expert, the world of Carbondale never provided an adequate outlet. The situation added to the strain between her and John as their personalities attracted nearly everyone they met, and the involvements that often followed fed tension between them.

"Their life was just a three-ring circus," says Baber, "with all that was going on, with people constantly in the house all the time, parties all the time, trouble and activity, not just in the marriage but in everything."

Says Pat Gray, "They made a lot of us think of [Edward Albee's play, *Who's Afraid of*] *Virginia Woolf[?]*. He loved Joan, no question. She was the love of his life. And he appreciated her talent. She matched him wit for wit." But, she qualifies, "I think a lot of times Joan was responding to things that John did. I don't know that she ever instigated, but she always matched it."

Reminiscent of the San Francisco vase-breaking incident, Baber says, "She would just needle him and needle him until he'd just snap."

One of the issues to which Joan was responding was John's involvement with other women. "He was enormously loving," says Gray. "But he was chronically unfaithful to Joan all their married life." Perhaps generously, she says, "I think of it as just another of his creative enthusiasms."

The jealousy such involvements occasioned certainly sharpened their difficulties. When in 1968, John was working on *The Wreckage of Agathon*, a novel he'd begun the previous year, he took refuge at Baber's for three days after a fight. Baber remembers him typing away for hours straight at the dining room table. "It was snowing very heavily," Baber recalls, "and he came over to hide out from Joan. He said something about having slugged her [and that] it kind of felt good." But then he seemed horrified "and said, like, 'Oh my God, I've hit her!' John and Joan would have these rifts," Baber says. "Then they'd patch up and be really sweet to each other."

In fact, John's injuries, which were much more common than for most, probably weren't usually inflicted by Joan but resulted from his own tendency toward physical carelessness. He had a long history of minor injuries that he liked to wear like badges of physical toughness. At the same time, they must have seemed to him emblematic—if not just consequence—of the guilt he professed.

Meanwhile, the openness that had led John to invite Alex Paul to the chicken coop, that had brought students and people from all over to Boskeydell for varying periods of time, also brought his sister Sandy and her family in 1967. And with them came more difficulties.

John stayed in close touch with his family, and when he learned that Sandy's marriage was foundering he invited her and her husband to come to Carbondale for a fresh start. Neither had professional ties or any apparent direction, so John suggested that David attend SIU to get his college degree. At the same time, they could set their lives straight in a comfortable, supportive atmosphere.

So, they came with their young daughter and rented a house in town big enough to sublease two rooms. Thus they could have some income while David, Sandy's husband, attended school. In January 1968, Greg, the son of John's aunt Millie and the minister with whom she had an affair, also came to SIU and rented one of Sandy and David's rooms. He admits he was jealous of the home Alex Paul had made for himself in the chicken coop, but he did have a private entrance at Sandy and David's and was grateful for the opportunity. He enrolled in the music school and also spent a good deal of time at Boskeydell, where he could get his hands into some of the farm life there and where he also witnessed close up some of the battles between John and Joan.

Like everyone else who knew her, Greg was impressed by Joan's intelligence and even remembers John's saying at times that she was smarter than he was. He also remembers a generosity that John demonstrated toward her, even in the heated aftermaths of their fights, that wasn't reciprocated. For Greg, the difference in their reactions was one of the things that made him comfortable and trusting of his cousin.

> There was a time when they were going back and forth, Joan saying, "You fool, you jerk," things like that, and Bud talking back. Then Bud left the room, and I remember Joan coming over to me and saying, "Well, that Bud, he's sick you know." Then she referred to something he'd said about inviting someone else to bed with them. And she just went on about how sick John was, and how he wasn't all there.
>
> Then she left the room and [Bud returned and] I was alone with [him], and he came over and said, "You know, Joan is really a terrific person." And he talked about how she had a lot of medical problems, some bad pain, and someone would come to the door and she'd be gracious and put all that pain aside and let them in. He'd go on about how terrific she was. Literally this was the same fight, the same afternoon.

The pain she suffered wasn't made up. She'd had several miscarriages through the years and was plagued by adhesions that had troubled her since their days in San Francisco. In 1967, she went to St. Louis for surgery, which removed the worst, but the growths persisted and continued to cause debilitating periodic spasms.

Greg is quick to point out, however, "I really did love Joan when I was there. When she wasn't in that mode—taking off on John, or something—she was really enjoyable. . . . I was something of a music student at the time, studying voice, and I can remember her accompanying me on the piano, her just being good, healthy company. She enjoyed being witty, had a bit of an off-beat take on things. And when she didn't have an ugly ax to grind, she was darn good company."

Sandy and David, however, relied on John to help them settle in Carbondale, and Joan seemed to resent the intrusion foisted on her. She had never liked Sandy's bubbly cheer in the first place. John did get Sandy involved in the Wakefield production, where she played the White Angel in the last of the Wakefield plays, and David, of course, enrolled at the university. But for Joan, their presence was one more irritation.

As they grew, Joel and Lucy were far from oblivious to their parents' dissension. In keeping with their parents' temperaments (and the times), both were given more freedom and access to physical space than most children. A beautiful blond girl, Lucy grew to be "very stubborn and mercurial," according to Baber, whose wife was her first violin teacher. Once, when his wife was out of the country, Baber stood in to give young Lucy, who was about six at the time, a violin lesson. "I was talking to her," he recalls, "and she threw the violin over her head. I think," he went on, "she was already in rebellion from all the garbage that was going on between John and Joan."

On another occasion when she was twelve, upset at her parents' arguments, she emptied all the gin she could find into the swimming pool they had built. Then she and the Rileys' daughter, Cynthia, spent the night sleeping in the field, and in the morning walked to the Vergettes—where Joel was staying with Marcus—for refuge.

Still, by both Joel's and Lucy's accounts, their parents gave them a rich childhood. Music, art, literature, and the conversation of highly educated people surrounded them constantly. Joan was usually there for them as they grew up, and since John did most of his writing at home he was likewise never far. He rode horses with them, played with them, helped teach them music, and showed them around the countryside, all of which they came to value.

Notwithstanding the turmoil that seemed always around, Brent Riley says of John, "He was basically a sweet person. . . . He was so compassionate. He'd say something at a dinner party, worry about it all week, then apologize later, and the person would say, 'What?'—not even remembering the incident." But she also notes, "He had a hellion side to him—an upstate farm boy whose brains were too big to be contained there" and, as everyone who was ever close to him quickly learned, "a sense of guilt that would sink a ship."

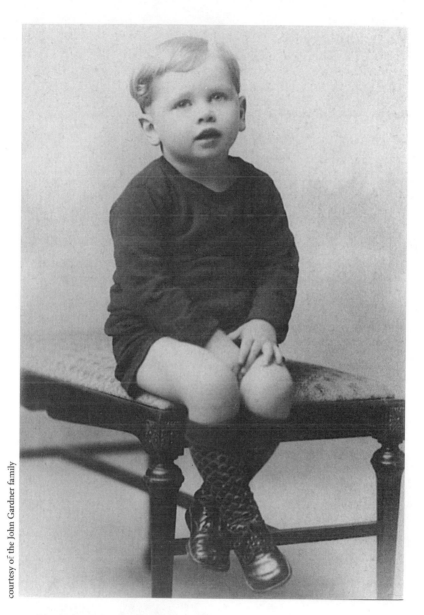

Buddy (John Jr.), age two and a half, 1935

Gilbert, age two; Priscilla holding Sandy, age six months; John Sr.;
Bud (John Jr.), age seven, 1940

Bud (John Jr.), in
Eagle Scout uniform
(Troop 7), in front of
Presbyterian Church
in Batavia, 1946

Bud's graduation photo, Batavia High School, 1950

Joan, John, Priscilla, and John Sr. at Joan and John's wedding, in Batavia, June 16, 1953

Jack Berry, John's hometown friend and college roommate, with Joan and John in Batavia around the time of their wedding, 1953

*Lucy and John
at Bread Loaf, 1975*

Joel Gardner

Joan at Bread Loaf, 1975

Joel Gardner

Joel Gardner

Joel at Bread Loaf, 1975

Liz Rosenberg in Baltimore, where she was in graduate school at Johns Hopkins, 1976

Joel Gardner

courtesy of the John Gardner family

John and Liz in California in December 1978, where he had been invited back to Chico State

Joel Gardner

John with his Harley, 1982

Joel Gardner

*John and Susan
Thornton, a month
before their wedding,
August 1982*

John in Bloomington, Indiana, where he had gone for an appearance at Indiana University, 1979

7

Rules

Sooner or later even the rules which keep a man alive—
keep his kind alive—come up for nearer inspection, so
to speak, and every generation—and every man of it—is
alone.

—*The Sunlight Dialogues*

SPURRED BY the acceptance of *The Resurrection* while
he was in San Francisco and the hope that New
American Library would also publish *Nickel Mountain,* John had continued to work on that novel, as well as on
"Squirrels." He'd also extended both the critical essay he had
been drafting on moral fiction and the critical biography of
Chaucer. The Chaucer manuscript had grown to a thousand
pages when he came to Carbondale, but it was still a long way
from done.

By his second year in Carbondale, he was involved in writing
a completely new novel, and that had grown to take up more and
more of his attention. It began with a murder in a monastery,
where one of the monks had been killed, apparently by another.

A police detective was investigating, and as Gardner worked at it the detective became more and more the center of his interest. After several different tries, in January 1966 he threw out the monk and the monastery entirely and centered the novel on the policeman, whom he made chief of police in Batavia, setting him against an apparent drifter from the youth culture who defaced a public street by scrawling LOVE on it.

For the police chief's character, he went back to "A Little Night Music," the story the *Northwest Review* had published in 1961. He also brought back two characters he had created in *The Resurrection* for minor roles. About the same time, his interest in epics and ancient literature had led him to scholar A. Leo Oppenheim's study of Babylonia, *Ancient Mesopotamia: Portrait of a Dead Civilization*, which focused for him the differences between ideas at the roots of Western values and corresponding ideas of ancient Babylonian culture. Using passages from that book, he structured his novel with four "dialogues" between the police chief and his young antagonist, the Sunlight Man, which serve to comment on the story as it unfolds, elaborating the larger philosophical argument that drives the novel.

The Babylonian idea was that there are no perfect, predetermined principles ordained by gods. There are no commandments issued from on high, but what commandments there are exist at the very foundations of our understanding. There is no afterlife we know of, and the individual, with no choice but to act, can only attend what results. Meantime, the good ruler is not limited by his rational faculties only, but is informed as well by intuition and omens.

The Sunlight Man is steeped in Babylonian values of spontaneity, which at one extreme lead to anarchy. The police chief, on the other hand, is a force for Western Judeo-Christian values, which promote planning and order. That opposition of planning and spontaneity is at the center of much of Gardner's fiction in various versions, as it was of public discussion at the time, amid the pressures of the Vietnam War and the youth culture. In the novel, he used characters based on members of his family and others he knew in Batavia to work out the philosophical positions he wanted to explore. So the Sunlight Man, who combined some of Gardner himself with his uncle George Preston, who dabbled in magic, and a healthy slice of Disney cartoon characters, was revealed finally to be a disaffected member of the town's leading family.

The Sunlight Man has returned to Batavia after many years away, bringing with him a set of ideas that oppose family, town, and society as a whole. Chief Clumly (the name itself seems cartoonish, as are some of the other events and characters), embroiled in a murder mystery and arson that has upset the whole town, must meet the Sunlight Man—who he knows is involved—at midnight first in a church, then at the cemetery, then in a square tent, and finally at the historic home of the venerable leading family. At the cemetery, the Sunlight Man summarizes for Clumly the *Gilgamesh* epic, in which the hero learns that death has no meaning. At its conclusion, he says: "Why act at all then? you may ask . . . Because action is life. . . . Once one's said it, that one must act, one must ask oneself, shall I act within the cultural order I do not believe in but with which I am engaged . . . or shall I act within the cosmic order I *do* believe in, at least in principle, an order indifferent to man?"

Thus, the characters play out their fates against the Babylonian-inspired interpretations of the Sunlight Man, in which the individual has little value against the social whole.

Gardner talked about these ideas with Eddie Epstein regularly, and by the end of 1966 he had sent more than four hundred pages of the unfinished draft to his editor at New American Library with an outline and description of the rest. By 1967, he had a thousand pages; a year later, the manuscript was finished. But *The Sunlight Dialogues*, as he titled it, was long and complicated, which made it a tough sell for any publisher, especially since the author was relatively unknown. By April 1969, it had been rejected by Farrar, Straus and Giroux, Houghton Mifflin, and Macmillan. The rejections were unpleasantly familiar for Gardner, but they certainly weren't going to slow him down; there was too much to do. Between teaching and work on his other projects, he was thinking that if he could write a smaller novel that would be popular, it might open a way for *The Sunlight Dialogues*. And so, in August, he began another.

Inspired by Plutarch, he initially titled it "The Last Days of the Seer" and set it in the period of the Roman Empire. He readily acknowledged his sources—"I used Plutarch heavily. I love Plutarch"—and indeed, one critic detailed twenty-three separate passages taken directly from Plutarch's *Lives of the Noble Grecians and Romans,* some almost word for word. For instance, Plutarch writes, "Aesop, who wrote the fables, being then in Sardis upon Croesus's invitation, and very much esteemed, was concerned that Solon was ill received, and gave him this advice: 'Solon, let your converse with kings be either short or seasonable.' 'Nay, rather,' replied Solon, 'either short or reasonable.'" Gardner, relating the scene, writes in contemporary style:

Aesop, the man who writes the fables, was in Sardis at the time of Kroesos's invitation—an old friend of Solon's —and he was troubled that Solon was so ill received as a result of his own mulishness. "Solon," said he, "when a man gives advice to kings he should make it pert and seasonable."

Solon nodded as if abashed and said softly, feebly, for he was well up in years: "Or short and reasonable. Or curt and treasonable. Or tart and please-him-able."

Just as Gardner seeks to retrieve Plutarch's lightly humorous touch here, the other passages he copies retain the same tones as the original relative to their contexts. His point seems mainly to call into his novel the same attitudes and textures Plutarch achieved in the original. But central to his own aesthetic interests, he commented in an interview, "The nice thing about Plutarch, of course, is that he was already revising history. . . . writing pseudo-history, which was not the naked truth. That is to say, he had people living at the same time who, in fact, had died hundreds of years apart, and that's handy."

Such collapsing of time and speculation, Gardner maintained, is a common device. "Fiction is like that," he said. "It follows with what ought to have happened after what happened *did* happen."

His other source of inspiration for the novel was the existentialist philosophy of Sartre. Just as he borrowed heavily from Plutarch, at least one passage in the novel is almost a direct translation from a passage in Sartre's *Being and Nothingness*. He objected to Sartre's conclusions, declaring his ideas "a horror intellectually, figuratively, and morally." At the same time, he acknowledged, "He's a wonderful writer, and anything he says you believe, at least for the moment, because of the way he says it."

He retitled this new novel *The Wreckage of Agathon*, after the name of the central character, whom he patterned after himself. Animated by a contemporary sense of male-female consciousness and relations, the story centers on a plot to overthrow the sitting governor and foment revolution. In that way, it reflects the political turmoil of its time and the issues of personal freedom against institutional authority, which domestic political struggles highlighted. In the novel, the conflicts lead not only to Agathon's personal "wreckage" as he languishes in jail but also to wreckage around him, which is a consequence of his ideas. Thus, the intersecting plots and concerns strike contemporary notes, as did the voice of Agathon in his self-involved ravings.

As he did again and again in his fiction, Gardner also confronted his brother's death. Here Agathon is haunted by the guilt he feels for the trampling of his brother under the hooves of Agathon's own horse. If the accident is not a central fact of Agathon's character, it at least contributes to his tangled, benighted frame of mind, a condition that is at the heart of the story—as Gardner's own feelings of guilt were to his identity.

From the beginning, however, Gardner distanced himself from the novel, saying more vigorously over the coming years that it was not a good book, that it was full of mistakes. He told students that it was in some ways a response to Updike's *Couples*, which was on best-seller lists at the time, but it seems likely that his negative assessment grew as much as anything from discomfort he felt about his relations with people he had used as models for characters. As in most of his fiction, he'd described actual behavior and thinking of people he knew well. In *The Resurrection*, for instance, friends, often barely altered, are the basis of characters. But the friends who found themselves in that novel were mainly amused when they saw the results. The same approach in *Agathon*, however, would have been awkward for those involved.

The most obvious models for this new novel were a couple he and Joan had met when they first went shopping for a house in 1966. The Russells had come from Stanford University in California where Bob had taught health education and Lenore primary and adult education. They had five sons, and when they moved to Carbondale they found a big house in town. But when it turned out not to be adequate for them, they put it on the market in 1966 to look for something more suitable. John and Joan, who also liked big, rambling houses, came to see it, and though the house wasn't what they wanted either, the two couples immediately connected.

Bob's specialty was teaching about alcoholism and problems with death and dying, subjects that engendered long discussions among the four over dinners. When Sandy and David came to Carbondale, entanglements grew as David enrolled in some of Bob's classes and the Russells' older son became a regular babysitter for Lucy and Joel.

More compelling than any common interest, however, was the chemistry between John and Lenore. Her habit of leaning forward to focus intently on her listener and touching him as she made her point attracted many men, including John, and his reaction would certainly have encouraged Joan to invite Bob's attentions. The result was two concurrent affairs. Though they only lasted a couple of months, such experience can't be simply walled off and ignored.

The Russells became central models for characters in the novel. Agathon, whom John patterned after himself, is embroiled in an affair with Iona (modeled after Lenore) while Tuka (modeled after Joan) gets involved with Dorkis (drawn after Bob Russell). Gardner's portrait of Tuka could not have pleased Joan. Though Agathon credits her with "a mind like lightning," and another chapter begins with his proclaiming, as Gardner often did, "This much is clear: I loved my wife," he also details acts of rudeness on her part. Other characters are similarly patterned after the Gardners' friends, and the portraits and interactions no doubt precipitated some embarrassment when Harper and Row published it in 1970.

In the end, all of that was only a small corner of the turmoil that surrounded the Gardners. Though disorder had been rare around Carbondale, which was a sleepy, conservative town prior to John and Joan's arrival (in fact, the only bookstore in town then was run by the Baptist Church), a few years later, as in many college towns, all that changed.

Originally a small teaching college, Southern Illinois University had grown to some fifteen thousand students by 1965. In the early years of that decade, the Vietnam War raged and baby boomers filled colleges in record numbers. The year before Gardner arrived, civil rights protesters picketed a restaurant for hiring Negroes solely for kitchen work, and threatened boycotts. In the spring of 1966, a traditional panty raid led to name calling and taunting of police, followed by trash burning in the street and the arrest of six students who allegedly set the fire. Student protests mounted over the next days in June, until one drew a crowd of some two thousand that was broken up by police swinging riot sticks. In the next two years, demonstrations for Afro-American rights, for student rights, and in defiance of the war increased. The university had decided on major expansion, and by 1970 the student population had grown to twenty-three thousand. The huge influx fed the volatile political atmosphere of the time as more and more disturbances broke out over the decade, changing both the university and the town.

Like most of his colleagues, Gardner remained largely apart from political activity, but it was nearly impossible not to be involved on some level. His own attitudes had been honed in rural, Republican country, where people hewed to conventions steeped in long tradition, and in a 1978 interview, he readily proclaimed, "I'm a law and order guy."

But having always rebelled against institutional authority, he sympathized with students in many ways, and Epstein recalls a different slant to their conversations when Gardner was working on *The Sunlight Dialogues:* "John was . . . talking about the necessity for spontaneity and freedom, whereas my taste was toward order. . . . So we stood for differing opinions on human nature."

It wasn't necessarily that Gardner changed his mind over the years. One can certainly be for "law and order" and at the same time value spontaneity and freedom. But the larger point is that despite proclamations that led many to think him argumentative and arrogant, not much for him was set in stone. Fundamentally, he was a social person. As a child, members of his large family had always been around; as an adult, he had never lived alone. Mainly, it seemed, he wanted to be liked, and not offend. Intellectual argument was a sport that attracted him as a way of exploring his own thinking and for whatever entertainment might ensue.

In the many interviews he gave as he became well known, he more than once took what seemed to be (and sometimes were) different sides of the same issue, depending on the questioner— saying in one interview, for instance, that *Finnegan's Wake* was "the greatest novel of the twentieth century" and, a year later, that he was "bored to tears" by it, seeing "nothing but smart-aleckiness and arrogance." Perhaps most significantly, his positions were informed by his bent toward iconoclasm and ideas outside the mainstream, which resulted in inconsistency, if not outright contradiction, in some of his statements.

His sympathy with the less privileged, however, was strong and consistent. Barry Sanders, who joined the Southern Illinois Peace Committee, says, "John was . . . on the outside," but despite the differences in political commitment, "he was always very sympathetic about minorities, and very outspoken in his sympathy." In fact, Sanders goes on, "There was a moment, in the fall of '66, when a young black student of his, whom he liked a lot, was beaten by police in a demonstration and lost an eye. That galvanized him briefly, and he got involved in supporting the Black Studies Center. At the moment when that young man was sent to the hospital, I think he changed his mind about what was and was not appropriate."

Sanders also points out that in the teaching they did together, Gardner invariably emphasized the essentially political nature of the medieval ballads. For much as he opposed the disruptive tac-tics of radical elements, strong populist sympathies made him quick to note that the ballads had been composed by ordinary working people as opposed to aristocrats. "John was always clear about explaining them in terms of political stance," Sanders says.

In 1967, Gardner did add his signature to a letter protesting the policy the university implemented (as several universities did at the time) of notifying draft boards of students with below-passing grades, which then led to their being drafted into the army. The letter deplored the "moral vacuum" the action evi-denced. Having his own classical idea of the definition of "moral," however, Gardner wouldn't sign unless the phrase was removed. When it finally was, he signed.

He was also upset at the clearly anti-Semitic edge to some of the local opposition to the antiwar movement. In one case, the father of one of the movement's leaders was a rabbi. The stu-dent's car was stolen and set afire in the woods, with a cross on fire in front of it. Anti-Semitic graffiti was scrawled around it, and the student received hate mail calling him a "nigger-loving kike."

When Sanders told Gardner about it, "John was livid," he says. The anger didn't directly lead to visible action in that case, but the sentiments that were aroused clearly informed his writing and teaching. And in the last years of the decade, as the conflicts intensified further, he was further pulled in.

Involved regularly with people and circumstances outside academics and the university, as Epstein says, "He was inter-ested in town life for his writing." And in 1968, no doubt stirred at least in part by Joel and Lucy, grown to nine and six and in elementary school, he decided to run for the community school board. The decision brought him and Joan into close touch with the world that had nothing to do with the university and led to a friendship that lasted for the rest of the time he was in Carbondale.

Bill Burns, who had long been near the center of political activities both in Chicago (where he had lived during the fifties after his college years at SIU) and then in Carbondale, had been president of the student body at SIU when he was a student there. In Chicago he had worked for city aldermen against the established Democratic organization, and he later served as president of the Independent Voters of Illinois, the major Chicago organization opposing the entrenched Democratic organization. Since moving back to Carbondale in 1961, he had worked for the establishment of branch banking as part of a major urban renewal project.

Burns remembers many nights at Boskeydell with Bordeaux wine, discussing politics and religion. "We had extensive conversations, till late evenings, about history, theology, political theory. . . . John had similar views on God, the universe, religion, virtue . . ."

Though they were "straighter," says Burns, and much less given to most of the wilder elements that seemed to go with the Gardners, he and his wife regularly exchanged visits with John and Joan. Burns too emphasizes John's sympathy with the disenfranchised. "He . . . had affinity for goodness and virtue," says Burns. "He was a very principled man." Moreover, Burns says, "He was too forgiving . . . [and] overly tolerant of the other side. . . . He was immediately taken in by people who were good and kind and friendly [and] had the capacity for believing people were better than they were."

In Gardner's statement to the local paper, accompanied by a picture in which he looks typically boyish, with his medium-length hair well trimmed, he advocated more emphasis on reading and suggested an alliance with SIU to foster that. Says Burns, "He had very idealistic, and to some extent impractical views on education."

The newspaper also notes that he was the only one of the five candidates to advocate more sex education in the schools. It was a statement that could not have been popular in the small southern Illinois town where he was a relative newcomer, and his suggestion that New York State had a more favorable approach would have been even less popular. Not surprisingly, he was not elected.

His candidacy and the election didn't precipitate any of the conflicts antiwar activity did, but political activism was in the air everywhere as action against the war mounted and Carbondale became a national flashpoint. In the spring of 1968, encouraged also by nonstudents who came to foment unrest, student protest at SIU turned violent. On May 7, a bomb exploded in the agriculture building; students took over the president's office and were finally driven out by police. Then, in June 1969, after another year of protests and demonstrations, which saw more than a dozen attempted bombings and arson fires, Old Main, the original building of the university and its traditional center, was burned down by protesters who saw it as the visible symbol of established, entrenched values, values they saw as the source of the Vietnam tragedy. When the university accepted a grant to open the only Vietnam Study Center in the country, a center that was moving from the University of Michigan in response to protests there, demonstrations mounted further. And in May 1970, when U.S. troops were sent into Cambodia to root out North Vietnamese forces there, campuses all over the country erupted in riotous protests and closed, as students insisted that normal everyday business could not continue and that universities particularly must direct all resources toward stopping the war.

Demonstrations at SIU that May included takeovers of campus buildings, riots downtown, and the mobilization of six hundred National Guardsmen and local and state police. The guardsmen and local officers mainly comprised people from the community, but the state police were from other places, and they moved aggressively to break up the march, throwing tear gas cannisters and swinging riot sticks. One house was burned down by a fire thus started. Demonstrators, meanwhile, broke windows of shops downtown. Many students ran into nearby dorms, but the state police set off tear gas inside the dorms too. When students streamed out, some were beaten; over 350 were arrested.

The riot was quelled but not the circumstances that had created it. Community leaders and others around warned the university to control its students, while self-proclaimed vigilante groups threatened to ride into town with shotguns, burn down dorms, and take control.

At this point, Gardner called several people he knew in the Carbondale community along with several others from the university, to come to a meeting at the farm, the first of two or three that went on there. They met there because it was outside city limits, and Carbondale had been completely shut down. Members of the History, Philosophy, and Psychology Departments also attended, the point being to find a way to reach some understanding that might diffuse the tension between university and townspeople. Joan's teaching in different places had made her known outside the university, and, says Jerry Osbourne, she took the most active part in directing the meetings. "[John] may've called people and invited them to the meeting, but Joan was the mover who ran things. She really ran the meetings at the house." On the other hand, observes Osbourne, "John, as he often did, watched people carefully and listened to them talk to each other."

Nothing tangible resulted, but as Epstein notes about John's overall political grounding, "His interest was to reconcile forces."

A frequent target of antiwar fury was the ROTC. Headquartered in the same building as the English Department, whose faculty had a reputation for being sympathetic to antiwar radicals, there seemed a real threat to the building that housed both. In hopes of forestalling trouble, some of the professors joined in nighttime patrols of the campus, an activity that seemed clearly dangerous at the time but just as surely necessary. Finally, the university decided to close down on May 12.

Though such political issues didn't get Gardner engaged much unless they touched him personally, he had always been quick to confront any bureaucracy that threatened the individual and his imagination. Thus, when the Illinois String Quartet of which Baber was a part, was faced with severe restriction by established interests in the music school, he was ignited.

The school had long supported both a string quartet and a woodwind quintet drawn from the faculty, both of which performed a few local concerts each year. However, under the leadership of violinist Myron Kartman, who had come from the more liberal and artistic environment of Antioch College in 1967, the quartet had begun reaching well beyond Carbondale. The changes had begun when cellist Peter Spurbeck had taken a position with the Memphis symphony, which meant traveling on the train between there and Carbondale to play in both places. Says Kartman, "This was very much resented by the old guard. They hated Pete for doing this. They thought he should stay right there in Carbondale. They accused him of neglecting his job and complained to higher-ups."

The result was that Spurbeck was forced to resign from the university, and Kartman, who had been recruited to upgrade the program, brought in David Cowley, another accomplished cellist he knew. With Cowley, the quartet had significantly more accomplished musicianship than it had known, and Kartman began seeking larger audiences for them. Meantime, Baber composed some music for the quartet that was recorded professionally, and the group began to draw more attention. Kartman arranged a concert at the Phillips Collection in Washington, D.C., where they played to enthusiastic reviews, and a trip to New York City was planned for the next year.

But the growing notoriety didn't sit well with the "old guard" —mainly the woodwind quintet—which seemed threatened by the success of this new group and had been instrumental in forcing out Spurbeck. Says Kartman, "The woodwind quintet used to spend most of their rehearsal talking about how they could crucify the string quartet."

Kartman called the dispute petty and childish, but the result was pressure for the quartet to curb its traveling and expansion.

When Gardner heard about the problem, he was outraged at what he saw as the stifling of artistic expansion. Known around the university as a rising young star himself, he had no hesitation in approaching the highest levels of the bureaucracy. In this case, the chancellor, Robert McVicker, was a member of the same Presbyterian church the Gardners attended, and John appealed directly to him. The result of their meetings was an arrangement that moved the quartet out of the music school and funded it directly through the chancellor's office as an arm of university public relations. It was no longer subject, then, to constraints the old guard put on it.

At the same time, Kartman, an equally outspoken opponent of what he saw as entrenched provincial interests, had come under fire himself. At the time, all students were required to attend a certain number of "cultural" events. At one of these, Kartman had dismissed an auditorium full of loud and inattentive students who were disrupting a concert that they were attending to fulfill the requirement. He simply wanted to permit those who had come to listen to be able to do so and to let the others go their own way, but he was called to the dean to account for his dismissal of the resistant students, which was counter to stated policy.

When Gardner heard about it, he was incensed and put Kartman in touch with officials of the American Association of University Professors, the union that safeguards faculty positions and professors' academic freedom. The result was that the threat to Kartman was removed, but the opposition to his and others' ambitions in the quartet ultimately led to its end, despite its accomplishments. Cellist Cowley was fired, and the second violinist quit in protest. Kartman left in June 1969 for another position.

Gardner's reputation as a powerful promoter of art and a supporter of young people opposed to the status quo continued to grow. Though fiction and art were always his central concern, and his adult life had been spent in the university, his interests had never stopped there, nor at the end of the campus. He once told Epstein that the office he wanted to run for was county coroner, because the coroner "was always being paid off by people who had killed people, just to ignore things." It was the kind of provocative statement Gardner was known for making, but there was a good deal of conviction behind it.

By THE SPRING OF 1969, Gardner had published one novel and finished two more. Those were strictly adjunct to his professorial position, as what counted for that was his academic work; but his critical publications were more than substantial.

At the age of thirty-six, he was coeditor of an important fiction anthology, editor of a major critical journal, and author of a book of criticism and almost a dozen articles on medieval studies. He had finally completed his biographical-critical manuscript on Chaucer, having revised it to focus on the theme of love in Chaucer's poetry, and the manuscript had been accepted by Yale University Press, subject to revisions. Meantime, he was modernizing Malory's *Morte d'Arthur* and a group of other medieval poems, as well as writing commentaries on them.

If that weren't enough, he had also written a CliffsNotes study guide for *Le Morte D'Arthur*, another for the *Gawain* poet, and had begun one for the poetry of Chaucer. Moreover, he had undertaken a new project stirred by his interest in medieval ballads —a series of thirteen radio programs on the ballad tradition that would be distributed through the educational radio network. Meanwhile, his teaching had been publicly praised by many, including his department chairman.

His prodigious academic record led to promotion from associate to full professor in December of that year. Among other things, this meant a significant salary raise, which was more than welcome. Though John didn't think about it much, Joan was an exuberant spender, and money was always in short supply. To earn a little extra in 1969, John had had to teach a summer class.

When the class was finished in August, he went to New York and met with David Segal, an editor at Harper and Row, and brought with him his unpublished novels. Segal was Bill Gass's editor, and John brought with him all his unpublished novels except "The Old Men." Segal liked *Agathon* enough to buy it, and in October the contract was sealed. When it came out the following June, despite Gardner's own critical assessment, the reviews and attention it garnered were much more significant than they had been for his earlier books.

In a September article in the *New York Times*, reviewer Christopher Lehmann-Haupt was effusive in his praise, calling it "a novel transcending history and effectively embracing all of it, a philosophical drama that accurately describes the wreckage of the 20th century as well as of Agathon, and a highly original work of imagination."

Two months later, novelist Paul West was more critical in the *New York Times Book Review*. Impatient with Agathon's ranting, he didn't feel it was well enough supported by the situations Gardner created. Still, he remarked on the character's vividness and pointed out analogies to contemporary political circumstances, which made the novel relevant. And with that sort of attention, not to mention favorable reviews in *Time* (a "sharp and provoking little anti-historical novel," the review termed it) and elsewhere, the novel achieved significant notice. In many ways, as Gardner had hoped, it helped open the way for his longer, more difficult fiction.

When he met with Segal that August, however, Gardner had talked about another novel idea that Segal was most interested in. It was a story he had been telling to Joel and Lucy for at least a year. He hadn't written it yet, but he'd started on it, and as Gardner explained the idea to Segal it seemed much more exciting to him than the new novel or any of the others Gardner wanted to have published.

The idea, Gardner said to an interviewer much later, had come first from his *Beowulf* class. "I told the kids that the three monsters in *Beowulf* are very symbolic, and Grendel [the first one] is symbolic of the rational soul gone perverse. Somebody asked me in the class if that was just old-fashioned Christian talk, or was it possible in the modern world for the rational soul to go perverse. And I said, 'Sure, Sartre's Existentialism is perverse rationality.' As soon as I said it, I realized what I was going to do, and I began planning *Grendel*."

His interest in philosophy led him to connect Sartre and the Anglo-Saxon monster more surely the more he thought about it. In fact, he voiced in another interview, "I finally worked out an interpretation that I believe in, where Grendel is a cosmic principle of intellectual disorder. He liked unreason, in the same way that Jean-Paul Sartre likes unreason." And that insight, he said, "gave me the idea of telling the *Beowulf* story from Grendel's point of view, using Grendel to represent Sartre's philosophical position and showing how it came about." He went on, "a lot of *Grendel* is borrowed from sections of Sartre's *Being and Nothingness*. The first major experience in Grendel's life, when he meets human beings for the first time, is all from *Being and Nothingness*."

Gardner found a voice for Grendel that also utilizes some of the alliterative qualities drawn from medieval tradition and sounds absolutely contemporary. One of "Cain's clan" (according to *Beowulf*) emerged from the exile to which God sentenced Cain for the murder of his brother, and Grendel's condition as the hyperconscious rational monster—completely alone, part Disney cartoon, part contemporary everyman, a permanent stranger driven to wreak horror on the human community— must have seemed to Gardner an embodiment of archetype, if not analogous to his own condition. Indeed, it was the troubled condition to which living with his own unresolved guilt had brought him.

From the first, he envisioned twelve chapters, each corresponding to one of the astrological houses. The use of such astrological symbolism also made the work current, as the ancient tradition was undergoing new waves of popularity, especially among the young. At the same time, the pre-Christian world invoked by astrology perfectly suited the universe Beowulf and Grendel inhabited. If the structure was consciously planned, the character, as in all fiction, developed in ways its author didn't anticipate.

"I wanted Grendel to be a creature trapped in determinism by his own nature," Gardner explained later, "because he refuses fate, he says no. . . . I wanted to present him just as a monster— dark, wrong." He continued, "I started out thinking I was going to do a sort of tirade against the intellectual stuff you get in the universities—this locked in, systematic thought. But then, in order to make him an interesting character, I had to become more and more sympathetic." Ultimately, Gardner realized, "he wants to punish himself for what he feels to be an inadequate state of being."

In this way, Gardner constructed a consciousness that seemed exactly right for the times, and not coincidentally a mirror of his own idea of himself as a kind of monster—unpunished and unredeemed.

He worked steadily at the novel, and in May 1969 applied for and received a grant from the school to work on it. But as often happened, the commotion around him got in the way again. Restless one late August night, he saddled his horse and went for a ride, but the horse stumbled or jerked, and threw him off. The fall cracked his head, and when he finally got to the hospital he found he had fractured his skull and had a concussion.

He would recover, but he was advised to slow down and take it easy for a while. For Gardner, though, there was no such thing as taking it easy. As with his broken arms in San Francisco, physical injuries weren't allowed to get in the way of the work he was set on. Back home, the grass and weeds needed to be mowed down, so on one of the days between his writing nights, he hauled out the riding mower to do the job. Not content to cut just the lawn around the house, he went over as much of the farm as he could. Mowing in the hot August sun, he grew weak and dizzy, and when he finally finished he went inside and collapsed with sunstroke.

While he was recovering Joan offered to help by continuing to type the story as he dictated. "But he kept repeating himself, over and over," she remembers. "Then he had a hell of a headache and wandered away. I just kept on typing."

Not surprisingly, the chapter she worked on, the eighth, came out quite stylistically different from the rest. But Gardner insisted that was just fine. He told Joan her chapter read like a TV or movie script and was just right for its place in the novel.

He continued working over the winter, into the next spring, and by summer 1970 the manuscript was finished. It was much shorter than his other novels, and its monster hero, redolent with contemporary consciousness, made it fiction unlike anything else he'd written.

Segal, now at Knopf, immediately offered a contract to publish first *Grendel* and then *The Sunlight Dialogues,* a book he had turned down when he was at Harper & Row and one he still didn't want to publish. But John insisted that it be part of any deal with *Grendel,* and so Segal agreed. The advance, for John and Joan, was substantial—some ten thousand dollars. Finally, it seemed that all the years of writing fiction were beginning to pay off.

The previous winter, he had also been been offered the Distinguished Professor Award from the University of Detroit, which came with an invitation to spend the fall of 1970 there as a visiting professor, and several thousand more dollars. Conceived by John Mahoney, the new dean of the liberal arts school, the award had been inaugurated two years earlier with the semester-long residency of English theater luminary, Sir Tyrone Guthrie. The next year, poet, critic, and fiction writer Samuel Hazo had occupied the position. Though Gardner had nothing like the renown of either Guthrie or Hazo, his reputation as a rising young star with loads of energy was spreading, and the offer was a decided step in recognition.

With *The Wreckage of Agathon* awaiting publication and *Grendel* finished, in August the whole family moved north to Detroit and into an apartment that the university kept nearby for visitors. On the first floor of a large U-shaped complex, an easy walk to campus, the 1920s vintage apartment was light and spacious, with a large living room, kitchen, dining room, and two bedrooms, all with high ceilings and dark woodwork. The neighborhood abutted Palmer Woods and had been an elegant district in the 1910s and 1920s, though like many such areas in major cities it had declined in value and appeal as the white population migrated to the suburbs. Now the area was predominately black and poor. The immediate environs of the school, however, were something of an island of greater integration. Still, when Joan took Joel and Lucy around in search of a school for them, they wound up enrolling at the neighborhood elementary school, where they were the only white children in their classes.

Lucy doesn't recall the difference much affecting them. She does remember that the children in Detroit played games she and Joel didn't know. "There was one where kids would squat around this basketball-sized hole they had dug," she remembers, "and poise the knifepoint of a switchblade on the inside of the lower arm, then flip it off with the other hand to make it stick a certain way in dirt."

It was hardly the kind of childhood game middle-class children were used to, but Lucy states, "No one ever got cut—there wasn't anything ominous—just different." Mainly, she remembers thinking, the game and the kids' style were "memorable, cool."

The university itself was a small Jesuit Catholic school, with just over a thousand full-time students, though it had many more part-time students who worked as well. The large number who also had outside jobs meant that many students were older than the usual eighteen- to twenty-two-year-olds.

Gardner taught a graduate seminar in Anglo-Saxon and an undergraduate class in modern literature that focused specifically on experimental fiction. Though he continued to avoid teaching creative writing classes, he was always interested in students' work, and one aspect of the literature class involved having students write creatively. He brought samples of their work to the Anglo-Saxon class from time to time, and at least one of his graduate students remembers the work to have been particularly well achieved.

On two or three occasions he also brought novelist Joyce Carol Oates to his classes, along with her husband, critic and editor Ray Smith. Since soliciting her work for what was called *Mount Shasta Selections* ten years earlier, he had stayed in touch with Oates as her novels and career advanced. She had also taught literary criticism at the university. Now she was teaching just across the river in Windsor, Canada.

Still, he discouraged students who were interested in writing from applying to any of the graduate writing programs that had begun to proliferate. Tom Porter, a professor with whom Gardner became particularly friendly, says, "He would have people who would want to become writers, and they'd want to go off to Iowa or someplace, and he'd say, 'Forget it. Go to St. Louis and work with Bill Gass, or go to SUNY Buffalo and get in touch with [Leslie] Fiedler.' . . . He really thought that if you wanted to be a writer, do it his way. Go and get a degree in some aspect of English and keep writing and find people who are interested in writing and set up some sort of salon if you want. And he talked about places that worked that way."

Though the quality of the student fiction Gardner brought to his class may not have been a result of his teaching, as always he deeply affected many students who found him inspirational. Which doesn't mean he was a wonderful teacher for everyone.

Margaret Pigott, a student in the Anglo-Saxon class and now a professor of medieval literature at Oakland University, says, "We all loved him dearly. . . . he had wonderful ideas, and he was extremely enthusiastic about writing. But the class was rather boring. All we did was translate. We never talked about the poems."

Pigott affirms, however, that his style of making very personal connections with students was powerful, as he and Joan created the same open, social atmosphere that they had in Carbondale. "They were party people," says Pigott, "and it seemed like they had a party nearly every other day—of course we were all invited—sometimes right after class. And always on the weekend they had people over."

Colleagues and students' friends were always part of the scene, and on several weekends they had houseguests from other places as well. Porter remembers that it "was pretty much an open house [as] evenings would extend into the mornings." Gardner "tended to play guru on occasion," says Porter. "There were those who sat at his feet. There were often little rings [of students] around him at the apartment." He adds, however, "There wasn't anything pompous about it. He was interested in them and interested in their ambitions."

Gardner had a pack of Tarot cards that he'd bring out to tell fortunes "which were mostly fishing expeditions," Porter recalls. "He'd have an impression of a person and he'd test the waters by reading the cards for them." It was all part of the general ambience of the time, and "there was never anything malicious about it. It was just John's curiosity."

The result of the whole thing, says Pigott, was that "because of them we had the best social life ever." In fact, she says, "[the] Gardners produced the best social life the university ever saw. . . . Everyone was entranced by [John] because he was so different."

Besides the social activity at their apartment, there were the attractions of the city, which meant a cultural and artistic world that hadn't been available since they left San Francisco. When they weren't entertaining at home, John and Joan and the children went to concerts and plays and other shows.

There were other social affairs to which they were invited as well, of course, and on at least two weekends, the family left the city entirely, once to go to Batavia for John's parents' anniversary and to visit the country of northern Michigan.

For her part, Joan often sat in on the Anglo-Saxon class. Always a striking hostess and cook, she was as much a social promoter as John. "They always had buffet suppers and she did exotic things," says Pigott. "She was a terrific cook . . . way ahead, in her culinary sense."

At parties and other occasions, she sometimes played the piano and did occasional performances, along with managing the household and children. As seems to have been the case from the beginning, "Joan was really mother," Porter says, referring not to her role with the children but with John. "She dressed him and kept him on schedule and that sort of thing."

Meantime, "John surrounded himself with his coterie of people. He'd find a couple of people who he thought had tremendous talent and he'd bring them home and they'd practically live there. They'd sleep on the floor."

One of those who joined the Gardners' orbit was a Vietnam veteran who was a graduate teaching assistant and in the Anglo-Saxon class. Gene Rudzewicz was also interested in writing fiction, and John offered enthusiastic encouragement. As with other students he got to know, both Rudzewicz and his roommate, Ken Fizette, were drawn into the whirlpool Gardner seemed to create wherever he went.

Joan particularly connected with Rudzewicz, who began spending more and more time with the family. A quiet—even shy—man, he was living in Detroit and working a factory job. The relationship among all of them grew closer and closer. In October, when the whole family drove to Batavia for John's parents' anniversary, both Fizette and Rudzewicz (and another graduate student) went along as well.

The intensity began to make Ken Fizette uncomfortable, he

later told Pigott, but the four of them forged a closeness that made them almost a single unit. Rudzewicz especially, encouraged by both John and Joan, became almost part of the family.

John urged him to keep writing and to pursue the literary life he wanted. But Rudzewicz also knew he had to make a living, and fiction writing didn't hold much promise of economic reward. Despite John's prodding, and the attractions of the lively, unstructured, endlessly interesting life the Gardners enjoyed, he felt he couldn't break his ties to his everyday life, no matter how mundane it might be.

Says Lucy, "Gene felt he needed some kind of safety net. Dad felt he was wasting his life doing that and [that] he should make the leap. But Gene was more practical."

John, meanwhile, was stimulated to try yet another new direction while he was in Detroit. Whether it was the setting and its availability, or something else entirely, he was struck by the idea of making a movie. Joan went out and rented cameras and other moviemaking equipment, and they went to work. With Fizette, Rudzewicz, and others, they made two shorts, teaching themselves how to work the equipment. Then John conceived a full-length project.

In Palmer Woods, which was close to their apartment, was an old mansion, originally built by one of the Fisher brothers who designed automobile bodies. "It was a classic 1920s multimillionaire mansion," remembers Porter, "with fifty bedrooms, a ballroom, an indoor swimming pool." And Mahoney, who was dean, agrees it was "a palatial place" though "sort of a white elephant."

No one lived there, and Gardner learned that he could use it for the movie. The story he invented for the film never became entirely clear as it developed, though Mahoney says it wasn't "shot on the run," and Gardner stayed ahead of shooting in his composition.

"The plot was typical John," says Porter, "in that one could not predict the angle from which he was going to continue to move through the scenario. . . . It was a kind of Frankenstein monster movie" with a murder, and a mystery. Gardner was receptive to ideas that people offered, says Pigott, but she also notes, "It was his project. He wrote it all. He was very serious about it. Mainly," she says, "It was great fun."

As usual, everyone around got involved in the project. Rudzewicz joined with his brother, the two starring as clumsy detectives. Fizette was a gardener, while Joel and Lucy were "hidden children." Besides them, Joan, and Porter, there were another dozen in the cast, including students. And the disarray that always accompanied Gardner was an integral part of it. "He had me playing a chauffeur," says Porter. "And he had me take off my glasses, at which point I drove this car . . . through a very narrow gate and knocked the driver's side rear view mirror off. That didn't render me too popular, but I told him, without my glasses . . ."

The movie was never completed for any release, but the whole enterprise embodied the exuberance and fun of most of Gardner's creations. As Mahoney says, "It was a hilarious time. . . . I just remember the film was hilarious. . . . He was a very infectious guy. And he was a performer."

When the Gardners left in mid-December, Fizette drove with them and Rudzewicz back to Carbondale, the first of many visits there. In Detroit, those who had been touched by their energy were sorry to see them leave. But John was never one to look back.

8

The Epic Conversation

We sail between nonsense and terrible absurdity.

—Jason and Medeia

BACK IN CARBONDALE in the winter of 1970 to 1971, John absorbed the changes both the town and the university had undergone in the five years since he'd moved there. Political and social turmoil still festered. The influx of thousands more young people, the Vietnam War, and traditional community values made a volatile mixture. His fiction had always engaged details of the larger world. Certainly *The Wreckage of Agathon* and *The Sunlight Dialogues* treated political issues that reflected directly on current circumstances. In *Agathon,* however, the universe was decidedly distant and metaphoric. *Sunlight*'s world of Batavia was a place he knew, but had since left behind. Home in Carbondale now, he infused his stories with the changed political atmosphere of the time.

Like *Sunlight,* "Pastoral Care" describes people and circumstances with which he was closely familiar. The story's protagonist is a minister patterned after the Presbyterian minister of the

Gardners' own church, a man he and Joan knew well. In the story, the minister is trying to come to terms with the disruptions fueled by the war and the burgeoning counterculture. Caught between lust for one of his congregants and demands to serve all of them, he is confronted by the moral pressures brought on by a radical-looking Vietnam veteran. The veteran shows up at a church service, disappears, then returns to tell the minister that he was particularly struck by the sermon's affirmation of the need to turn away from materialist concerns, to not give in to lust, to eschew pride and "come to terms with world powers."

The minister is sympathetic to the antiauthority bent of the young man and sees similarities between primary religious teachings and some counterculture proclamations. But his sympathy alienates him from townspeople. After being reprimanded by a leading congregant for being seen even talking with the anonymous veteran, the minister leaves town on a train and is approached by a doctor interested in a homosexual liaison. In the end, the train crashes, and another young man, described in classical images of the devil, appears distraught at the death in the crash of his pregnant wife. His last cry is for a priest, not a doctor. The minister responds, realizing "the fall [as from grace] is endless" and, echoing one of Gardner's essential tenets, that "all systems fail." Finally, he decides, "I force myself to continue. I have no choice."

The story suggests parallels between the story of Jesus' railing against the temple and contemporary youth who were likewise denouncing what they saw as corrupt institutions. Furthermore, the crash of the train carrying the minister and his lust away and the death of the devil figure's pregnant wife point to an entirely different world that is about to emerge. In the end, the minister, quite secular though steeped in Christianity, finds no solution, no right way to be. He can only "continue"—which is Gardner's own personal view. It was a year before the story was published in the small literary magazine, *Audience,* but it stands as the most complete expression in Gardner's fiction of the circumstances around him at the time.

Working as usual on several things at once, he kept few records, but evidence suggests that the story was begun just after Christmas 1970. It was then that news came from New York that David Segal, the editor who was John's longtime advocate and who had paved the way for the publication of his novels had died suddenly of a heart attack.

Segal had followed John's career from Harper and Row, where Segal had bought *The Wreckage of Agathon,* to Knopf, where he had bought *The Sunlight Dialogues.* He had seen and liked *Nickel Mountain,* but he especially enjoyed *Grendel,* which he bought with the intention of bringing it out the next fall. Though their relationship had never been personal, John had liked him and felt profoundly indebted to him for his championing of his novels. When he heard of Segal's death, he was distraught.

As he had come to do in times of upset, when he heard, he went out to the barn, saddled his horse, and went riding. But this time, he didn't come back in a few hours. The next day, Joan got a call from the hospital reporting that her husband had been admitted and was being treated for a head wound. As he had done in August the year before, John had fractured his skull and sustained a concussion, apparently from falling off the horse. He could go home the next day, but he would have to rest.

The day after the phone call, he was released, and as soon as he got home he went right on working. But his distress at Segal's death wouldn't fade. In March, he boarded a plane for New York and went to Segal's Upper West Side apartment. Segal's wife, novelist Lore, whom he had never met, answered the bell. She remembers the incident vividly. "I opened the door," she says, "and outside stands the most beautiful man I've ever seen—or [someone] looking like no man I've ever seen—with silver hair down to his shoulders, and an upturned nose and bright blue eyes. And he comes in. And he stays. For a week."

He came to offer comfort and no doubt to ease his own sense of loss by sharing its pain. He confided in Lore the ongoing conflicts he had with Joan but also stated that by no means was he breaking with her. Before he left, he insisted that Lore and her two young children come to visit Boskeydell. She was taken aback, but he insisted that their coming to visit would be a fine idea. Such response to his editor's death, especially the visit to Lore, seems extreme, but as she points out, gestures that most saw as extreme were the norm for Gardner. "They're so out of proportion with the way people usually behave," she says. But "John had absolutely no inhibitions about things. . . . He didn't do things that were probable. He did what occurred to him as a nice idea. He didn't ask if this is a reasonable thing for a grown-up to do. He satisfied his immediate imagination."

In late July 1971, then, she came to Carbondale with her two school-aged children. It was unbearably hot, as it often is there at that time of year, and as a Manhattanite planted in rural Illinois she felt completely out of her element. But her children settled in upstairs at the Boskeydell farm house with Joel and Lucy, and Lore was given a couch in an alcove off the kitchen for sleeping quarters. As always, there was a steady flow of visitors and the telephone rang steadily. At one point the phone was simply left unhooked to stop the constant ringing.

Lore recalls that John told her at the time that he hadn't been writing at all for four months. Surprised to hear that from such a notoriously prolific writer, she asked, "How can you bear it? But he said, 'No problem.'" And one night, he went to work again.

"Somewhere around the third day of our visit," she says, "he brought out his typewriter, set it down on the far side of the kitchen table and began to type. . . . It seemed to me he typed twenty-four hours, day and night." She remembers going to sleep with him typing in the kitchen, on the other side of the door. "Every once in a while, he'd reach behind him for a pillow and put his head on it and go to sleep for a bit. Then I'd wake up again and hear this sound of typing. It seems to me he finished that book in days. . . . I know that he essentially wrote that book for the second part of the eight or nine days that we were there."

He may have been writing "Pastoral Care," or one of the other stories eventually collected in *The King's Indian,* if not the title novella itself. If it was in fact a novel—Lore thought it was *Nickel Mountain*—it would have been a new version of that manuscript, which David Segal had told him Knopf was interested in. Regardless, the sense of charmed unreality that began for Lore in New York and persisted for her during the visit to Carbondale continued through their leaving and visits afterward.

"I remember the day we left," she wrote. "The train originated in Carbondale around 5 A.M. The night before, we sent the children to sleep in their street clothes. John and Joan and I never went to bed. The four Gardners came to see the three Segals off. In the car, John complained of David's dying, of the world's indifference to the several unpublished novels in his drawers. Nobody knew that *Grendel* was about to make John Gardner a name and that every one of his early novels would eventually be published."

The first copies of *Grendel* in fact arrived while Lore was there. "I read it with a thrill of astonishment," she wrote of its impact. An excerpt appeared in *Esquire*'s September 1971 issue, and the book was released to the public. Reviews appeared in every major national venue and more than three dozen periodicals in all. The praise was universal and effusive.

"An extraordinary achievement," reviewer Richard Locke termed it in a daily *New York Times,* concluding that "John Gardner has become a major contemporary American writer." In a full-length Sunday *Times* review, Keith Mano said the novel was "myth itself: permeated with revelation, with dark instincts, with swimming, riotous universals. . . . The special profundity of Gardner's vision . . . is so thought-fertile that it shunts even his fine poet's prose to a second importance." In the end, he calls the book "wholly a blessing." In *Newsweek,* Peter Prescott called it "absolutely marvelous: witty, intelligent, delightful," concluding, "I cannot recommend it too highly."

Like many who were introduced to Gardner's work with *Grendel,* Prescott would continue to read his work and follow his career closely as Gardner rose to achieve all the success and renown even the most optimistic had not predicted. But a decade later, Prescott would also become the agent of some of Gardner's most trying moments. In the months that followed *Grendel*'s publication however, all Gardner's ambitions seemed to bear fruit as the novel was showered with acclaim.

Gardner, though, was not there to receive the honors. The previous summer of 1970, he had gone with the family for two months to England, then to Ireland, where they'd visited Tom Kinsella, who was back home in Dublin. They went on to travel in western Europe, then returned to London. It had been a great vacation for the whole family, and that fall he had applied for a sabbatical leave, which had been granted for two quarters. Now in September 1971, the family left for a more extended London stay.

They rented a two-bedroom flat with large windows and plenty of room, just off Regent's Park near the London zoo. It was smaller than any of their previous houses, but with a big living room, a balcony off the kitchen, and carpeting throughout, there was plenty of space and comfort. Joel and Lucy shared one of the bedrooms and were enrolled in school there, Joel in the equivalent of sixth grade now, Lucy in fourth.

Since they'd been there the previous summer, London wasn't entirely foreign, and just as in Carbondale, a steady stream of friends and acquaintances came to visit for various lengths of time. Joyce Carol Oates and her husband, Ray Smith, were also in London that year, along with Stanley and Joan Elkin, Bill Gass, Robert Coover, and their families, all of whom visited regularly at the Gardners'. Helen Vendler was the guest of honor at one of their parties, where Oates met her for the first time. Eddie and Tegwin Epstein likewise came for a visit, as did the Howells, the Vergettes, and Howard Webb (the English Department chairman at SIU) and his family. Joan Elkin recalls that she and Stanley, who also spent various periods in England, saw the Gardners frequently that year, going out to dinner, and to each other's apartments. And in the summer, Lore Segal and her children rented an apartment Joan Gardner found for them in the same building.

At a bookstore in a nearby town, Elkin gave a reading of the entire novella he had finished, *The Making of Ashenden,* and Joan Elkin remembers that at the end of the story, when the protagonist Ashinton, in an absurd touch, is having sex with a bear, a group of teenagers walked into the store and stood in back, obviously captured by the scene, to the discomfort of the more serious adults. Both the Gardners and the Elkins had brought their children, and after the reading they all went to a big party where the Coovers were staying and spent the night at a nearby bed-and-breakfast.

If things around the Gardners were less wild and frenetic than in Carbondale, it was only a matter of scale. In October, a month after they had settled, John was showing Joel what he should do if he were somehow locked in the apartment and a fire broke out, or how to get in if he were locked out. The apartment was a floor above the ground, and John was demonstrating how Joel should climb in and out of one of the windows.

Says Joan Elkin, "He was being Spider-Man, clinging to the house. And he fell."

He was rushed to the hospital, where his leg was diagnosed as broken. It was another in the long string of physical damages he seemed to keep inviting — or that found him. In any case, none of it seemed to do more than temporarily delay whatever he was writing. It hardly slowed him.

Not surprisingly, London was much more hospitable to Joan's professional and cultural interests than Carbondale. There were the museums and the theater, and her music training enabled her to get a job in the spring teaching cello and violin quartets at a local school. In the summer she was employed to adjudicate a week of exams at the Royal Academy.

Gene Rudzewicz also came to visit, and with John's encouragement he stayed with them. Rudzewicz continued to grow even closer to all of them. He went on to share many of the practical burdens of parenting and householding that had been almost entirely Joan's responsibility, and the role that had begun with his first trip to Carbondale thus continued through that London visit and afterward back in Carbondale. Says Joan Elkin, "He idolized John. . . . He felt [John] should just write, just have time."

If the arrangement heightened difficulties between John and Joan, it also relieved John of some of the householding pressures he'd always avoided. And though, as Joan Elkin says of the Gardners, the constant sharp-edged banter they exchanged made "the two of them [remind] Stanley and me of Zelda and Scott Fitzgerald," in London, she recalls, they were getting along as well as ever. Once, in fact, the Elkins' daughter walked in on them when they were making love. "So they were apparently getting along fine," she says.

The Elkins had known John and Joan for more than a decade, and though John and Stanley had the generally friendly and mutually respectful relations of professional peers, John, particularly, felt more competitive with Stanley, as Elkin had had more success with his writing to this point. Only now, with the praise

Grendel was receiving, were their careers beginning to seem balanced. Socially, however, both Elkins liked Joan more. Says Joan Elkin, "Both Stanley and I were extremely fond of Joan. We thought she was one of the funniest ladies we'd ever known. . . . It was just one funny story after another, and I loved being with her. . . . [She was] so clever [and] smart. Stanley would say of some of John's work, I bet Joan wrote that." She offers a different view of John. "John was difficult," she says. "He was quiet. There was not a lot of anecdotal give and take with him."

It was a comment others who knew John also made—that there was no such thing as small talk with him. On the one hand, he was interested in the social dimensions of most everything the culture presented, but the conversations that engaged him were invariably those about art and ideas and writing. It wasn't that he was an antisocial drudge. He loved to have people around, and he clearly liked the cultural richness of London, which he knew pleased Joan far more than Carbondale. But his interests were mainly in larger ideas. And his intention was to write.

That September, Southern Illinois University Press had published his *Alliterative Morte Arthure,* which he had finished the previous spring and summer, in an edition that also included *The Owl and the Nightingale* and five other Middle English poems. The work of modernizing medieval classics seemed clearly useful—no modern rendering of these poems existed—and its creative requirements made it an interesting task. Moreover, the scholarly investigations justified the university grants that supported the family's sojourns in England. On their trip the previous summer, they'd been to York in central England, where they'd seen a production that was part of the annual staging there of the medieval mystery plays, and John had the idea of modernizing them and writing some commentary. Thus, the project was part of his sabbatical application.

In truth, however, he was growing tired of writing medieval criticism. The proposals he wrote were aimed mainly at getting the grants to help the family's finances and getting time free of teaching. Though he kept his hand in the whole enterprise of medieval literary criticism and edited a series of academic books on the subject for the SIU press, he devoted himself more and more to his fiction. He also began writing essays and book reviews that advanced his aesthetic, opportunities that began to arise more frequently now that *Grendel* was putting his name on the national literary map. He'd written a pair of lengthy essay-reviews on contemporary novels in the previous three or four years for the literary journal the *Southern Review;* now the *New York Times Book Review* began calling on him. The same month *Grendel* came out, he wrote to praise John Cheever's latest novel in the *Review,* and in the next year the prestigious newspaper, his largest forum to date, solicited two more reviews and a longer essay on the current state of fiction. That article, "The Way We Write Now," appeared in the summer, and it articulated his view of contemporary fiction while taking American novelists to task for valuing style and technique over the human complexities of characters. Rooted in his belief that fiction had a serious function far beyond entertainment, it was a position he'd been staking out whenever he had the chance.

In the article, Gardner criticizes Updike's *Couples* for "abandoning close analysis and dramatic inevitability in favor of, simply, a way of being." He concludes, "There's the problem in all of our finest contemporary fiction, I think. It's the reason for the thin, unglued quality in even the most dazzling technical performances. Whether you write about dragons or businessmen, it's in the careful scrutiny of cleanly apprehended characters, their conflicts and ultimate escape from immaturity, that the novel makes up its solid truths, finds courage to defend the good and attack the simpleminded."

But most of his first six months in London were devoted to the other major project that he'd described on his sabbatical application. That project had begun with "The Epic Conversation," the book he had started when he'd been at San Francisco State, arguing that each of the classic epics was responding to a previous epic. "It seems to me that the Homer of the *Iliad* sets down a sort of code of life," he said in a later interview, "and the Homer of the *Odyssey* says, 'Yeah but—' *The Odyssey* is an answer, very definitely, to *The Iliad*." This dialogue continues, he argued, at least through James Joyce, who was "constantly and consciously echoing the epic tradition."

"The Epic Conversation" had never coalesced, though, and so, he went on, "I decided that instead of writing about what the epics do, I'd do my own epic in which I'd use materials from all the others. Do it as art instead of criticism."

About the same time he had begun "The Epic Conversation," he had also started a translation of the classic Latin epic *The Argonautica*. Now, he decided, he would write his own epic. "It's sort of a mock epic poem," he said, "but so is *The Argonautica.*"

He undertook to tell the complete story of Jason (of the Golden Fleece) and Medea in an epic of his own. He wrote the long first draft, eventually over five hundred pages when it was published, in the months before coming to London. The whole thing, he said later, came to him mostly in sleep. It was the sort of claim, in keeping with the times, promoting the myth of the mysterious writer, to which Gardner was given. "I would go to sleep and dream the stuff and wake up and write it down, then revise and revise until it made some kind of sense," he said.

In another interview, he explained that the whole project really began with his reading Euripides years earlier. "At first I skimmed through Euripides, shook my head, then decided to drop and add passages to portray Medeia as positively as I could." But then he began to feel that the translations of Euripides were inadequate. He continued, "I decided to use Apollonius' *Argonautica* as a primary source and I wound up translating line after line. . . . As I recall it, I was at the point of the, well, 'kickoff,' when Medeia was preparing to murder her children, and I decided to go back to Euripides in Greek and see if there was anything I could keep. It was awesome, a magical moment. I was knocked off my feet by the sheer brilliance of his play."

In June, he'd written a research proposal for what he tentatively titled "Jason: An Epic Poem" and he had received a grant from the university for typing, as well as for magazine submissions and expenses in Europe. The project, his application said, intended to "explore theory about the direct and conscious dialectics in the epics of Homer, Apollonius, and Virgil."

He'd written poems since high school or before, and amid all his other work he'd also continued at least sporadic involvement with serious verse. The poetry he wrote was more conventionally formal than most serious poetry of the time, often using traditional rhyme schemes and meters. But the skill and intelligence it manifested were certainly noted by editors. Beginning with publications in student magazines, he'd continued to write and publish occasional poems in some of the most prestigious literary periodicals—*Perspective,* the *Southern Review,* the *Kenyon Review,* the *Hudson Review*—up through the spring 1970 issues. Thus, when he went to work on his epic poem, he was hardly a neophyte.

The epic, however, was a different enterprise. For one thing, it was much longer. Like fiction, it told a story that explored and illustrated human character, but it required certain established conventions—a catalog of events and circumstances, epic similes, and a hero who pits himself against supernatural forces and emerges victorious. For his, Gardner fashioned an approximately six-stress line, which he termed "sprung hexameter." "It obviously varies," he said, "but most of the poem is cadenced, six-stress verse."

With gods and heroes from the Greek classics actively participating, he rendered his story of love and heroism in a language that mixes contemporary diction with older, anachronistic phrasing. In the end, he was well aware that there was something at least a little odd, even humorous, in the exercise. "I didn't really mean for things to get serious until the final book," he said. "I meant it to be kind of a romp. I assume I'm writing for . . . people who aren't very thoroughly educated in the classics, and what I want to do ultimately is bring all the myths together, everything from Oedipus to Aeneas to whatever."

The work collapses time, mixing references to works and events from the classical Greek era to the contemporary, and at the same time is sprinkled with neologisms Gardner coins. Most important, it addresses the whole question of the function of art and language—ideas at the center of Gardner's concern. In one passage, he writes more directly about the artist than he had in any other work to that point:

> The true artist, who speaks with justice,
> who rules words in the fear of God,
> is like morning light at sunrise filling a cloudless sky,
> making the grass of the earth sparkle after rain.
> But false artists are like desert thorns
> whose fruit no man gathers with his hand;
> no man touches them
> unless it's with iron or the shaft of a spear,
> and then they are burnt in the fire.

In the poem, Jason cleaves to reason and intellect at the expense of love and art, showing himself to be a "false" artist. "Spinning his web of words," he justifies abandonment of wife, comrades, and other misdeeds, all of which bring on his own psychological downfall. Finally, though, the poem becomes an affirmation of the essential power of imaginative art—a force Jason doesn't see—in both personal and social life.

During that fall and winter in London, he worked steadily and intensely at it. When the family took a short trip to Paris, he brought it along and found time to scrawl notes and lines on whatever scraps were available between visiting the sights. When he finished it in the following spring or early summer, he was so pleased with what he'd accomplished that he began plotting another.

During the same period, he also worked on another Carbondale story. Using characters modeled on Epstein and himself, "The Temptation of St. Ivo" revisits discussions that informed *The Sunlight Dialogues* and dramatizes directly their ongoing philosophical argument about the fundamental principles by which one should behave — obey rules and support order or violate them in the name of freedom and risk chaos? In the story, the narrator, Brother Nicholas (patterned after Epstein), believes in strictly adhering to rules, and is continually upset by the apparent ease and success of Brother Ivo, who blithely goes his own way, breaking rules and tempting Nicholas to do the same.

Meantime, with the rest of the family happily settled in London, no one was in any particular hurry to leave. In February, Joan had another operation to scrape the remaining adhesions from her lower spine, and arrangements had to be made through SIU for the insurance to cover the expenses. At the same time, John wrote to ask that his leave be extended through spring and to be excused from teaching in the summer. With *Grendel* gaining more and more notice — it came out in England in July 1972 — *The Sunlight Dialogues* scheduled for publication at the end of the year, and the new *Jason and Medeia* also ready, he had no interest in to going back to teach. Though he was off the payroll through spring and summer, there suddenly was money and time that neither he nor Joan had seen since they'd been together. John's success kept mounting.

In the spring, he was awarded a five-thousand-dollar grant from the National Endowment for the Arts for his writing, and a fifteen-hundred-dollar advance from Knopf for publication of *Jason and Medeia*, with the understanding that the book would be "lavishly illustrated." The idea of having his novels illustrated was something he'd long nursed, and he'd persuaded David Segal to have *Grendel* illustrated with drawings at the beginning of each chapter. For *The Sunlight Dialogues,* he arranged for artist John Napper, with whom he had become friends when Napper came to Carbondale as a visiting professor, to do drawings for the dust jacket and for scenes in the text.

An oil painter trained at the Royal Academy of Art in London by a pupil of Degas, Napper had lived in England and France for seventeen years. His paintings had been featured in several shows in Europe, and many had been sold there, as he accumulated a reputation that led to the invitation to come to Carbondale in 1968. He and Gardner got along immediately. Napper was a voracious reader and very interested in teaching. He was also a guitarist, and so the two spent time playing music together as well.

After Napper returned to England, John had written him about illustrating his novel. But Napper's father had been an illustrator, and Napper wasn't interested in that work. Gardner persisted, however, and sent chapters from the novel to try and interest him. Napper read them, then the whole manuscript, and changed his mind. In the autumn of 1972 he came back to the States and went with Gardner to Batavia, where he sketched for three weeks, producing drawing after drawing of common daily objects in houses there, which were later incorporated into the novel.

In an interview just a few months after the book was published, Gardner insisted that the illustrations were not simply decoration or "visual ideas." "The error," he said, referring to the notion that illustrations in a novel are superfluous, "is the implicit assumption that all grown-up fiction is realistic and self-importantly solemn, so that illustration must be irrelevant. Another error is that illustrations merely illustrate."

Rather, significant illustrations—like Napper's—were "fictions" of their own, which "freeze complex emotions into charged images," and so comment on and counterpoint the novel. "Thus [Gustave] Dore gave Dante's hell new dimensions and [John] Tenniel transformed Lewis Carroll's *Wonderland.*" Placing the idea in an abandoned tradition, Gardner wanted to repopularize the "illustrated novel."

Ultimately, Napper made a set of thirteen lithographs, each of which got a full page in the text, with originals published in a limited edition of one hundred signed and numbered sets. In January 1973, Napper was given a show with his drawings at a New York City gallery.

That previous August, the Gardners had left the Regent's Park flat and headed back home. They stopped in New York for a few days where John met with Georges Borchardt, his agent now, and with editor Robert Gottlieb, who had taken over editing John's books when Segal had died. Though *Grendel* hadn't been a big seller in hardback, with its critical success, a three-novel contract, and his other writings, John had become "an important literary writer," as Gottlieb puts it.

Certainly Gardner liked visiting Manhattan and Knopf with his newly achieved literary notoriety, but he had always been a small-town boy for whom the charms of the city were limited. And the business of working with his editor, though he may have enjoyed the occasion of the meeting and got along with him well enough, was one of such limitations. Gottlieb worked with him by mail, on the phone, and occasionally in person, to revise and prepare his novels. The conversations weren't at all contentious, Gottlieb says, but "on every book there was endless discussion of various things. John wasn't a particular rewriter. Some writers are at their best when they're rewriting—that's what they really enjoy. He wasn't like that. He didn't particularly enjoy the editorial process. So it was more of a negotiation than a collaboration. I don't mean it was in any way difficult or unpleasant. We always had the most amicable relations, as I recall. But that wasn't the part of the process he liked."

Though his style was different from Segal's, Gottlieb was equally "superb" as an editor, Gardner said in a later interview. "Bob works differently from David. David would produce a carefully written analysis of everything in the book; Bob works more from the seat of his pants. His remarks are incisive and immediate; but they're brief, not elaborately spelled out. What's invaluable about Bob is that he works exactly by my standards. We've talked at length about what I should be trying to do, and in that respect, we agree to the letter."

With the final manuscript finished then after the New York visit, the family drove upstate to Batavia, and when they got back to Carbondale, Boskeydell resumed its customary liveliness as normal life resumed—however far from "normal" that may have seemed to most.

9

Illinois Tales

> I could tell you a tale, if ye'd understand from the outset
> it has no purpose to it, no shape or form or discipline but
> the tucket and boom of its highflown language . . .
>
> —*The King's Indian*

W HEN I GOT THERE it was late, it was raining, and I came in last. The only place for me to sit was on a piano bench across the door from where I came in. There was a young guy reading poetry, which John made some comment about, and a big metal coffee urn on the dining room table. Joan was there at the time. He was wearing jeans and a white shirt. After the guy had finished reading his poetry, [John] turned to me. I had brought three or four of my manuscripts, of novels I had written, and put them on the table, and he asked what this was.

He looked them over and said, "obviously you can write, why are you here?" And I said, "Yeah, I can write pages, but there's a lot I can learn about voice and rhythm." He immediately responded to voice and rhythm and said, "Oh, I can teach you that."

When Charles Johnson came to Boskeydell for Gardner's professional writing class on a rainy night in September 1972, the English Department was in the process of making creative writing a separate concentration. Though he had avoided teaching it most of the time he'd been there, he had taken on one class three years earlier; then, the year before he'd gone to England, he'd told John Howell that he was tired of teaching medieval literature and wanted to go back to teaching fiction writing. From England, he'd written department chair Howard Webb the same thing, but Webb wasn't receptive to the idea, having no one else as qualified to teach medieval literature. Creative writing as part of formal English curricula was surging in popularity in universities everywhere, though, and John had always been known to be good at it. Now, the success of *Grendel* and the upcoming publication of *The Sunlight Dialogues*, along with a few years of respite from the demands of student writers, all helped rekindle his enthusiasm.

For his part, Johnson was exactly the kind of student John took to immediately. He shared with John a seemingly bottomless fountain of energy, and they had other things in common. For one, Johnson was a graduate student with an M.A. in philosophy and was interested in continuing toward a Ph.D. It was a discipline that had attracted John since his first undergraduate days, and his fiction was, of course, seriously engaged with its ideas. In fact, *The Resurrection* had been criticized by some for having characters that were no more than actors of philosophical ideas.

Johnson was also a cartoonist, though he was much more successful and committed to it than John had been. At the time they met, he had published over a hundred drawings, had one book out, another due, and was hosting a national educational television series, *Charley's Pad*, a drawing program. Gardner looked over the comic art books and individual drawings Johnson had brought, commenting, "Well, that's all just preparation for your writing."

Needless to say, the remark was discouraging to Johnson. "I didn't see it as that," he says, "not those seven years of passion I'd put into being a cartoonist."

But with the same dedication Gardner had to writing, the two were a natural match. And thirty years later, after four novels, his last the winner of a National Book Award, Johnson quickly credits Gardner's influence:

> There is no writer on earth who has affected me more than John.
>
> One thing I've always taken to heart is the absolute and total commitment to art. Something else I found in John that I responded to very strongly—he was a polymath. He wrote in all these different categories of creative expression, he played the French horn . . . and all of that appealed to me. Because one of the things that I was about as a cartoonist was drawing in lots of different styles. . . . That was one of the things that was so exciting about John. We could be talking and move from philosophy to talking about short fiction writers, and he'd start talking about music.

It was clear at that first meeting that Johnson was no ordinary student. He wanted to work with Gardner individually and

Gardner agreed to work with Johnson at his office and asked him whether he wanted to concentrate on revising one of the novels he'd written or start a new one. Johnson said he wanted to start something new. "So I wrote a new chapter," Johnson says, "and he got real enthusiastic; and we were skating from that point on to the end of the book."

The book became Johnson's first published novel, *Faith and the Good Thing*, and Gardner had an excerpt published in a literary tabloid he supervised in the winter quarter. That term, John was a Visiting Professor at Northwestern, just north of Chicago, some six hours away, where he taught a class called "Narrative Forms" which took up some contemporary novels. Three years later, when Johnson's novel was published, he met Gardner in New York City at Lore Segal's. They all went to a play they decided they didn't like, and they walked out of it partway through—but not before John walked up and down the orchestra aisles passing out leaflets he had brought advertising Johnson's novel. The enthusiasm was a crucial boost for Johnson, and Gardner was delighted to be able to offer it.

That first fall of 1972, when Johnson had gone over to Boskeydell one night with a new chapter of his novel, he saw the first advance copy of *The Sunlight Dialogues* on a table near the door. When it was officially published in December, the reviews were even more glowing and widespread than those for *Grendel* had been. In the *New York Times*, Christopher Lehmann-Haupt called Gardner "a major American writer whose promise for the future now seems unlimited." It may have seemed usual book review excess, but such praise was repeated by every major outlet —more than two dozen publications. As the new year dawned, Gardner's fourth novel, 673 pages long, climbed onto the *New*

York Times best-seller list where it would remain for sixteen weeks. Not yet forty years old, after working intensively at his fiction for twenty years, Gardner experienced waves of sweeping success.

Jason and Medeia was scheduled to come out later that spring, and in December, after twenty years of writing and rewriting and expanding his first undergraduate story from Washington University, he would see *Nickel Mountain* published. Requests to review books and write articles began coming regularly from major national publications. He hired the first of several personal secretaries to manage the mounting schedule of readings and conferences. In the spring of 1973 he was also awarded a Guggenheim grant, one of only a handful given each year and the most prestigious award an American writer could receive. The money that resulted from the award and from his novel's success would be enough to let him take off teaching completely in the next year.

The money also led to changes in the Boskeydell house and grounds. Two major additions were made to the house, one of which was a square wooden tower with a winding staircase, extending one story higher than the existing house and culminating in a small windowed study at the top where John could retreat to write. The style was a reflection of his medieval interests. Its greater privacy might have supplanted the study on the second floor, but because he never managed to put in a heating and cooling system that worked well the tower study was always too hot in summer and too cold in the winter. Even so, like the ceramic dragon installed in the tree in front, the visual aesthetics easily outweighed more pedestrian concerns.

On the other side of the house, a concrete patio and swimming pool were built adjacent to a new patio room. The room had windows on three sides, a wet bar, and two sides of the room were lined with water beds, in part to accommodate whatever guests might be there. In addition, the Gardners traded in their Chevrolets for a Mercedes-Benz (the first of three they would own) and an antique Essex. John Howell remembers the Essex John drove with Vergette one night to Howell's, which, like the medieval-style robe he liked to wear at readings, reflected his penchant for showmanship. "John obviously spent his money in a hurry," Howell remarks. "He bought [the Essex] for about twenty thousand dollars. It is a model that is cut out of 1924. John liked to get dressed up [and] I remember he and Nicholas came up to the house . . . dressed up in Edwardian clothes and driving their Essex."

Part of that taste for the elaborate, recalls Ed Epstein, likewise led to the "Southern Illinois Hunt Club," which John and Vergette formed. Mainly, says Epstein, it meant the two of them getting dressed up in some facsimile of British hunting gear, "sitting against a tree and drinking bourbon."

With the new additions, the house itself was even better equipped to receive the company that both Gardners always drew. A steady flow of people was welcomed at any time, whether invited or not. Charles Johnson, in fact, remembers a young man who lived there who said that "John had taken him on as an apprentice." Says Johnson, "He was one of a coterie of aspiring writers around John."

Neither the success nor the liquor, however, changed anything about his work habits. He'd been at it too long to go about it any differently. Nor did it visibly change much about his daily surface. His temperament had always been shaded by a darker side, colored, as everyone close to him knew, by the loss of Gilbert. What with the ever-present problems with Joan, including her medical problems, which surely compounded the difficulties, it was a darkness no doubt fed also by the gin that he drank as copiously as ever, late into nights. And the solitary business of writing offered plenty of breeding ground for it.

The infidelities that Pat Gray has commented on surely played a role as well, and partly as a sort of guilty reaction to his own affairs, it seemed, he'd continued to encourage Gene Rudzewicz as he became a more or less fixed member of the household. Though Rudzewicz's contributions took pressure off John, the arrangement could only have deepened the chasm between John and Joan.

Says Lore Segal, " Gene moved in and took on all the jobs that John didn't do. . . . He took the children to school, picked them up, made sure their shoes were watertight. In the beginning, it was a very sort of utopian arrangement." But, she points out, such arrangements rarely remain "utopian." As Rudzewicz became increasingly sympathetic to Joan, he grew resentful of all John didn't do for her and the children, and he came to emphasize John's faults more and more. "There was a way John acquiesced," says Segal, "but broken-heartedly—to the situation which he himself not only condoned, but maybe initiated." Meantime, John "sat in his study up in his attic, yearning for fun that went on below."

Since 1973, he'd been deeply involved with the newest secretary he'd hired. Tall and slender, with long dark hair, Nancy

Longwell was twenty years his junior and a product of the youth culture of the time. With her long dresses and quiet demeanor, she drew John powerfully. To complicate matters further, she'd fallen in love with him. Troubled by the difficulty of her position as the "other woman," however, she left in the fall, returned briefly in December and again in February, then left again in March.

In Boston, where she had gone to escape the difficulties John presented, she became deeply involved with an Indian guru and made plans to go to India. That summer, she went on a spiritual pilgrimage and returned, John told his friend John Howell later, with leprosy, which she had incurred while working at a leper colony. Still in love with her, John told Howell that he had crawled into bed with her at the hospital, hoping to catch the disease.

WAVES OF LITERARY success rarely continue unbroken, and they certainly didn't for John. The New York literary press, to which he'd always felt a somewhat jealous outsider, was decidedly less laudatory of *Jason and Medeia* when it came out in the summer of 1973. Johnson, in fact, recalls being at Boskeydell one day after John had received some critical reviews of the book.

"He sat alone in the house that day at the long, mead-hall-size table in his dining room," Johnson wrote in a memoir, "drinking whiskey from a Mason jar and editing a movie his family and friends had written and performed [a satire on Westerns that they were calling 'The Midwesterner']."

Cautiously, Johnson asked what he thought of the reviews. "He replied quietly, hardly looking up from his editing machine.

'They just want to keep you from going to heaven,'" he told Johnson.

It was hard to be immune from the criticism. Still, invitations to read and lecture came from all over the country, along with other marks of his achievements. Often enough, they came from former colleagues, and John must have enjoyed playing the role of the returning prodigal son.

Though engaging and personable and intense as ever, he did seem, to some old friends, changed in his demeanor. In November 1973, he took his family to Carleton College in southern Minnesota where his old Oberlin colleague George Soule was now a professor. For a symposium titled "Myth, Society, and the Search for Meaning," he gave a talk that sounded an old theme, identifying Jean-Paul Sartre as the intellectual model for Grendel, the force of philosophical darkness and nihilism.

But the Gardner Soule met was new. The families had dinner together, and Soule remembers, "It was a different John from the one I'd known. He was trying to be as affable as he could. . . . He'd just been in New York and was flush with money from *Sunlight*. He'd bought French horns . . . and [the children] carried them into our house." Lucy, in the way of many young children who haven't been much restrained, "marched into the house, turned to her parents and said, 'This isn't very big'—which sort of set the tone for the visit."

When it came time for dinner, Soule remembers, "John wouldn't eat any of our food. He had little wads of yin and yang things in his pocket, that he'd take out and eat [a result of Nancy Longwell's influence and the macrobiotic diet she had introduced him to]. Then next day, he gave a convocation address, in a spangled suit . . . the general thesis of which was that we all have to love one another and be kind to one another . . . delivered . . . in the most aggressive way you could imagine. As if he wanted to beat us all up. It was incredible."

John had always had a missionary streak, going back to his childhood days when he'd led mock church services with his cousins. And even among senior colleagues, he evinced a certainty and fervor that many remarked. Still, the aggressiveness Soule notes was more than a step beyond what those who knew him were used to. For all the respect his intellect had always commanded, coupled with the compassion and general goodwill friends and acquaintances always noted, his pronouncements couldn't help but offend some. And the strain between him and Joan added to the discomfort.

Their old friend from California, Eric Solomon, recalls their visiting San Francisco in 1975:

> It was a very bad evening. I did not recognize this guy or what had happened between him and Joan. She was down . . . bitter, and obviously unhappy. He was affecting his pipe . . . quite boastful about everything he was accomplishing and all the places he was going and the awards he was winning. . . . They stayed three or four hours, and toward the end of the evening he asked me what I thought of his most recent book. I said, "Well John, you're writing so fast I'm about two behind." And that was it. He left, insulted, and I was not sad to see him go. I'm sure it was a response to his own sense of how successful and self-important he was.

Jerry Handler concurs. "Once he became famous, I became aware that he was a pontificator. He would pontificate on any subject imaginable—things he didn't know anything about.

Now, he did know about a lot of things, but . . . the more famous he got, the more he'd pontificate."

Even familiy members were struck by the change. John's cousin, Bill Gardner, also remembers a visit from John in the summer of that same year, and feeling virtually assaulted. Talking about his stature, Bill remembers his saying, "I'm not *one* of the best, I'm *the* best!"

As his reputation grew, the intensity of his enthusiasms, coupled with his distaste for convention and restraint, also led him to clash with authorities, as it had over the years. This time, it was SIU's president, hoping to take advantage of Gardner's prestige, with whom he collided. In winter 1973, President David Derge had asked John to write a history of the university for a respected academic journal, hoping that the article might draw the kind of attention that would lead to financial gifts from proud alumni. When he saw Gardner's proposed article however, the casual tone that made it so readable drew a picture of the region that an enthusiastic booster might not find attractive.

Commenting on the million-dollar-plus house the trustees were having built for the president, with a trustee's nephew as the architect, Gardner wrote, "Moral shortsightedness is a way of life in parts of southern Illinois." He went on to describe circumstances that fed conflicts in the area: "To the extent that poverty makes men angry—snipers in Cairo [a town in far southern Illinois], teen-agers mugging old ladies in the lost little village of Makanda because there's nothing else to do, or farmers with squeezed-shut faces brooding on a life of betrayals . . . a good many people in southern Illinois are isolated even from each other: black versus white, farmer versus professor, even campus policemen against the more countrified state police."

Along with this, however, he praised other aspects of life in Carbondale just as strongly: "There are . . . reasons [to live here]. One is the chance to raise one's children where the air is clean and there are animals and plants for a child to get to know . . . the chance to work in peace." And of the university he noted that "the freedom teachers have at SIU to create new programs or pursue far-out if not outlandish ideas is extraordinary."

But Derge wrote to Gardner that the article wouldn't do. Committed to his point of view, however, John refused to concede to any real changes and wrote back that he'd revise the tone a little, but not much. When it was published in the academic journal, *Change*, in April 1974, it earned praise from others around SIU, but Gardner, never satisfied, went on to parody Derge in the novella he was working on, in which Captain Dirge appears as an essentially pompous and gullible scholar who heads the illusory ship that is the story's setting.

Far more troubling than any skirmishes or complications that shadowed his professional success, however, were the serious health problems of those closest to him. All the years they lived in Carbondale, Joan continued to suffer pain that was more and more debilitating. She had seen doctors and psychiatrists in the area, in St. Louis, and in London, but the adhesions that were first discovered in 1967 flared up regularly. On top of this, in the winter of 1973, John's closest friend, Nick Vergette, was diagnosed with lung cancer. He was seemingly in good health when he was diagnosed, and Joan says, "He glowed with health and vitality, always looking young right up until his last year."

But over the months, his body struggled, trying his jovial nature, as the cancer took its toll. Charles Johnson recalls being invited with his wife to dinner at Boskeydell with the Vergettes that last year, when Nick was coughing badly. Though he never stopped working, his energy lessened, and toward the end, instead of large sculptures, he took to working only on a small scale, painting small mushrooms and lemons. John himself grew angry, frustrated at medicine's inability to help him. In the end, Vergette's kidneys failed, and at the age of fifty, in February 1974, as John's own success was reaching a pinnacle, Vergette died in his bed at home.

In the months that followed, Gardner sought to memorialize him in the only way he knew. *The King's Indian,* the collection of stories published later that year, whose title novella he was working on at the time, is dedicated to Vergette. The Vergette house is on the dust jacket of the hardback; a drawing of Vergette is one of the book's illustrations; and toward the end of the novella, Vergette enters directly: "A fifty-year-old sculptor with terminal disease sits painting with infinite patience and total concentration a pale yellow lemon on a field of white. With each light stroke added, the lemon shows more its inclination to vanish."

The vanishing, which is Vergette's death, cut all of the Gardners deeply. For John it again made intimate the specter of mortality whose breath he had long felt. The novella itself manifests a major issue Gardner sought to address and one that Vergette's death highlighted—the significance of art in culture, and what fiction should be, given the inexorable fact of life's shortness.

The topic emerges amid Gardner's traditional concerns— conflicts between order and disorder and between what is real and what is illusory. In the end, the novella stands as a metafiction, a fabulation, that, like the work of John Barth, to whose *Sotweed Factor* it makes reference, and other metafictionists

Gardner later attacked, points to the artifacted nature of fiction. But as in some of his pronouncements and other writings, the novella takes the idea of the unreal nature of fiction to a different point, underlining the essential generative force of the imagination, which combines with reason in the making of art.

He writes near the end of the novella in regard to his central character:

> Dr. Luther Flint has been raised from mere artifice— a ventriloquist's dummy!—to a touching spokesman for all criminal, all pseudo-artistic minds. . . .
>
> But I haven't interrupted this flow of things imagined for mere chat about the plot. This house we're in is a strange one, reader . . . and I hope it's one you find congenial, and sufficiently gewgawed and cluttered but not unduly snug. Take my word, in any case, that I haven't built it as a cynical trick, one more bad joke of exhausted art.

This is the precise accusation he leveled at Barth and other metafictionists. Gardner's own tale, on the other hand, is "not a toy but a queer, cranky monument, a collage: a celebration of all literature and life; an environmental sculpture, a funeral crypt."

In a 1977 interview, Gardner spoke of the novella's composition: "At the time . . . my best friend—who was a super sculptor and artist—was dying and I couldn't handle it. I wanted to write about it, though not directly, and particularly because my friend participated so splendidly in the field of art, particularly American art, I wanted to write about art too."

At the memorial service for Vergette, John read the poem he

had written in his honor, simply titled, "Nicholas Vergette: 1923–1974." Evoking at one point Auden's elegy to Yeats ("The dogs howled. It rained. We should have expected it. / He became once more like the clay he himself had fashioned or discarded"), the poem recalls Vergette's art, and their friendship, with snapshots of the sculptor:

> and we'd sink out of thought for a moment, gaze down
> at a gray gin and tonic . . .
>
> . . . .
>
>   a man all alone in his living room,
> staring at the embers in his fireplace . . .
>
> . . . .
>
> His faith was in stones, and in his own bright mottled
>   imitations of stones;
> in bronze, wood, plastic; in towering forms, in squat
>   forms, in walls . . .

Right after he died, John and Joan took Vergette's widow, Helen, and son, Marcus, who were as close to them as family, to tour the Greek islands for a month. Though nothing could remedy such loss, the generosity was characteristic, however grandiose the gesture may have seemed to others.

When they returned, John's crowded schedule resumed without a break. He had been selected to be the subject of a half-hour documentary for a nationally broadcast public television series titled *American Originals.* Featuring profiles of artists at work and at home, the show brought a film crew to Boskeydell and began with shots of Gardner riding his horse, while the sky thundered in the background and he talked about *Grendel* in a voice-over. The quasi-mythic image captured a persona he loved to project, and the filming continued with a "party" staged at the Rileys', to round out the view. Joe Liberto, one of John's former students, played piano in the background, amid general party conversation, spotlighting one where Joan made fun of a Japanese bonsai tree with her customary biting wit. The whole invention was intended to feel natural, and, indeed, the picture it drew seemed a reasonable slice of the world John had gathered about him.

In August, Gardner readied himself for another conference. This, however, was more than the usual literary visit. He had been invited to be on the faculty of the Bread Loaf Writers' Conference in the Vermont mountains. Begun as a summer English writing program of Middlebury College in 1926, Bread Loaf is the oldest and one of the best known of literary writing conferences. Since 1927, it had been attended regularly by Robert Frost for thirty-five years, and his presence and invitation had brought many of America's most famous writers to his vision of a "literary summer camp." Over the years, the list of authors who had come to teach selected students read like a "Who's Who" of twentieth-century American literature: Harriet Monroe, John Farrar, Stephen Vincent Benet, Sinclair Lewis, Archibald Macleish, John Crowe Ransom, Wallace Stegner, Saul Bellow, Adrienne Rich, Ralph Ellison, Anne Sexton, and Nelson Algren, to mention some of the most prominent. For Gardner, who had always felt on the outside of (if not downright antagonistic toward) the world of established contemporary writers, the invitation was another imprimatur of the status he had achieved.

He arrived with Joan a day late that first year and, drunk,

drove their Mercedes into a ditch the first night. This wildness, of course, was part of his appeal, especially to the students with whom he always felt close, and from the first his presence was magnetic. He became a center among his colleagues in his annual appearances thereafter. Author Jay Parini knew him there and recalls the comments of many through the years, saying, "He was a very powerful character and energetic teacher and personality. He talked a lot, and fast. . . . [It was a] verbal landslide at times."

His intensity and outgoing nature spread among writers and students both. That first year, Hilma Wolitzer, who was only a fellow then—the lowest of the tuition-paid positions in the Bread Loaf hierarchy—gave a reading from her first novel and has since written of the importance of Gardner's presence: "I had been very, very nervous about reading my work in public and felt quite ill beforehand—I didn't know whether I'd faint or throw up or have a heart attack or do something else to disgrace myself besides the reading itself. And I think that because John was there in support of a fellow, on an afternoon when a lot of staff people tended to take naps, was wonderful. At the end, he stood up and said, 'Bravo.' That he had such an enthusiastic and public response cured my stage fright instantly. . . . And he continued to be very supportive."

Poet Chris Merrill had written very little fiction, and he remembers screwing up his courage and approaching Gardner at the 1977 conference.

"He could be found most days holding court in the barn," Merrill says, "the informal gathering place. But he was alone the afternoon I asked him to look at my sketch.

" 'I'll read,' he said in a weary voice, 'till I get bored.' "

After reading the first paragraph, he motioned Merrill to sit down and said, "You're a writer."

Then, relates Merrill, "He sat back in his chair, lit his pipe, and started talking to me. He talked for the next four and a half hours, patiently giving me instructions about the sacred nature of my art, the religious devotion it requires of its servants. . . . What stays with me is the care and attention he showered on a twenty-two-year-old apprentice to the craft. He was serious, intense: writing was everything to him."

The missionary fervor that attracted so many wasn't, of course, equally appreciated by everyone. Joan Elkin especially remembers Stanley's annoyance at the attention John drew. Stanley had, after all, first served on the Bread Loaf faculty in 1964 and frequently thereafter. He had published several novels, achieving recognition earlier than Gardner, and was equally revered as a raconteur. Not surprisingly, says Joan Elkin, as Gardner's renown grew, "Stanley felt competitive with John. Once at Bread Loaf," she relates, "we were sitting in front of the huge fireplace in the barn and talking to some people gathered there, and Stanley turned around, saw a huge crowd of people all sitting facing one way, and there in front was the guru, John Gardner. It infuriated Stanley."

Like some other old friends, both Elkins were put off by the changes that John's fame seemed to have wrought in him. Says Joan Elkin, "He was very sweet before his fame—but after, the sweetness and innocence was gone. The fact that so many people were sitting at his feet—at Bread Loaf—would have been something he would have totally rejected before *Grendel.* He would have thought it ridiculous. But now he seemed to feel he deserved it; that he could give advice, that he could tell people what to do."

Stanley's jealousy is something that commonly afflicts writers, and this was hardly the first time Gardner's theatrical habits and penchant for making proclamations put off contemporaries even as they attracted students.

Meantime, opportunities to travel and to move elsewhere flowed in. Officials at SIU knew that they would have to offer him more to make it worth his while to remain in Carbondale. In the fall of 1974, he was nominated for the position of artist in residence, a position only Buckminster Fuller, their most prominent and nationally known faculty member had held. But John's days at SIU were nearing an end.

The previous April, a reading invitation had taken him and Joan to Bennington College in Vermont. They were met at the nearby airport in Albany, New York, by novelist and critic Alan Cheuse, who had loved *The Sunlight Dialogues* and had written a glowing review of it for *The Nation*. John arrived from another reading, long white-blond hair spilling over the black leather coat he often wore, and they all drove to dinner at novelist Nicholas Delbanco's house, halfway between the airport and the college. Delbanco was ten years younger, his upper-middle-class English background and degree from Harvard on a different order from Gardner's more modest roots, and he had already published seven novels. But Gardner was much more famous at the time, and despite the apparent differences they hit it off from the start, as did Joan and Delbanco's wife.

Their arrival that first night was typical. They got to the

Delbancos' about two hours late. As Delbanco recalled in a later memoir: "It was not his fault, in fact; it was Albany airport's, and the fog's. But somehow in the ensuing years, there would always be some such disruption. A car would fail to start or end up in a ditch, a snowstorm would come out of nowhere, a wallet would be lost."

As always, both Gardners made distinctively striking impressions: "Joan Gardner wore expensive clothing and fistfuls of jewelry; the novelist wore blue jeans and a black leather vest," Delbanco wrote.

But they all liked to drink, and talk.

"I've never seen anyone drink as much as John drank," comments Cheuse, and Delbanco concurs, "He emptied a quart of vodka before he sat to eat."

"Around midnight," Cheuse goes on, "and several fifths of vodka later, we ate; and then we kept on talking and drinking. At 4:30 A.M., I loaded them back into my VW Beetle and, with only the powerful odor of John's pipe tobacco to keep me a single strand sober, drove the back roads back to Bennington, mostly on the left-hand side of the road, with Joan passed out in the backseat next to John, and Josephine Carson [the other novelist colleague with them at the Delbancos'] awake and frightened enough into sobriety to scream most of the way about our impending head-on collision."

When Delbanco had pleaded the previous night that he had to get up and teach a class on Virginia Woolf the next morning, John had assured him that he would come and help. When Cheuse arrived at the motel to pick him up at eight, neither had slept more than a couple of hours, but John was outside puffing on his pipe. The class went until lunch, and Delbanco did most of the talking; but afterward, "with characteristic hyperbole," as Delbanco says, John asserted "that it was the best talk he'd ever heard. At least on any author after Malory."

Then, says Cheuse, John had "another class after lunch, and then a cocktail party, and then dinner, with more drinks, and then the reading (of his story, "Pastoral Care") . . . then another party. . . . At around two this next morning, he turned to Nicholas and me and announced with great passion that he loved the students here and loved Vermont and if we were interested would send us his [curriculum vitae] so that we could find a place for him to teach here." Delbanco had, in fact, asked John if he wanted a job there; as "secretary" of the department, he had the power to hire new faculty when administration permitted an opening. But he also knew Gardner was an established star, and so he was surprised when Gardner expressed interest.

By the time John left, he says, "We'd spent about thirty of thirty-six hours together." On the one hand, the whole experience "is not so uncharacteristic of the way John sort of swallowed people whole, with open arms in his embrace." But John's interest in moving back east and teaching in the new writing program at Bennington was genuine, and Delbanco was certainly enthusiastic about having such a famous and energetic colleague that he had liked so well. The Delbancos had also carefully pointed out the local symphony and good school system, which made the area more appealing, especially to Joan, who had never liked life in Carbondale. "Thus," says Delbanco, "it was one of those happy accidents."

Four days after the visit, John's curriculum vitae and letter came to confirm his interest, and Delbanco and Cheuse went to see what could be arranged. Gail Thain Parker, Bennington's president (at the time the youngest female college president in America), first told Delbanco and Cheuse that she did have one position available but that she had given it to the Science Department. She'd never heard of Gardner and asked about him. When they told her about his importance and value, she changed her mind and gave the open position to them for Gardner instead.

Thus, Gardner got the position. He then went on to apply for, and was awarded, a Hadley fellowship, which would pay him to teach at Bennington the following year as well. By fall, the whole family had moved to Vermont.

10

Old Bennington

To all that would tyrannize—the flag and religion and the domination of men—the novel smiled sweetly, like a loving wife, and . . . she hunted for the image and, with delight, jumped it: *smiled sweetly and let a little fart.*

—*October Light*

ROM THE BEGINNING, the move to Bennington was expected to be permanent, but because John needed to keep the insurance that came with his SIU job he couldn't afford to sever official ties there. With the help of John Howell and the cooperation of some officials, he arranged to conduct selected classes by going over student work by mail and visiting Carbondale to meet students in person at the end of the semester. Thus, he could officially remain on the staff at SIU while teaching at Bennington.

At his new job, he worked with Delbanco on designing a creative writing program, and the two saw each other almost daily, both professionally and socially. They visited each other's classes, conferred about students, and read and commented on each other's fiction.

"So we had a couple years of being very tight colleagues," Delbanco says. And he quickly testifies to Gardner's influence. "His first question to me always was, 'What are you working on?' He really was just passionate about making sure that art mattered to me as much as it did to him."

Especially he remembers their ongoing wrangles about subtleties of language and diction that were both entertaining and in some ways instructive—whether Sherbrooke, in Delbanco's trilogy, for instance, should be spelled with an *e* at the end. Gardner had insisted it would not be in American usage. The argument went on until Gardner found a bottle of Sherbrook scotch, labeled without the final *e* as proof. "That's the kind of thing that lasts for me," Delbanco says. "Saying *this* matters. And staying with it until it was solved."

It was understood when Gardner was hired that he wouldn't be there until October. For the entire month of September, in a trip sponsored by the U.S. government, he would be touring Japan with the family, to meet writers and officials there. Lucy remembers the whole trip as a great adventure, beginning with the long flight to Tokyo. Gardner kept downing the airplane cocktails; by the time he landed he was thoroughly drunk, and Joan was angered by the habitual indulgence. Just getting him through the airport with their luggage was a struggle. But once they were settled, "Dad was treated like a famous author everywhere he went," Lucy recalls, "and everyone thought we were so fascinating because we were so blond and white."

Their itinerary took John to meet with writers and officials in Tokyo, Sapporo, Nagoya, Kyoto, Hokkaidō, and Osaka. On trips overseas, the family had always sought accommodations and circumstances that were part of the indigenous culture, as opposed to seeking the familiarly American. For Lucy, Tokyo was disappointing, as it felt to her like any big American city, right down to the McDonald's restaurant that had been opened there.

The lush, green city of Kyoto was another matter, however. There, she and Joan went to a school where they took an all-day class in kimono tying and came home with kimonos. In the industrial city of Osaka, they visited a more American-style site — the World Expo amusement park. Its roller coaster was promoted as "the biggest, fastest and safest in the world," so John of course had to ride it. But when he got off, says Lucy, "He was white as sheet. He just held his chest and said, 'I just realized I'm old enough to have a heart attack.' And as far as I know he never went on a roller coaster again."

Since physical recklessness was a habit with him, his reaction to the roller-coaster ride was unusual. But while it may have discouraged him from trying a roller coaster again, the experience did nothing to dampen his general physical exuberance. It was partly a result of his disregard for anything ordinary, both physically and intellectually, and it was expressed in the certainty he projected, which some took as arrogance. In his travels to foreign countries and dealing with other languages, for instance, he manifested a bravado that could seem childish.

Says Lucy, in a comment very similar to one that Liz Rosenberg made about a trip she and John took to Europe a few years later, "He convinced himself everywhere that he could learn the language immediately. He'd always attempt to speak the language wherever we went." He had learned some Latin and Greek, and some of the Romance languages, but his knowledge was far from fluent. His enthusiasm however, overcame any obstacles lack of fluency presented. "We went everywhere with stacks of Berlitz books," Lucy says, "and everyone in the family got a lot of pleasure out of trying to speak the language."

In interviews and conversations with Japanese media, he sounded notes he had raised in numerous domestic interviews, explaining what good fiction should be and who the important writers were. Not much he said was new, but some questions led him to speak to the relationship between social and political circumstances and literature, a subject he hadn't addressed in other public statements. In one interview, he said that one effect of the Vietnam War had been that conventional realism had lost its meaning. Hence, he went on, in his own work he tried to "get rid of everyday reality and get to the heart of guilt, violation and anarchism immediately."

Whether or not readers would agree that his fiction accomplishes that, the connection between literary ideas and sociopolitical factors was not a notion he had ever expressed. But his ongoing desire to be understood and appreciated had always led him to seek common ground with his audience. Sometimes, as occurred more than once in conversations reported in the U.S. media in coming years, this resulted in inconsistencies, if not direct contradictions; he would praise a writer in one place, for example, whom he had criticized in another.

In a broadcast interview produced by the U.S. Information Agency (which sponsored the trip) before and during the visit, he praised Donald Barthelme, one of the most noted writers of playful, nonrealistic stories, whose method and writing are nothing like Gardner's idea of good fiction, and who had at other times been a target of his censure. In a 1972 essay for the *New York Times Book Review*, he had written that Barthelme's work "has less first-rate humor than his admirers claim," and that he "avoids style at any cost, and also avoids psychological or moral analysis, escaping despair by America's oldest, still commonest trick . . . childishness." It's hardly a description, one would think, of fiction deemed praiseworthy. Similarly, in an interview in the Japanese *Asahi Journal,* he named Saul Bellow and Eudora Welty as his favorite American writers, though in another journal, *Dimisura,* he criticizes Bellow's *Herzog* and *Humboldt's Gift* for self-indulgent sermonizing by their narrators. The inconsistency applies to statements about his own novels as well. For instance, he told one interviewer that he wrote *Grendel* in the early sixties, against the "mainstream of realism," though we know that it was in 1969, when antirealistic metafiction was at the peak of critical fashion that the first of *Grendel* was written.

These could be taken as pedantic quibbles, but critics did (and do) fault him for such inconsistencies as examples of unclear thinking. When challenged, he would say that he simply changed his mind sometimes, that he gave so many interviews he couldn't necessarily remember what he said in each. Occasionally, though, he admitted misjudgments. Of his criticism of Joseph Heller, for instance, in *On Moral Fiction* a year later, he said, "I think I underestimated *Something Happened*. . . . I think I was unfair."

There's no question that he gave many interviews. But the desire to be *liked,* to be sympathetically understood, seemed to figure in some of his responses. And by now, with a literary reputation escalated to star status, an ever wider audience attended his pronouncements.

In August, his *Construction of the Wakefield Cycle in Old English* had been brought out by Southern Illinois University Press with *The Construction of Christian Poetry in Old English* to be published the following spring. He had been working at these medieval criticism books over the year, and while he was finishing the novella that would highlight his latest collection he was also working hard on the Chaucer biography that he had been crafting for nearly a decade. The extensive manuscript was, however, more than Knopf wanted to publish, and at his editor's suggestion, John broke it into two books. One, which Knopf would publish, would be a biography aimed at a general audience; the other would be a critical appraisal for a more scholarly press.

Thus settled in Bennington at the end of October, John once again turned his attention to teaching and writing. In December, Knopf published *The King's Indian: Stories and Tales,* featuring the title novella and five other stories he had published in the last few years in leading magazines, both general and literary—the *Atlantic Monthly, Esquire, Tri-Quarterly*—as well as in the lesser-known *Audience* and *Fantastic Science Fiction and Fantasy.*

"The Ravages of Spring," published in the last, was a product of his interest in the unrealistic, exaggerated stories inspired by early Disney cartoons. Marked by the old, anachronistic voice of the narrator, like the book's title story, it was a tale, one of the forms he and Lennis Dunlap had discussed years before in *Forms of Fiction,* and not seen in literary fiction of the time. The center of the collection—three fairy tales—exhibited another version of the form.

More than three dozen reviews, in all the major venues, assessed Gardner's latest fiction, finding it worthy and most of them applauding the title novella especially. *Time* magazine had nothing but praise in its full-length review, and *Partisan Review* called it "the best thing Gardner has done so far." In the *New Republic,* novelist William Kennedy called Gardner "a writer of enormous range and inventiveness" and the novella "unforgettable." Reviewer Alan Friedman in the *New York Times Book Review* agreed: "The undeniable power of [Gardner's] imagination transcends the question of his method altogether."

Still, the praise wasn't entirely universal. In the *New York Review of Books,* Thomas Edwards praised Gardner's "great gifts for language and moral atmosphere" but found the novella "irksome in its reaching for the outrageous, the crazy, the (I'm afraid it must be said) cute." Nonetheless, the overall tenor of reviews confirmed Gardner's stature as one of the country's most important writers.

In late February, he and Joan bought a big house in Old Bennington, right in the center of town and catty-corner from the Congregational church, in front of the graveyard where Robert Frost was buried. As usual, the Gardner house became a center of social activity.

"We had party after party, and dinner after dinner there," Delbanco recalls. They were frequent guests, as the Gardners were at their house, and Joel and Lucy regularly baby-sat the Delbancos' two younger children. Charles Johnson and his wife came for a Thanksgiving visit; Lore Segal spent Christmas there with her children; and the list of visitors went on, as it had in Carbondale and before.

John went back to work on what he hoped would be a major novel that he had begun in Carbondale. It would embody the world that he had left there and, like his other fiction, would undertake fundamental questions of what is real and what is not, of who we are and what we know. The central character would be an alcoholic detective who is focused on an attractive young woman someone (the detective himself?) is pursuing or who is pursuing him. The confusions of identity and purpose at the novel's center would take many revisions to perfect. John would work on it intensely until he reached an impasse; then he'd set it aside and turn to other projects.

One of those side projects was a collection of the stories he had been writing every Christmas for his and friends' children. The centerpiece, "Dragon, Dragon," was informed by his engagement with medieval myth. Its common fairy-tale elements had the underdog—in this case the smallest and least powerful-seeming of three brothers—triumphing. It's an old idea, but the conversational style laced with contemporary asides creates incongruities that make the story truly funny for adults as well as children. When a poor cobbler approaches the dragon's lair, for instance, he is shaken by the monster's roar and says, "I merely thought you might be interested in looking at some of our brushes. Or if you'd prefer . . . I could leave our catalogue with you and I could drop by again, say, early next week."

The dry humor enlivening the stories delighted the Knopf editors who were pleased to bring it out in October. And that winter *Dragon, Dragon and Other Tales* was chosen in 1975 by the *New York Times* as Outstanding Book of the Year.

As the year progressed, Gardner involved himself in yet

another novel that he'd begun before leaving Carbondale. This was to be his "bicentennial novel," for publication in 1976. To help establish its historical context, he used quotations from Revolutionay War–era patriots to set off each chapter. Against the backdrop of the traditional conflict between conservative and liberal ideologies, it engaged political issues more specifically than any of his previous works.

Gardner dedicated the novel to his father. Its central character, James Page, an old Vermont farmer bitterly distrustful of the modern world and its technology, is a type his father— and Gardner himself—would be well familiar with. But James Page is not modeled after Gardner's father, and in a later interview Gardner pointed out that neither the landscape nor the people of Vermont is anything like western New York where he grew up.

October Light itself begins just after James has taken his shotgun and blown up the TV, which Sally Abbott, his elderly sister who lives with him, had been incessantly (in his view) watching. Then he locks his sister in her room. Sally reads a book she has found, *The Smugglers of Lost Souls' Rock,* and, adding to Gardner's cartoonish plot, this novel within a novel is a trashy pulp novel, with missing pages. It makes fun of the whole enterprise of tale telling, as well as suggesting the fragmentary nature of fiction and the consciousness that generates it.

Much of the pulp novel came from conversations with Joan, who contributed substantially to character and plot development. John, always quick to acknowledge her hand, specifically credited her on the novel's acknowledgments page.

In an interview the year after the book came out, he said of the pulp novel's origin, "Long before I had even contemplated what became the 'outside' novel, Joan teased me, saying: 'Why don't you write something popular, some kind of garbage-philosophy novel that will make a lot of money?' This took place at a party when I was pretty drunk, and so I left the room, went upstairs and hacked out the first chapter of something I called 'The Smugglers of Lost Souls Rock.'" He read it to others at the party and remembered Joan's "laughing and insisting it would sell."

Joan says that John's story of the pulp novel's beginning is pure invention but that they did talk about *Smugglers* regularly in the days to come. For his part, John Gardner said, "All the sentences of the final work are mine, but she would suggest ideas and plot developments and whatever."

Says John Howell of the original manuscript, "She used to write funny things in the margins . . . and . . . they may have collaborated on some wacky things." Specifically, he says, Mr. Nit, "who hooks up all the electric eels [is] based on a local psychologist who . . . was working at . . . a mental institution for this area. He was rewarding people for using the bathroom and so on by giving them tokens. He had written this stuff up nationally. He and John would sit, drink, and talk. John claimed to me that [the psychologist] had done such a thing [connecting electric eels to test their effect]. . . . When he told me this I could barely believe it, . . . [but] John loved the idea so he stuck it in the novel."

In both the novel and interviews Gardner acknowledges sources of other ideas, particularly Delbanco's new novel, *Possession,* which he read in manuscript. From it, he said later, some of the conflict between James Page and his sister, Sally Abbott, emerged. Most important, though, the sibling conflict is mirrored in crucial ways by the inner novel, which manifests issues that Gardner's fiction always addressed—the clash between order and anarchy and between tradition and the new world that threatens it.

Like *King's Indian, October Light* stands clearly as a metafiction, an invention that is neither an imitation nor a direct picture of the world we live in. Though he spoke often against fiction that undercuts the real world and so trivializes serious fiction that engages real issues, he would argue that his point was never the unreality of fiction. Though he was constructing a wildly nonrealistic world, its universe and characters behaved in ways completely consistent with the facts of the world he had established, and so illuminated human nature, extending our understanding of what it means to be human.

In mid-February of 1976, he finished the novel, and Knopf scheduled publication for December, just in time for it to be the "bicentennial novel" he envisioned. When it came out, it was hailed with as much, if not more, acclaim than anything he had written.

"Lavishly talented," the *Village Voice* review gushed, "clearly his best book since *Grendel.*" *Time* agreed, calling it "his best novel to date." And in the Midwest, the *Milwaukee Journal* reviewer called it "Brilliantly conceived. . . . Moving, comic, desperate and beautiful."

For ten weeks it was on the *New York Times* best-seller list and became a Book-of-the-Month Club selection. Then, in January 1977, it won the annual National Book Critic's Circle Award for Fiction. For any writer, that prize and the National Book Award, were the highest honors a book could receive. Knopf knew the prize meant a major boost for sales and a suite for the celebration was set aside for Gardner at the Algonquin Hotel, one of New York's most famous literary landmarks.

He was flown to New York for the ceremony and dinner, which was attended by a roomful of authors, publishers, and connected luminaries, and he invited Nick Delbanco and his wife, Elena, to meet him there. Everyone dressed in their best for the occasion, but Gardner wore the same jeans and ragged sweater that Delbanco remembers his having worn in Bennington for several days before. When he arrived at the hotel after the ceremony with no credit card or any cash, carrying only the typewriter and briefcase he had brought from Vermont ("reeling," Delbanco wrote), the clerk wouldn't admit him, not believing he could possibly be the famous writer Knopf was hosting.

When the clerk was finally persuaded, Gardner went up to the suite with the Delbancos, where they were greeted with flowers and fruit and champagne. They ordered brandy, and Gardner sat on the couch, which, Delbanco wrote, "was vast; [and he] sank in its plush lushness." Then something that could only be seen as almost supernatural occurred: "Mice scrambled from his feet [and] . . . in that quick first instant I thought they had emerged from his boots."

The contrast between Gardner's ragged dress against the Algonquin's plush surroundings and the ceremony and dinner that Knopf hosted, struck Delbanco memorably. "The image," he wrote, "remains and retains its power to shock." For in that moment, "I saw his power in the process of collapse."

When the phone in the hotel room rang, John answered,

"Hello, Gardner." At home he always answered, "Hello, Gardners'," the plural acknowledging the presence of other family members who were always around. In his brief introduction to Gardner's *Stillness; and Shadows,* Delbanco noted the difference: "He seemed forlorn; the brandy and Book Critics Circle had no power to invigorate. He was white and tired and, for all our efforts at support, alone."

The aloneness embodied by that image had reached a peak that fall, coinciding with the height of his literary reputation. Despite his success and the move to Bennington, which both he and Joan had found serendipitous in most ways, relations between them had only deteriorated, and the events that followed were dramatic.

None of the characters in *October Light* is a portrait of Joan any more than their marriage is a model for any relations in the novel. But Gardner had always used autobiographical detail in his fiction. Most of the characters in *The Sunlight Dialogues,* for instance, are portraits of people he knew in and around Batavia, rendered as accurately as he could. Sally Abbott in *October Light,* he said, was in part based on a woman he knew there. In one passage in the novel, he describes the failing of a relationship that seems to have been his own and whose autobiographical closeness friends confirm. The passage, in the inner novel, details a dream conversation with a dream woman to whom the male character is explaining the troubles between him and his wife in answer to the question "What happened?" The male responds:

> Long drunken talks late at night, each of us trying to explain to the other, both of us feeling imprisoned and be-

trayed. Arguments; fights . . . It was horrible; stupid. I never wanted to hurt her. I just wanted to live. . . .

Do you love me, she was always asking . . . sometimes angrily crying, and I honestly don't know. . . . I would storm off and leave her sometimes, late at night, when I'd drunk myself stupid and I knew there was bound to be a fight, or else we'd already have had the fight.

Since living in San Francisco, both John and Joan had seen various psychiatrists and counselors in trying to work out their differences. In Carbondale, at one point, they had taken regular time to talk specifically about issues between them as part of therapy. They would go to the porch with martinis, tell stories, and take turns typing them out. But the problems always resurfaced and only gathered force over the years. Now, after twenty-three years of living together, the conflicts seemed insoluble. And that fall they had come to a head.

For one thing, Gene Rudzewicz was living with them again in Bennington, back in his role as "a member of the family." He'd become closer and closer since John and Joan had met him in Detroit, and John had long encouraged him to give up the pedestrian life that he found so unsatisfying there and devote himself to writing in Carbondale, or somewhere. The first year the Gardners were in Bennington, Rudzewicz had been violently assaulted in Detroit. With the encouragement of both John and Joan, he had moved to Bennington to live with them.

At the same time, John had become involved with another lover. This was much more than a casual fling, even more serious than his involvement with Nancy Longwell.

He had first met Liz Rosenberg in the fall of 1975 in Nick

Delbanco's Shakespeare class. Delbanco had told him about his exceptional student, and he had also mentioned John to her. Still, of their introduction, Delbanco quickly says, "I certainly wasn't doing this in the spirit of 'Have I got a girl for you.' He came to my Shakespeare class and talked. She said something smart, and I brought her up afterwards. It was that sort of thing, not, 'Come out to dinner with the man you're about to run off with.'"

In fact, the enormous differences in their backgrounds would seem to have precluded any more than a brief fling at most. To begin with, Liz was twenty-two years younger. She had been born and raised in the Jewish culture of suburban Long Island, which was a far cry from John's rural, upstate Presbyterian farm world.

But both had parents with literary interests that they passed on to their children. Liz's parents were both enthusiastic readers, and in high school her father had won a prize in an essay contest. She also had an uncle, Anton Rosenberg, who counted Allen Ginsberg and some of the other Beat poets as friends. A Greenwich Village artist, Rosenberg had owned a gallery there and was one of the "angelheaded hipsters" Ginsberg mentions in "Howl." He was also a model for one of Jack Kerouac's characters in *The Dharma Bums*. Though Liz didn't see him more than a half-dozen times after childhood, she remembers him well as an eccentric whose talent she still respects.

More important, she was vibrant and energetic, and as Delbanco had said, very smart. She was working toward a degree specializing in fiction writing and certainly knew of Gardner's huge reputation. In the beginning, though, she was less than enthusiastic about meeting him.

"I first heard about him," she says, "when they wrote him up in the Bennington College paper. I remember he had on a long black robe with a big silver medallion and that Lord Fauntleroy page-boy haircut, and I thought, 'What a jerk, I'd better stay away from him.' So I did the first year. But all the students raved about him, especially my ex-boyfriend who loved his class on the epic."

She signed up for his class in Anglo-Saxon but dropped it. Then, while attending Delbanco's Shakespeare class her second year, he introduced her to Gardner, not once, but two or three different times, as she recalls, until it became a sort of joke between her and Gardner. At one of those meetings, she remembers, "John said, 'Why did you drop my class?' and I was surprised he'd even noticed."

That wasn't the only time she'd thought better of her first impression. "The first time I heard John singing in the halls, he sang 'Amazing Grace,' and his voice was so sweet and pure I really thought, 'I must be wrong, he can't be a jerk.' And when I met him in Nick Delbanco's office and heard him speak, he had that same sweet tenor; and I thought again, 'I must be wrong about him.'"

In the spring of 1976, she signed up for his fiction workshop, "but," she says, "after the first few classes, he said or did something that bothered me and I went to Nick and said I want to drop this class—maybe I can get an independent study or something. Nick was really vehement that I not drop the class. . . . Ben Bellit, my adviser, also told me not to drop the class, and even Alan Cheuse said, 'Stick it out, the man is brilliant.'"

Cheuse suggested she meet and talk with him, which she

agreed to do. In preparation, she says, "I read and reread" an essay he had written that he passed out for the class. It would be published in a critical journal the next year, part of the new book he was assembling, something he had been writing off and on for ten years. Spawned from frustration at rejections of his fiction and stored away, the new book took up his passion directly: what fiction should do and how it should be accomplished.

Like much of his writing, it aimed to reach beyond academic specialists. Now that he was beginning to attract the broader audience he had always wanted, he plunged into the idea the only way he knew—full speed ahead, with everything he could muster. And at this point, what he could muster, and the impact it made, was considerable.

11

Moral Fiction

As you know, the picture of my childhood that I've just
set down is a lie.

—*On Moral Fiction*

SOMETIME DURING the spring semester of 1976,
Gardner passed out to his class his essay "Death by
Art; or, 'Some Men Will Kill You with a Six-Gun,
Some Men with a Pen,'" which was due to be published that
summer. In one sense, it was an outgrowth of the same impulse
that he expressed in his old college journal entries praising and
condemning classic authors in typically reductive student terms.
Over the years, spurred by the frustrations authors have often
felt at what seems to them lesser writing that gets recognized and
celebrated, he'd written more extensively on the subject. In 1965,
he'd gone on to compose a full, book-length manuscript articu-
lating his ideas of what good fiction comprises.

Like much of his writing, it was stored in a box while he
tended to other projects. But now, as his ideas were attended in
national venues, he took up the manuscript again. The first of

several essays on the subject came out in the fall of 1976, with more following in the succeeding months.

Central to his ideas was Tolstoy's concept of the moral nature of good art. Gardner had been convinced of it since college when he first read Tolstoy's nineteenth-century classic *What Is Art?* Tolstoy had asserted that "ideas expressed in art can have an effect on behavior," that "art instructs" and that "nature follows craft." At the heart of Gardner's idea of moral, taken from Tolstoy, was the idea that good fiction "affirms life."

"Death by Art" contained these central ideas, as Gardner argued against what he saw as the pervasive pessimism that dominated contemporary fiction. Such pessimism, he argued, was in the end an incomplete gesture, an easy trope that was finally no more than simple escape from the real complications that serious fiction must engage if it is moral.

The essay also launched attacks on some of his most respected contemporaries, and by name—Donald Barthelme, John Barth, Saul Bellow—calling their fiction "second rate." As he went on to extend his thinking in further essays, the debate he stirred about the position and value of fiction grew in importance to dominate national discussion of the subject. On the one hand, such attention was just the thing he had always wanted. On the other, however, the response he inspired made him a target of critics and writers, occupying him, not necessarily happily, everywhere he went.

When she went to meet him, Liz argued against his criticism of pervasive negativity in contemporary fiction and "in favor of writing darkly if dark is what you feel." Mainly though, she was taken by the serious attention he gave to her own thinking. Their first long conversation led to another and turned into ongoing weekly discussions at Friday afternoon meetings that continued through the spring. After a while, he began showing her his own new fiction for comment, as their meetings became much more than teacher-student discussions, despite Gardner's far greater experience and achievements. "Always I felt honored that he would be interested in my opinions," she says.

Over the summer and early fall, their relationship grew closer, and as the situation wound tighter things between John and Joan became increasingly harsh and tangled. Their habituated conflicts had become even more consistently volatile well before Liz entered the picture, and as John got more deeply involved with her he began to to seek refuge at Delbanco's more often.

"It was pretty operatic stuff," says Delbanco. "John and Joan were neither secretive nor reticent people. There was lots of screaming and throwing of dishes and midnight visits to explain themselves. John would stay for a while, and Joan would come over and demand he come back. . . . It was the usual sturm und drang of marriage breaking up."

However "usual" time and distance may have made the dramatics seem, the circumstances were more painful for John than anything he'd confronted since Gilbert's death. He would stay at Delbanco's for three or four weeks at a time, then go home to Joan for a while, then return to Delbanco's at three or four in the morning. Ultimately, he decided he just couldn't live in the same town that Joan did. At the end of October, he determined, he would move out of Bennington and leave the college.

He had never before lived alone, nor even gone off by himself for any period. But living with Joan had become impossible.

Still, he felt lost without the support that the ongoing presence of other people—especially women—provided. Though Liz was only a student, and so much younger, she had a mind as quick as Joan's, with a powerful literary insight Joan didn't have. She had supported him completely in the last months, as they had fallen in love. He would leave with her.

Despite the ire between them, however, Joan had become pregnant in the spring and only John could have been the father. Over the years, she had had a number of miscarriages, and neither she nor John could countenance abortion. Now, the very day John had determined to leave while their friend Carl Dennis was visiting, she miscarried again. Even so, that October night, as he had planned, he called Liz and told her to pack her things and meet him at the back gate of the college.

With only some books, manuscripts he was working on, and a few clothes, he picked her up and they drove toward Williamstown, Massachusetts, where she was to take her qualifying exams for graduate school the very next morning. It was a short drive from Bennington, but they had left late, and when they got there, with no place to stay, they found a place to stop and slept in the car. Both wanted to be open about their relationship, and so, after she finished the exam, they drove first to Batavia to tell John's parents. After that, they planned to come back and visit Liz's family on Long Island, who they knew would be a much "tougher sell," as Liz termed it.

The visits were brief, and when they returned to Vermont, Liz moved back to her dorm while John went to the cabin he had found to rent close to the Delbancos, near Cambridge, New York, some twenty miles from the Vermont border. Liz planned to graduate in December and would join him at the Cambridge cabin as soon as she could. They did not want to raise eyebrows around Bennington, but in such a relatively small and close college community that would not be easy.

"The night I ran off," she says, "my best friend and exboyfriend noticed me not in my room and began a late night frantic campus search for me, combing the grass of the Commons and so on. I kept where I was a mystery and didn't discuss it with anyone. One young man I knew followed my car apparently, all the way to Cambridge, and in that way found out where I was living."

They settled together in the cabin, and Liz's companionship was undoubtedly a great comfort. But Gardner was bitterly unhappy. "He began suffering intense guilt pangs starting a little before Christmas," Liz says. "It must have been a shock to his system, after almost twenty-five years of marriage, not to be with Joan on the holidays—and not to be with his kids, even worse."

Besides being depressed about his broken family, serious trouble with Lucy's kidneys had also developed just after their return from Japan. In her seventh-grade gym class, Lucy had severely broken her ankle in an accident on the trampoline, and during surgery her blood pressure had dropped dramatically, leading to the discovery that her kidneys were failing. The trouble was still unresolved.

"It was a source of immense grief and rage," says Liz. "Lucy was really his darling in those last years he lived at home." By January she recalls, "Things . . . had gotten quite . . . dreary. He seemed depressed and uncertain and very guilty about what he'd done." They decided that their living together wasn't working for either. So, Liz says, "We both thought it best [that] he and I . . . have time alone to see if we really wanted to be together or not."

At the same time, she got a job offer from the *New Yorker* to work for writer Ved Mehta. It was the kind of opportunity an aspiring writer dreamed of, and so Liz moved to the city and took it up. She sublet an apartment in Greenwich Village, and as the winter wore on, she and John talked only occasionally. "I think at one point I asked him not to call for a while," she says. "It seemed to do more harm than good. And I thought he really needed time and space for clarity about his own life."

Seriously depressed, Gardner suddenly found he literally couldn't even raise his arms above the level of his elbows. He sought the help of a psychiatrist, and in the next two months he got his arms to function again. In May, he wrote Liz a long letter saying how much he wanted them to be together, and called her right afterward. After a long talk, she was convinced. She gave notice to Mehta, and went back to the cabin in Cambridge.

When Gardner left Bennington, he found two other one-semester teaching positions for the spring of 1977. One was at Williams College, in the northwest corner of Massachusetts; the other was at Skidmore, in New York, west of Bennington. The cabin in Cambridge was between them, and he drove some sixty miles to Williams on one day and the same distance in the other direction to Skidmore on alternate days. The commuting was surely a strain, but it didn't seem to cut into his teaching and writing in the least.

Fiction writer Anne Calcagno met him while she was a second-year student at Willams, and at a time when no other teacher had encouraged her she was positively inspired by the encouragement and attention a famous writer gave to her work. She remembers him vividly from the first class:

> Gardner appeared with his long white hair and set us to writing in-class exercises. . . . After we wrote these, he read them, called us into his office, and then asked three or four of us to read them out loud. Miraculously, I was one of the people chosen.
>
> [He] seemed to select students he favored quite quickly, and once he did, he treated each like gold. He tended to every single amateur piece of writing I wrote from then on with [unusual] concern. . . . When he gave, he gave 1 million percent. He sparked a flint in my chest, I tell you. . . . It was an amazing experience.

Not surprisingly, his growing stature in no way affected personal habits that had solidified over the years. He paid no more attention than he ever had to his grooming or to what and when he ate, and he continued to drink as much as always. Whatever disorderly tendencies he'd always had were made worse by the upheaval.

In June, he went to Austria with Liz for three weeks, to give three lectures on American literature at Salzburg. From the Albany airport, he made a desperate call to Alan Cheuse, asking Cheuse to race over to his house and bring some clean shirts to the airport. John had forgotten to take any. But when Cheuse dutifully hurried to his house, he found nothing but dirty shirts wherever he looked. John would have to manage with what he had. So the trip went on, and with the help of a laundry they found there, John managed to appear a respectable author.

In the fall, Liz began graduate school at Johns Hopkins University in Baltimore, working on an M.F.A. in fiction writing and John looked for a job nearby. He heard then from Susan Shreve, a professor at George Mason University in Washington, D.C., whom he'd met at Bread Loaf where she'd been a fellow. When an award that year relieved her from teaching, she was asked to find the highest-profile replacement she could. She hadn't worked with Gardner at Bread Loaf, but she had seen him read at Bennington, as well as at the Library of Congress in Washington, and so she called to see if there was any chance he might be available. When he jumped at the chance, she was delighted.

Michael Kelley, another professor at George Mason, had written a book about fifteenth-century English drama, which he'd hoped John might publish in the Medieval Criticism series of Southern Illinois University Press. John hadn't thought the manuscript was ready yet and had made various suggestions for revision, the two corresponding several times about Kelley's book. Thus, when Gardner came as Shreve's replacement, he went first to Kelley's house in nearby Fairfax, Virginia, where he would stay until he found an apartment.

John arrived to a party thrown in his honor, and afterward he went home with Kelley.

The Mercedes and other benefits John's literary success had brought were gone, the money largely having been spent. What little remained of it was left for the family in Bennington along with everything else, or tied up by lawyers, against expenses for Joan and the family. He had never been interested in material things anyway, but now he was considerably poorer than at any time he had lived with Joan. When he moved in with the Kelleys, all he had was his IBM Selectric typewriter, a few clothes, and an old two-door Plymouth Valiant he had bought with nine hundred dollars that Liz had given him when he first left Bennington.

When he'd gone with Liz to buy the car, the salesman recognized Gardner and was amazed to see him at a used-car lot. "Mr. Gardner," he said, "if you don't mind my asking—what is a man of your stature doing in a place like this?" The phrase "a man of your stature" thus became an ongoing joke between him and Liz as Gardner's tenuous financial circumstances continued.

"I also gave him one of my sweaters to wear," Liz says of that first winter. "I mean, the man had nothing. He felt he deserved nothing, I suspect. I think for a long time he felt he'd been robbed of all his worldly possessions. I think he half felt he deserved to lose them—or that they were never rightly his, that he was a poor farm kid who shouldn't have wanted them."

When he arrived at Kelley's that first night, he stayed on the couch on the main floor of the two-story house. Kelley himself had just been abandoned by his wife, who had left him and their three-year-old son, Owen. Owen had been born with epilepsy and other difficulties as a result of a birth accident, and Kelley's wife, saying she just couldn't imagine taking care of both him and Kelley, had left them and was on her way to England. Thus, he and John immediately discovered they had more than professional interests in common.

After the first night, Liz came over and went with John to look for places for him to live. After a day of looking, Kelley told him that he had an unused room in the basement that John could use. John had explained that most weekends he would be up in

Baltimore with Liz, anyway, and so the arrangement seemed a good idea to all.

"I set him up on a typing table down there, and an office chair, and he was in heaven," says Kelley. And from the beginning, he goes on, "We hit it off like brothers. . . . I was an only child and never got much support. . . . He was like an older brother I never had."

The next week, Kelley's wife stopped by with a cousin of hers, to pick up things her cousin might want. It came as a surprise to Kelley, and the painful incident cemented a friendship both John and Kelley badly needed.

"My wife . . . is going through the house," recalls Kelley, "picking up what she's going to give to the cousin . . . saying, 'You can have *this*,' and I'm saying, 'No way . . . I need that for Owen.' . . . John's downstairs without [their] knowing this, and when they left, I'm practically in tears. I get a beer and John comes upstairs and says, 'God, you handled that so well. I couldn't handle that, putting up with that shit they were giving you. You handled it so well. Well, let's have a drink. Don't worry about those fuckers. We're good people.' . . . He was just wonderful."

Though he himself had never been much at home management, during his stay that fall John taught Kelley to cook fried chicken, to make shirred eggs, and enough other things to keep up the household. Mainly, though, Kelley says, "He was a big fan of Doritos," and they often nourished themselves on chips and Molson beer. "I bought the food and he'd give me half the money, or one week he'd buy the beer and I didn't charge him for rent. But he paid for what he ate and drank and we had a real party. . . . We partied all through the semester."

Perhaps most important, he gave Kelley important help with Owen. Says Kelley, "This was the first time I was a bachelor. . . . I was walking through the house and I was still not used to Owen, and he was always in my way. John would say, 'He's just a kid.' . . . "He was enamored of my son . . . and Owen fell entirely in John's thrall. John would sit sometimes at the dinner table and Owen would be sitting in his lap the whole time. John would just bounce him on his knee. He was just a beautiful sight."

At one point, a TV crew came over to videotape John for a project about teaching that the National Endowment for the Arts had funded. Toward the end of the filming, Owen was brought back by a baby-sitter, "and he sees this place . . . with all these strangers all around. He spies this TV [monitor] on the floor with Gardner on it, and . . . goes right over to the screen and kisses it."

Kelley's mother also came over frequently on weekends to help with Owen, and on one occasion she was awakened by John and Liz making noise in the bathroom. She was outraged at the "immorality" and complained to Kelley. But he told his mother he wasn't going to tell John to leave; she would just have to get used to it.

John was often gone for lectures and readings, and Kelley helped him by proofreading pages of *On Moral Fiction*, which Basic Books was readying for spring release. John had hoped Knopf would publish it, along with his novels, but though his editor, Gottlieb, who also headed the company then, liked John's fiction and certainly valued the attention his books brought to the press, he foresaw trouble from this one.

"There were various people [Gardner criticized] in that book, whom we published," he says, "and I felt it was inappropriate for me to be giving editorial opinions about books which I was involved with. There was a real conflict of interest there."

Gardner told him that he had to be specific about the writing he thought failed, to name names, in order to make his points clear. But Gottlieb was well aware of the trouble that John's sallies could cause, and he turned it down for Knopf.

At this point, however, John had no trouble finding another publisher; and the arrangement with Kelley worked well for both too. As if in a preview of controversies the book would engender, talks with Kelley gave John an opportunity to further argue out its ideas.

"We didn't agree about a lot of things about literature," Kelley says. "He used to say, 'If you'd only read *this*,' and I'd say, 'Well, I never read anything you've written. I've tried but I've never gone through very far.'" Amazingly, Kelley's unfamiliarity with Gardner's work was never an obstacle between them. "You're the only person who ever liked me and never read my stuff," Kelley remembers Gardner saying. "Maybe that's why," Kelley answered. "We'd just be funny with each other," he says now.

As he was proofing, Kelley warned him as Gottlieb had, and as Liz would also, that accusing well-known writers, by name, of writing inferior fiction "is going to get you in trouble with these people." But Gardner was adamant that he wouldn't be able to make his point convincingly without specific examples.

"Then in the middle of this thing," Kelley says, "he said, 'I really got a fever . . . and chills, and I don't feel well. I think I've got the flu. I don't have any other symptoms, but I really don't want to make Owen sick.' Then he said, 'I think I'll go stay with Liz and see a doctor up there.'"

Wherever he went, John usually preferred to ride the motorcycle he'd bought soon after moving in with Kelley. After years of Joan's forceful objections to any idea of his having one, he'd bought the first when he moved to Cambridge. It may have been a kind of consolation in his new situation, as unhappy as it was in many ways. And, of course, his indifference to physical danger was a lifelong trademark.

Kelley remembers a morning when he and John were leaving for school at the same time. "It was raining and we weren't coming back at the same time, so . . . I said, 'Take the Valiant.' He said, 'Nah,' got on the motorcycle, and I followed him. We were on this wet street in the rain, and he was wearing his helmet and gear. Someone coming from the residential street swerved and ran John off, and he fell off his motorcycle. I slammed on my brakes right behind him, and he was kind of shaking and had this big cut on his leg. I said, 'You hit your head right on the car.' And he said, 'I'm okay. That's why you wear a helmet. I know how to fall.'"

It wasn't the first time he'd fallen; nor would it be the last.

But feeling sick now, he didn't want to drive the bike to Baltimore, and because the Valiant wasn't entirely reliable he decided to take the train. It was almost Thanksgiving, and he'd planned to go up to Baltimore for the holiday anyway. Liz's parents were coming down, and when he got settled in and the holiday came, they took Liz and John out to dinner. The next day, her father felt a bit sick, and John only got worse. Both had apparently contracted food poisoning at their dinner out. It turned out not to be too serious, and after a day or two Liz's father recovered. John, however, showed no signs of getting better. Though he refused to be concerned about his health, he was clearly sick—he hadn't had a bowel movement in a week—and Liz insisted he go to Johns Hopkins Hospital. As he didn't have an insurance card, he was admitted to one of the large public wards. A battery of tests was begun. Liz particularly remembers that though John never complained about physical discomfort, the colonoscopy that was administered "was very painful for him—it shocked him."

When the tests came back, their findings were clear: he had cancer of the colon.

Kelley called, and John told him he had cancer, and of his plight. "I'm on this terrible ward, it's like a charity ward," he said.

Kelley asked who his doctor was, and John said that it seemed to be some intern. Like Liz, who'd also insisted that John get a private doctor, Kelley was upset that no one knew the famous author and that he was shunted to the side with other anonymous patients. Kelley asked John for his insurance number, saying he would make some calls and get the attention of a good doctor. But John told Kelley that he didn't have an insurance card, that Joan had always handled such things. When Kelley called Joan and told her the story, he got no help and discovered that her rancor burned as hotly as ever.

Kelley was shocked but got in touch with his own doctor, who in turn contacted a colleague who specialized in John's disease. As a result, John got moved to a private room.

"This is really slick," John told Kelley. "I got this private room with this French painting, this Matisse. I got this fantastic surgeon who operated on President Eisenhower. How'd you do all that?"

Kelley just said, "John, I live in the real world."

Despite John's pleasure with his improved situation, his condition was grave. Liz remembers talking to him about the diagnosis and asking him what he'd heard of the prognosis. "He told me he looked at the prognosis written on his chart and it said something like 'probable death.'"

He and Liz met with the surgeon, who "was not very sanguine when he described the location of the tumor—very hard to reach and so on," she says. "I also remember [the doctor treating him] saying, 'This must be quite a shock.' He said, 'John, the tumor is . . .' and John said, 'Malignant.'"

His treatment would involve two operations—the first, in December, would remove the large tumor that had grown. The second would involve a resectioning, in which part of the colon would be cut out and the remaining reattached. It was a relatively new procedure that had been done just six times before. Only one of those patients survived.

Liz came every day that December of 1977 and stayed with him as much as she could, leaving only to go to her classes, or when she was otherwise forced to leave. The night nurses were almost always sympathetic, and when she could she slept in the hospital bed with him. "I basically never left his side," she says. "We would go into the bathroom sometimes to make love. I was there every night. . . . As long as I sat there with him, I somehow believed he could not die, that I could keep him from dying. . . . I was so afraid of his dying. He seemed like almost the whole world to me."

Despite the gravity, John was uncomplaining and carried on with a stoic forbearance. He often had nightmares, but Liz recalls that he was always calm during the day. He volunteered for any experimental protocol available, feeling, she says, that "since he was going to die anyway, he might as well be of use to someone." It was an attitude that endeared him to all the doctors and nurses who attended him.

In the meantime, as long as he could, he was determined to do what he knew. He took notes toward a novel about Rasputin he'd gotten the idea to write. He began typing up his extensive notes for the instruction of young writers. Then, when he took a break from writing, he decided to take up painting.

During that month, Joan came to see him, with Lucy and Joel, only once. Liz particularly remembers that Joan "made no bones about being glad he was sick." She remarked about what she said were "dead flowers" Liz had left in the room—though Liz says she made a point of keeping fresh flowers there. Then she told Liz that the doctor had said the cancer had metastasized to John's liver.

Liz was stricken.

Joan had told everyone there that she was "the wife"; thus, the surgeon was unwilling to share medical details with Liz. When John was able, he instructed the surgeon to talk to Liz. Liz learned then that Joan hadn't told the truth, the cancer hadn't metastasized, and there were no traces of it beyond the colon. But Joan's anger, directed at Liz as well as at John, still raged.

The morning of the operation to remove the tumor, Liz was with him as he was being readied. She remembers him sitting up in bed at the bedside tray table, hooked up to IVs and typing as he waited. He was working on the instruction book of exercises and advice for writing fiction that he called his "black book," as it was gathered in a black binder. He'd been accumulating materials for this project since the 1950s. He referred to it, Liz says, as "his version of Chopin's études—what he could leave behind of use to young writers."

The operation to remove the large tumor took most of the day. By the time it was finished, the only one left in the waiting room was a woman whose husband was having a heart-transplant operation. But the tumor was removed, and the operation was deemed a success, though John would remain attached to a colostomy bag while waiting for the second operation, which would resection his colon.

As a Christmas present, Liz's parents sent a small tree to the hospital. Unfortunately, the tree carried ants, and in a few days they had spread throughout the room. The tree of course was removed, and the room cleaned of the insects, but their encounter with the "great outdoors" was also welcome relief from hospital sterility and the source of a good laugh as well.

On Christmas Day, John was alone when Nick Delbanco showed up in his room unannounced. He remembers John was paler than usual, but the real oddity to Delbanco was finding Gardner watching TV, a pastime John usually decried. Delbanco remembers teasing him and Gardner blushing in response. But Delbanco laughed and assured him his "secret addiction was safe."

More typical was the rest of the setting: "The medicine tray held his IBM Selectric, and his window ledge was heaped with erasable bond"—both good signs. John's engagement with his writing extended as he began to feel better. "The next time I visited him at Hopkins," Delbanco says, "he was sitting up in bed and busily at work—irritable almost at the interruption."

Delbanco remembers him talking about his struggle with the "Carbondale" novel he had begun before leaving SIU. He'd been having trouble with a particular paragraph, he said. But his frustration with the paragraph was part of the larger dissatisfaction he felt with his protagonist, complaining that his detective's "work was boring, his colleagues were boring, his clients were boring."

"The third time, Elena came too," Delbanco says, "and we could not find him; he was in the reaches of the hospital basement, having commandeered a Xerox machine." But that first time, says Delbanco, when he saw Gardner "reaching for his pipe, turning even this cell into a work space, I knew he would survive."

John had to cancel his spring semester classes at George Mason. To take his place, he called on James Dickey, whom he'd met on a visit to Reed College in Oregon the year before. Though Dickey had made his reputation as a poet, winning a National Book Award for his work in 1966, his 1970 novel, *Deliverance,* had been a best-seller that spawned a hugely popular movie. John certainly admired his success, as well as his work, and he and Dickey had hit it off from the beginning.

Though Dickey was from the Deep South, both were powerfully influenced by the rural, physical worlds they had grown up in. Their common ground stretched to aspects of personality and temperament as well. "Both men liked to hold court, to tell stories, to be the center of attention, to make things up, to make grand gestures," says Liz. "Both were the real thing in terms of creative genius."

Dickey liked to tease Liz, and Deb, his wife, who was often critical of him. During his many visits, Liz remembers him once bringing a novelty buzzer to shake her hand with, and at other times "showing off like a ten-year-old boy." Though John and others enjoyed the brash playfulness, not everyone was so appreciative.

Kelley was one who wasn't charmed. Of his first meeting with Dickey, he recalls:

He comes to my house, because I'm the one who knows Gardner, so I'm now the caretaker of Jim Dickey. He arrives with a young wife and a big old Cadillac car and a cowboy hat and a huge twelve-string guitar in a big case. The people across the street had this wild ass Labrador retriever that I couldn't stand, barking all the time, and they never kept it locked up. So Dickey arrives all drunk, his wife driving the car, at eight thirty or nine on a Sunday night, to meet me and get a preview of George Mason before class begins. I go out to greet him. And the big dog, named Snow, comes bounding out to meet him, barking. Dickey steps out of his car with the guitar in this hand and hits that dog under the chin and he's outta there. And I thought, "Whoa! I've got an entirely different situation here." John would have put out his hand and said, "Come on, doggie."

Dickey was thinking about living here, but I said, "Jim you don't want to live here." He said, "Well, I understand

John stayed here." And I said, "No, that's all right, Jim, I'll show you a real nice apartment right down the street."

Thus, Dickey found another place. But he and John thoroughly enjoyed each other. "With John," Liz says, "he was much calmer [than with me], more serious, earnest. [Dickey] really *talked* to him."

Dickey visited John frequently in the hospital, often with his wife, usually in the morning when Liz was at her classes. Despite the teasing and childishness, Liz is quick to say, "Really, it was all very endearing. . . . He was enormously generous and good to John."

The second operation, to resection John's colon, was scheduled for early February. He told Liz it would be a "simple" procedure, not like the lengthy operation to remove the tumor, and it did last only about two hours. Nonetheless, Liz recalls being "terrified." The operation went smoothly, though, and a week after Valentine's Day, he was released from Johns Hopkins Hospital.

12

A New House

The rest of the time what he felt was not anger but a
great, sodden depression.

—*Mickelsson's Ghosts*

OR MOST OF HIS recuperation that spring, John
stayed with Liz in Baltimore. By March, he felt well
enough to visit the class at George Mason that
Dickey had taken over. The lively conversation between the two
of them about the nature of good writing made great copy for an
article in the university newspaper. And at the beginning of
April, he went up to SUNY Binghamton, where he read for the
first time from the new Carbondale novel, which he'd decided to
call *Shadows*.

Later that month, he was interviewed for the *Wall Street Journal*, and he traveled to the University of Indiana at Valparaiso,
Brown University in Rhode Island, and East Tennessee University where he met with students and read and discussed his fiction. In May, he was one of the featured guests on the nightly
Dick Cavett Show on public televison.

Like the interview in the *Wall Street Journal* and several others at the time, his television appearance was occasioned by the publication of *On Moral Fiction* that spring of 1978. Though PBS audiences were much smaller than those of commercial networks, the audience for Cavett's more intellectual late-night fare was still far larger than most any literary writer got, and Cavett himself also seemed to be more sympathetic and better informed than the usual TV interviewer.

Interested in attracting as large an audience as he could, Cavett focused on the controversy Gardner's book provoked and started off by talking about Norman Mailer's "Evaluations: Quick and Expensive Comments on Talent in the Room," a chapter in his autobiographical *Advertisements for Myself*. The title referred to the harsh feelings among writers that public criticism by peers can cause. Such criticism can be "expensive," Mailer had said, because its subjects often retaliate with bad reviews and a sort of professional "blacklisting" that can significantly cut into a writer's opportunities if not reputation. Yet Cavett agreed with Gardner that unless specific examples are pointed out the argument isn't convincing.

Cavett's questioning seemed almost scripted as he led Gardner to reiterate Tolstoy's idea that "fiction teaches people how to behave" and that "life follows art" and gives us models to emulate. What had gone "wrong" with contemporary fiction, Gardner said, was its resignation to despair, its failure to truly "explore the world" and "find out really true things." This, he went on, was symptomatic of the loss of faith by fiction writers that novels are important. As he had argued in other interviews, "What fiction does at its very best is test out values. . . . A good book leads to a great affirmation. . . . A really good book tests ideas."

As an example, he pointed to Dostoyevsky's *Crime and Punishment,* which "makes a perfect laboratory experiment. . . . He makes up a situation [with] an absolutely accurate boy . . . and puts him through an experiment. In that experiment he finds out what holds, what doesn't hold. . . . Among contemporary writers it seems to me that there are hardly any that do that."

Some of his most praised contemporaries were, thus, "minor" writers because their fiction either was trivial entertainment (Barthelme and Vonnegut) or it succumbed to philosophical argument (Bellow). Though such fiction might be very good at what it did, its failure to engage real issues with lifelike characters ignores what only good art can address. Charged Gardner: "Teaching people to look at themselves . . . reminding them what they believe, takes pictures, takes painting, and the most powerful implement in the world for that is art. . . . When art begins to be only entertaining, only cynical, only ironic [as it has] . . . you get in trouble . . . in civilization, right down to the roots."

The chance to appeal to a large national audience was not to be taken lightly and Gardner's characteristic verbal firestorm was at full strength that night. Cavett remarked at the end of the half-hour segment that Gardner must have set a record for "number of words per second" heard on the show.

Thus, the sparks Gardner fanned with his proclamations kept flaring. In 1977, the year *before* the book was published, no less than twenty-five interviews appeared in various newspapers and magazines, compared with just eight the year before. Now questions about his ideas and the meaning of "moral" pursued him at every turn.

In a spring 1978 interview for the *Paris Review,* he was once again at pains to distinguish between "moralistic" writing, which

he said didactically espouses traditionally conservative positions, and fiction that is "moral." "I'm talking mainly," he said,
". . . about works of fiction that are moral in their process. . . .
Good works of fiction study values by testing them in imagined /
real situations, testing them hard, being absolutely fair to both
sides. The real moral writer is the opposite of the minister. . . .
The writer's job is to be radically open to persuasion . . . not be
committed to one side more than to the other—which is to say
that he wants to affirm life, not sneer at it. But he has to be absolutely fair."

The loaded adjective of the book's title that inflamed many in
the literary world also rang political bells well beyond it. He received solicitations from the American Nazi Party and from
evangelist Jerry Falwell on behalf of his archconservative, right-
wing group. Gardner was infuriated at being associated with
such antipathetic politics. It was true that his rural, Republican
sympathies made him more conservative than many writers and
academics, and his novels did argue for order and traditional
values against what he saw as destructive threats of anarchy. But
this in no way precluded the empathy he had always felt for disenfranchised groups or individuals. He insisted that the "testing"
moral fiction does through character and circumstance results
in demonstrations of life-affirming values (as in *Crime and Punishment*), which such empathy with the less privileged necessarily informs.

When John Barth learned that Gardner was living in Baltimore, he brought him to his fiction class at Johns Hopkins. He
wanted his students to benefit from hearing and questioning
Gardner, though he knew his own work was one of John's targets

in *On Moral Fiction*. At the class meeting Barth was professional and diplomatic; he certainly wasn't looking for any aesthetic confrontation. But John explained his notion of important fiction by calling Barth's work "secondary," as opposed to "primary fiction." The latter, he said, was fiction that engaged fundamental human questions and so made it "moral." Secondary fiction —like Barth's—served mainly to comment on the other. Forced to enjoin the argument, Barth, in a later article, termed Gardner's book a "self-serving, finally demagogical attack on his contemporaries." And the argument continued.

In one sense, Barth seemed to feel that his home ground of Baltimore was being invaded. Liz had enrolled in his fiction class that spring, though she felt awkward there. Whether it was because Barth knew she and Gardner were living together and so associated her with John and the aesthetic differences between them or because he didn't like the "Jewish realism" (as she termed it) that she was writing or simply because of personality differences, she felt he definitely picked on her.

Soon after an interview with Gardner in the *Baltimore Sun* came out, she remembers seeing Barth during a break in class and his complaining to her. "The man is insulting me in my home-town paper," she remembers he said about Gardner, his face bright red. In a fit of "impotent rage," she says, he punched the soda-pop machine where they were standing and broke off the tab of the can of soda so that he couldn't open it. "But he was too nice a man," she goes on, to really damage the property, himself, or anyone.

For Gardner's part, though his strident assertions set many against him, he saw no reason that they should affect personal relations. He'd been raised on the rowdy dinner-table arguments of childhood that had always been part of family gatherings. For him, spirited debates simply enlivened the atmosphere.

William Gass was one contemporary who took Gardner's arguments in the same spirit, and though he wrote from a very different aesthetic grounding the two remained friends, and always maintained their professional respect for each other. Both were exacting in their choices of language, but for Gardner, the values his characters and stories affirmed were primary. For Gass, if the language and fictional devices evoked their worlds accurately and logically, whatever value judgments followed were secondary. Gass was primarily interested in creating "beauty," he said. His fictions were "objects," which at their best manifested such beauty, and such creation for him was "moral" in its nature.

Nonetheless, Gardner said in an interview just after *On Moral Fiction* came out, "[Gass] changed my writing style because of his emphasis on language, that is, his brilliant use of it in books. . . . I'm sure I owe more to him than to any living writer."

However, other writers whom John targeted, like Barth, were offended. Says Gass, "We [he and Gardner] weren't close friends —we lived too far apart—but we were very companionable. I liked John a lot. I loved debating with him. He was a man of enormous energy. It just astonished me. While we didn't agree about a lot of things, it was great sport."

On the other hand, he notes, "He antagonized his colleagues. . . . Jack Hawkes was mad because he wasn't in the book. John Barth was very mad because he was. . . . Stanley [Elkin] got angry. It was as though [Gardner] were a member of the group and then he turned on them."

John clearly achieved the literary notoriety he'd sought, but the pressures it brought were never easy to bear. To some degree, the pressure was relieved by the success that fed it, but only in part, as John's own intense nature tended to compound stress exponentially.

In the "black book" he had been typing up in the hospital, some of which grew to become *On Becoming a Novelist*, he wrote about intensity as the necessary fuel for the best "moral fiction," and he shed light on the likely source of his own:

> After verbal sensitivity, accuracy of eye, and a measure of the special intelligence of the storyteller, what the writer probably needs most is an almost daemonic compulsiveness.
>
> A psychological wound is helpful, if it can be kept in partial control, to keep the novelist driven. Some fatal childhood accident for which one feels responsible and can never fully forgive oneself . . . insofar as guilt or shame bend the soul inward they are likely, under the right conditions . . . to serve the writer's project.

Anyone who knew him understood immediately that he was talking about the impact of Gilbert's accident on his own writing. For years he had tried to write about it. For years he had had nightmares and been haunted by it.

"Always, regularly, every day I used to have four or five flashes of that accident," he said in a later interview. "I'd be driving down the highway and I couldn't see what was coming because I'd have a memory flash."

In 1976, however, just before he discovered his cancer, he finally succeeded in writing the story. In the same interview, he said, "I haven't had that [kind of memory flash] once since I wrote the story. You really do ground your nightmares, you *name* them."

Most of his fiction had been largely autobiographical, and using techniques he had learned in more than twenty years of work, he told the story he knew so well directly and forcefully from the first sentence: "One day in April—a clear, blue day when there were crocuses in bloom—Jack Hawthorne ran over and killed his brother, David."

The story is about how Jack's personal anguish that followed found resolution in music and the lessons his mother sent him to. That is, he found relief and the promise of a worthwhile future in art. The *Atlantic Monthly* published "Redemption" in its May 1977 issue, and it was reprinted a year later in the volume *The Best American Short Stories*. Clearly, writing the story was a way of finally coming to terms with the horrifying sense of responsibility he felt, which he believed was fueling his "daemonic" drive. Not that his success with the story did anything to reduce his drive, but the story was a significant step toward settling the turmoil he had always felt.

By the time *On Moral Fiction* was published, invitations to read and lecture were coming from all over. Offers to teach also came from many corners. The timing was fortunate as the money that had been so plentiful when his novels were bestsellers had quickly disappeared with his family's dissolution. He never cared much about the money or what it could buy, leaving such pedestrian concerns to Joan; when he left her, he'd only taken a few personal belongings. But with medical expenses and the family still depending on him financially, he needed to keep a teaching job.

With Liz's help, his personal life had steadied, even if he was poorer than he'd ever been. At this point, he wanted to return to

upstate New York; his parents were getting older and he had always felt most at home in that area. He heard of an opening to
teach fiction at SUNY Buffalo, where the poetry program was
headed by Robert Creeley, one of the country's most noted contemporary poets. Buffalo was less than fifty miles from Batavia.
It seemed a perfect opportunity.

In the spring of 1978, he talked to officials there and the possibility seemed promising. The attention he drew with his novels
and now *On Moral Fiction* heightened his visibility, which would
unquestionably attract students to any university. John interviewed and it seemed certain he would be tendered an offer.

But the offer didn't materialize. The previous fall, *Speculum*,
the leading scholarly journal of medieval literature, carried an
appraisal of his *Life and Times of Chaucer*, the biography Knopf
had brought out in April 1977. The author of the article, medieval professor Sumner Ferris, harshly disparaged Gardner's
book as a "disservice to its author, publisher, and readers." The
work was "inadequate and unscholarly," he said, noting that it
contained errors of fact, dates, and chronology.

It was hardly the first time scholars had criticized one of
Gardner's books, but this instance was more serious and pointed.
Ferris accused Gardner of committing the "most serious scholarly offense" of having "closely paraphrased" the work of other
critics, without appropriate footnotes acknowledging the sources.
He cited sixteen examples of such uncredited paraphrases, a list,
he said, that did not purport to be complete. He noted that
Gardner was obviously "not intent on deceiving his readers,"
speculating that he may simply have been in too great hurry to
get another book into print. But the result, he suggested, was

nonetheless inexcusable. Ferris was taking Gardner to task for the very qualities of integrity upon which serious scholarship is based.

The whole affair might have been nothing more than a proverbial teapot tempest, an academic quibble ignored by all but specialists. But Gardner was now a central figure in any national discussion of art and literature, and *On Moral Fiction* had highlighted his position even further.

Peter Prescott, who had been writing about Gardner's fiction for *Newsweek* since he had first praised *Grendel,* was alerted to Ferris's critique. In a *Newsweek* article that April, he suggested that though the paraphrasing of an earlier critic's work wasn't necessarily plagiarism, it did raise the question. And since *On Moral Fiction* was "an essay denouncing American novelists for their failure to make a moral commitment to truth-telling," Ferris's questions went to the heart of the intellectual honesty on which the book's arguments depended.

Prescott had called Gardner to ask about Ferris's charges before he wrote about the issue, but Gardner had been quick to dismiss them. He had only sought to be a popularizer, he explained, drawing from what was known, nowhere claiming to have done original research. He had written the book with several histories of Chaucer in front of him, simply trying to enliven dry history others had set down.

"It wasn't done by mistake," Gardner said. "Whenever I paraphrased a part where an author had made a discovery of his own, I acknowledged it. The rest of the time I did not acknowledge it."

Despite his explanations, however, his unattributed, nearly

word-for-word paraphrases seemed inappropriate to most scholars and serious readers, and the title and stridency of *On Moral
Fiction* brought down the kind of scrutiny Prescott evinced. Now,
questions of plagiarism and the ethical use of others' work followed Gardner everywhere he went.

As critic Gregory Morris later said of Gardner's borrowings,
"In the end, all arguments seem hinged on the distinction one
draws between plagiarism and paraphrase, between theft and
artistic technique. That Gardner borrowed is unarguable. That
he borrowed in order to feed a greater, more imaginative vision
can, I think, be contended. In a very limited sense, all Gardner
may be faulted for is insufficient acknowledgments."

In the face of such questions, SUNY Buffalo officials made no
job offer to Gardner. Still, his notoriety was such that he received
another almost immediately. Binghamton, about three hours
northeast of New York City in the southeastern part of the state,
wasn't quite the familiar country that Buffalo was; nor did it
have a prestigious university writing program. But it wasn't that
far away either, and the state university branch there was committed to expanding the M.F.A. program in fiction. Novelist Jack
Vernon was directing creative writing there and remembers
when Gardner came to interview for a position: "I first met John
Gardner when he came to 'interview' at Binghamton in 1978; interview is in quotes because there was no doubt about the out-
come. Indeed, it was clear that he was interviewing us. John was
ready to make a move closer to home."

After the "interview," Vernon encountered the Gardner who
was familiar to most who knew him: "When the postreading re-
ceptions and parties were over, John, my wife Ann, and I sat and

talked until two or three in the morning, in our kitchen in the country four miles from campus. . . . Only weeks after his cancer operation, John was drinking gin straight, smoking as though to vent a volcano, and talking about everything—about the Olympian opening to the Book of Job, about writing, about not being afraid of death. At last we showed him to his room, and Ann and I went to bed, but we still heard him prowling about the house."

The job offer that followed included an appointment for Liz as an assistant professor in the program, and that fall they began teaching in the M.F.A. program at SUNY Binghamton, with a mandate to expand the program's visibility and reputation. He and Liz found a house to rent and settled in. John set about attending to the myriad projects he had in various stages.

Besides the fiction he was working on, another project that had grown to consume his attention was his ongoing collaboration with Joe Baber. They had been working sporadically, composing operas since they began back in Carbondale, with John writing the librettos and Baber the music. The first one, *Rumpelstiltskin*, had been finished in 1975, and in spring of 1977 it had been premiered in Lexington, Kentucky, where Baber taught at the university. By the end of 1976, John had finished a libretto based on Poe's story, *William Wilson*, for which composer Lou Calabro wrote the music; another, *Ivan the Fool*, was adapted from Tolstoy's story of the same name. In 1977, John wrote a libretto for *The Pied Piper of Hamelin*, and he and Baber also completed *Frankenstein*, which was produced in Lexington. That same year, *Rumpelstiltskin* was broadcast on National Public Radio.

In December 1978, the Philadelphia Opera Company mounted a production of *Rumpelstiltskin,* which he and Liz attended. In an interview the next year, he said he thought the production "horrible." Still, the company was well established, and for it to have undertaken such an enterprise at all was proof of the seriousness with which Gardner and Baber's work was regarded. In an interview in 1979, in fact, Gardner had said that he most wanted to be remembered as "the greatest librettist of the twentieth century." Though the remark might have seemed tongue-in-cheek to many, when asked about it later he made clear that he was serious, as were his ideas about the possibilities for opera. Though he had dedicated his life to fiction and medieval literature, his engagement with opera was far from casual.

"The glory of an opera," he said in that 1979 interview, "is that a really fine drama, one that expresses character, can be matched by a perfectly accentuated score. In too many operas, they nail a character to one place on the stage, literally. They abandon the possibilities of language. And in many cases, the translations are just wrong-headed."

Though his ambition as a librettist was gathering momentum, it was his fiction and literary work that had made his reputation and opened the doors to those other possibilities. Even so, controversies generated by Prescott's article and *On Moral Fiction* accompanied him wherever he went, and his own fiction continued to be measured by the terms he had been so stridently insisting.

In October 1978 he went to Cincinnati, where he appeared at a fiction festival with Bill Gass. It was there, in explaining his idea of what makes important fiction, that he first used a phrase that became the signature identity: "The theory I'm proposing says . . . that you create in the reader's mind a vivid and continuous dream. The reader sits down with his book just after breakfast, and immediately someone says, 'Hermione, aren't you coming to lunch?' One instant has passed although 200 pages have passed because the reader has been in a vivid and continuous dream, living a virtual life, making moral judgments in a virtual state."

The idea of creating a "vivid and continuous dream" with fiction is a formulation that has been linked with Gardner ever since, even as it has persisted beyond him. Likewise, the polemics that gave rise to the expression kept him "in the conversation" about fiction on a national scale, as was his ambition, he declared in an interview the following year.

But his personal troubles continued to mount. First there was the impending divorce itself, which had left the whole family in a state of upset. Then there were the financial problems exacerbated by it. Both he and Joan opted out of managing finances, and when they left Carbondale they asked John Howell to sell Boskeydell for them, telling him that he could keep a portion of the proceeds. But this congenial arrangement was not without complications. First, the real-estate agent told Howell that the old barn was worth more than the house. Furthermore, the farm was being foreclosed on because John and Joan had simply stopped making payments on the mortgage.

Nonetheless, Howell managed to find someone interested in buying the property. But when Joan met the prospective buyer, she decided she didn't like him and refused to sell. Though her stance seemed absurd to both Gardner and Howell, she remained adamant, and Howell washed his hands of the whole affair.

In early 1979, John got a notice from the IRS. Joan had always taken care of their taxes, as she had handled all their financial matters since their first years together. As John's writing became successful, the money they earned became more than substantial, and the taxes they owed were substantial too. But as Joan had grown angrier and their relationship deteriorated, she had simply quit tending their finances. For the years 1973 to 1978, he was informed, he owed about four hundred thousand dollars in unpaid taxes.

Needless to say, John was shocked. After years of ignoring financial matters, he realized he could no longer afford to. He called his cousin Bill, who had a law office in Buffalo, and Bill agreed to take on the matter. But whatever records existed were with Joan in Bennington. In April 1979, after talking to Bill, John knew he would have to go back there. The prospect unnerved him completely.

"He was frightened to go alone," says Bill. " 'She'll kill me, she'll kill me,' " he said, "and he wasn't speaking hyperbolically." Bill knew they had a history of going at each other physically but tried to reassure him. "I was trying to tell him he was exaggerating. [However,] he was at the level of really heavy-duty anxiety, and I don't know to this day whether there was any real basis for it."

When they got to Bennington, Bill walked up to the door of the old house on Monument Street with John, "expecting World War IV." But the explosion didn't occur. Instead, says Bill, "within five minutes, everybody had calmed down and John told me to pick him up in an hour and a half."

Bill went to a local coffee shop and returned to find everyone getting along. Gene was there too, of course, but John and Joan had reconciled as sweetly as had been their wont after many past fights. John left then with Bill, and though no permanent reunion seemed to be in the offing, at least for the evening, a peace prevailed.

Still, the IRS trouble didn't disappear. Two weeks later, Bill and John spent a full day together, going over records. Bill went to court then and persuaded the judge that John was indeed not responsible in any criminal way for tax delinquency and managed to have the criminal charges that had been filed dropped. But John still owed the four hundred thousand dollars in taxes. And he would have to pay.

One thing he did was to call his editor. Robert Gottlieb lent his author some money and arranged a contract for books he would write that would pay enough to cover the debts both to Gottlieb and to the IRS. One book would be based on the "black book" he had occupied himself with in the hospital. A writing primer, *The Art of Fiction* would also contain specific exercises he had collected in his years of teaching. Drawn from the same material, but more general in scope and without accompanying exercises would be another, published as *On Becoming a Novelist*. And of course there would be the novels. Thus, with a contract and a payment plan in place, John was able to assuage the IRS. There was, of course, still the divorce and the money it would cost in the final settlement, but an agreement seemed to be on the way. And in July, Lucy helped talk her parents into working out an arrangement they could both accept.

By now, Gardner was about as famous as a novelist can be in America. But it was almost as if the notoriety had come in inverse proportion to the personal satisfaction so many hope such fame might bring. In spring, he had received a call from Stephen Singular, who was planning to write a feature article for the *New York Times Magazine* on him and the controversy brought on by *On Moral Fiction*. Liz still remembers that as John spoke on the phone with Singular, he looked suddenly disturbed. Such an article meant a burst of publicity that fiction rarely received. But it also seemed clear to Gardner that Singular wanted to highlight a fight in terms that would appeal to a popular audience. And that he wanted to take Gardner down with it.

When Singular came to do his interview for the article, John and Liz were living in Lanesboro, Pennsylvania, a tiny town about half an hour south of the Binghamton campus near the Pennsylvania–New York border. They had moved there in the fall of 1979, after spending the first year in a Binghamton neighborhood that had been "too much a faculty ghetto," as John describes the area in *Mickelsson's Ghosts*. They'd found this house, about an hour away, on a motorcycle ride that fall. Like the big houses John had always lived in with Joan, this was an old, rambling frame structure. Its two stories had fifteen rooms, black marble fireplaces, parquet oak floors, carved oak cornices over the door frames, and "a kitchen the size of Rhode Island," as Singular put it. Trouble was, it cost twice as much to heat as to rent (the heating bill for one month the first winter was two thousand dollars) and it was much larger than they'd ever need. But the style ("an American Gothic church," as Singular described it) perfectly suited Gardner's taste, as well as Liz's.

Though Gardner had always been surrounded with people, most of whom found him friendly and easy to approach, Singular seemed set on knocking down an icon. From the beginning,

John experienced him as "a very unpleasant, aggressive young man," Liz said, as she did also. He came with a photographer, who took typical shots of the author at his typewriter, but Singular's description of Gardner was distinctly unflattering: "He is a small, potbellied man and his white hair falls over his shoulders, so he looks something like a pregnant woman trying to pass for a Hell's Angel."

The description was matched with a list of some of Gardner's notable literary accomplishments, including Robert Towers's *New York Times Book Review* commentary that had called him a "dazzling virtuoso among recent novelists: a plausible impersonator, ventriloquist, puppet-master and one-man band." The contrast between physical description and intellectual accomplishment was striking, as Singular no doubt intended. But Gardner detected genuine hostility and was upset further by what he felt was Singular's failure in the article to seriously engage the significant issues. For maximum effect he had quoted some of Gardner's critics, and the result deepened the storm gathered over John's pronouncements.

From John Barth: "There's something very self-serving about [Gardner's] argument. He's making a shrill pitch to the literary right wing that wants to repudiate all of modernism and jump back into the arms of their 19th-century literary grandfathers. . . . He's banging his betters over the head with terminology and, when the smoke clears, nobody is left in the room but Mr. Gardner himself."

Bernard Malamud was even harsher: "I find Gardner lacking in generosity and, sometimes, judgment."

And so was Joseph Heller: "Gardner is a pretentious young

man, talks a lot and has little of intelligence to say. He writes dull novels and dull carping criticism."

Singular even managed to draw harsh words from William Gass: "His greatest weaknesses are his glibness and his preachiness."

None of this was new. But this article was cast to draw interest from a more general audience than literary fiction usually reached, and, indeed, it may have succeeded. Despite his love for argument and seemingly unlimited capacity to engage it, this time Gardner may have taken on more than he bargained for.

13

Killing the Dragon

> The knight, killing the dragon, showed no faintest trace
> of pleasure, much less pride—not even interest.
>
> —*Freddy's Book*

THOUGH HIS DIVORCE was not yet finalized and the IRS debt was still outstanding, for John the worst seemed to be over. Settled with Liz, there were no new interferences with his work. That work focused more and more on the theme of art's ability to transcend the ordinary. He had written another story that the *Atlantic Monthly* published in the fall of 1979 in which music performs this transcendence. In "Amarand" (published as "Nimram" in his 1981 collection), a dying teen meets a symphony conductor on a plane. When she comes to hear him in concert, the music transports her beyond her ordinary life.

By the time the story was published, however, John was on to another favorite subject. In May the year before, he had been invited to Stockholm for the PEN International Conference. On the way, he and Liz befriended the poet Richard Howard, who was also invited. But once in Stockholm, John connected most with Swedish writer Lars Goren Berquist. "Thin and vaguely handsome and desperate looking," is how Liz describes him. Berquist was a heavy smoker, "full of nervous energy and enthusiasm for John's work." The two men hit it off immediately, and John and Liz spent an evening in Stockholm with Berquist, his wife, and John's Swedish translator.

Most important, however, the trip opened a whole new venue for John. They visited the old city of Uppsala, on the Fyrisan River in eastern Sweden. Founded near the sixth-century pagan capital and a thirteenth-century Gothic cathedral said to be the finest in Sweden, it became the customary site of kings' coronations. It is also home to Uppsala University, the oldest university in northern Europe, still considered among the finest, with a library of over one million volumes and twenty thousand manuscripts. John and Liz also visited a site of ancient runes inscribed on stone and took a "gorgeous and golden" boat ride, as Liz describes it, on the river.

When they returned to Binghamton, John immediately put what he had seen to work. By December 1978, he had finished "King Gustav, Lars and the Devil," a tale of some two hundred pages that he would incorporate into a full-length novel. One of his main sources, the seventeenth-century *Religio Medici* by Sir Thomas Browne, informed some of its philosophical themes as well as the working title of the novel—*Rude Heads That Staresquint.* In one passage, Browne comments on "vulgar heads that looke asquinte on the face of truth," which in the novel Gardner revises to "rude heads that stare asquinte at the sun." The title works as a central metaphor, with the main characters trying to see and understand the true nature of things, which are obscured by the chaos of rising urban culture and the work of the Devil.

Despite his pronouncements about the importance of writing believable fiction, much of John's own fiction, from *Grendel* to *October Light* to *The King's Indian* and beyond seems more like the metafiction he so often disparaged. Inhabited by ghosts and grotesque caricatures in novels within novels, all of it underlines the invented nature of art. And this new one was no exception, though his point was entirely different.

As critic Robert Morace explains, "Gardner suggests the retreat into art and the emphasis on technique that is so prevalent among the new fictionists is actually their abdication of the writer's responsibility to society." But "Gardner and the realists [referring specifically here to William Dean Howells and Frank Norris, to whose nineteenth-century novels the term was first applied, but including as well modern novelists of similar persuasion] have the same goal—truth in fiction," though their methods aren't the same.

"The realists," Morace says, "reacted against sentimentalism and espoused 'real life.' Gardner has reacted against the very different kind of realism implicit in, for example, Sartre, and has espoused the philosophical idealism that began to go out of fashion in the nineteenth century."

Using one of his techniques as an example, Morace notes that unlike popular metafictionists of the time, "Gardner uses parody as a means rather than an end in itself. . . . Moreover, he does not use parody to 'combat the content of familiar mythic or historical forms' [in Robert Coover's words] but rather to test the con-

temporary validity of the moral values embedded in older literary works and genres, and in so doing, to establish a sense of
moral continuity otherwise very little in evidence in 'disruptive
fiction' of the past decade. . . . It is [the] search for values that
Gardner finds missing from so much of today's fiction."

So, in *Freddy's Book* (as "Rude Heads That Staresquint" came
to be retitled), the absurdly fat and reclusive Freddy, another of
Gardner's cartoonlike figures, sets the story in motion by giving
a novel he has written to Professor Jack Winesap, a friend and
colleague of Freddy's father, Sven Agaard. Freddy's novel is about
the heroic exploits of Lars-Goren Berquist, a name John took
directly from his friend, who in the novel is a cousin of King
Gustav, the sixteenth-century king considered the founder of
the modern state. Gustav has been helped to his kingship by the
Devil, but the alliance is provisional at best, and at the end,
Gustav sends Lars to get rid of the Devil. Lars is accompanied by
Bishop Brask, an intellectual and nihilist who has been attracted
to the Devil from the beginning. Eventually, Brask climbs the
physical landscape of mountains and rocks that the Devil has become and kills him, thus inaugurating a new era when it seems
humans are wholly responsible for human fate.

Gardner uses *Freddy's Book* to comment on "psychohistory"
as opposed to the more conventionally understood version (one
that doesn't speculate about motives), as the two professors in
the first part of the novel, which leads to the tale of King Gustav
in the second part, enact a traditional opposition. The older historian, Agaard, whose son Freddy has written the novel, cham-
pions conventional academic rigor while his colleague, Jack
Winesap, the "psychohistorian" to whom Freddy has handed the

manuscript, is more genial and informal—"a mere poet of a historian," as he calls himself at one point. Lars is devoted to traditional values of loyalty (not coincidentally, he is the only character with a family), while Brask's thinking has led him to sink into immoral dark. Thus, in one view, the story comprises an argument for tradition against the chaos spawned by novelty.

In one draft, Gardner had discarded Freddy's slipping Winesap his manuscript, but at Liz's suggestion he restored it. He never completed Freddy's adventures, however, and though ideas in the two tales that make the book can be seen to reflect on each other, the story of the professors is abandoned entirely after it introduces Freddy's novel. The disconnection results in a disunity criticized by many reviewers. Still, in a prepublication review, *Library Journal* called it "one of Gardner's most subtly moving and persuasive fictions." And Ursula Le Guin, in the *Washington Post Book World*, praised it as "a brilliant novel . . . [that] left me mystified and satisfied to the highest degree."

But in the *New York Times Book Review*, John Romano tellingly suggested that the book evidenced Gardner's two sides —the fabulist and the moralist—clashing with each other, and the problems that result. Other influential reviews were harsher. In the *Saturday Review*, Thomas LeClair said the novel was "another of Gardner's tedious arguments for moral fiction" while the review in *Time* asserted that it "emphasizes ideas over incidents . . . [and] tells too little while arguing too much."

The very terms Gardner had used in his aesthetic judgments in *On Moral Fiction* and other reviews and essays now marked critical assessments of his own fiction, as his provocations looked to be biting back. In part, he seemed a victim of one of the very points he had made in his work as far back as *The Resurrection,* about the impossibility of living according to theory, for none of his longer fiction, since at least *The King's Indian,* appeared to conform to the standards for realism necessary to create the "vivid and continuous dream" essential for good fiction. The inconsistency was a point LeClair made specifically in his review of *Freddy.* The reflection of the critical ideas Gardner was promoting in his own fiction seemed blurry at best.

When interviewers asked about that directly, Gardner admitted that *Freddy* did violate his own rules. He would not go so far to say that the novel was somehow second rate, but he did concede it was his most "immoral" novel: "I wrote [*Freddy*] after *On Moral Fiction,* and I guess in an unconscious way I was trying to say what my earlier argument necessarily left out. That is to say, after publishing *On Moral Fiction* and . . . having people clap and say 'Hooray that somebody's finally said that' and so on, I wrote this other book which pretty much violates everything argued in the earlier book. . . . I think that the only thing in the book that's really moral is that as you read it you have a good time. It keeps you off the streets."

This statement seemed enough, and he didn't try to argue that the novel somehow fit his theory. But that didn't mean he was abandoning his idea of what good fiction should be. He had spent far too much time elaborating the principles.

In another interview about *Freddy's Book,* he said, "I feel very strongly that fiction, at its best, should work the way *On Moral Fiction* says it should work. I'm not denying, of course, the legitimate existence of other kinds of fiction, fictions that violate the rules. I'd only say they shouldn't be mistaken for great fiction."

But he also began qualifying the criticism he had leveled at many of his contemporaries. In a 1981 interview that ranged over other novelists' responses to his polemics, he said, "I think probably [Joseph] Heller ought to be a little mad at me because I think I was wrong; I think I made mistakes in my criticism of him." Of Stanley Elkin, another target, Gardner says he "is a brilliant writer—he has I think the finest imagination since William Blake, an absolutely incredible imagination." And John goes on to mention Bellow, Barthelme, Vonnegut, and Updike as well, making clear his respect for their work.

But the controversy continued, even two years later, when Gardner admitted in another interview that he had gone too far in *On Moral Fiction*, driven to some extent by jealousy. "I wrote that book in 1964," he said. "I had not yet been published. I was furious—just enraged at those guys with big reputations." But, he goes on, "Most of it I got wrong. . . . I'm ashamed of my mistakes, and it's full of them."

If the storm of responses *On Moral Fiction* had unleashed led him to soften some statements, there still didn't seem any change in the certainty of his attitudes. And his energy continued unflagging, not only for his fiction but for his other projects too. In addition to his continuing, if irregular, work on opera librettos, his engagement with theater had blossomed again.

In the summer of 1979 he met Jan Quakenbush, a playwright who made his living writing for an insurance company in nearby Montrose. They met at a poetry reading by Galway Kinnell at SUNY Binghamton. During a break in the reading, Quakenbush, who had seen one of his own plays produced in New York City and also in Scotland, introduced himself to John and told him he was trying to write a play but was stuck. Gardner invited him to come to his office at Binghamton to talk, and learned that in addition to writing plays, like John, Quakenbush also rode a Harley and had grown up on a farm. The two shared ideas about theater as well, and began a real friendship. After a dinner at John and Liz's house a few weeks later, the two persuaded Quakenbush and his wife to come with them to the local theater.

"It was community theater home-grown style," Quakenbush wrote, "on-stage cues loudly whispered, unabashed mugging to front-row friends, misplaced props, mottled make-up."

There were no more than a handful in the audience, but he was struck by Gardner's enthusiasm, observing: "During the production he would one minute be sitting quietly, feet planted on the floor, and the next, laughing loud enough for the actors to have heard—a friendly sound in a cave. He applauded loudly at the end."

Afterward in the lobby, he told Quakenbush that they should each write a better play.

"Try to beat me," he said.

The evening continued at John and Liz's, and John talked about his ideas for just that theater. He would tell the committee that ran the theater that he and Quakenbush would produce original plays for it—"Not crappy stuff. Original work. We could fix the place up," he said. "We could pack it with people [and the local theater committee] could take the gate."

It was another night of talk lubricated by plenty of wine, but when it came to writing, Gardner was always serious. In a few days, Quakenbush and Gardner finished their one-act plays (each insisting the other's was better) and went to the next meeting of the Susquehanna Choral Society—the group that ran the Laurel Street Theater.

Says Quakenbush, "Riding up on his motorcycle with his long white hair dropping over his black leather jacket, his appearance and manner must have come as a surprise to the members. . . . But his incredible enthusiasm and exuberant nature carried the moment . . . and the society agreed to carry our one-acts as a double bill."

Gardner wrote *Days of Vengeance* with his mother in mind, and the weekend after Thanksgiving, it debuted with the one-act play Quakenbush had written, *Eden's Rock*. Gardner acted in Quakenbush's play, and Priscilla, by then seventy-seven years old, came to play the role her son had written for her. Word of the famous author's involvement had got out, and the auditorium was filled to its capacity of two hundred or so. The local Binghamton paper sent a reporter who wrote about it as "the highlight of the fall drama season" (not that there was a lot of competition), and the success opened the way to more.

Immediately after the first show, John challenged Quakenbush to another competition, to write a new Christmas play to meet a contest deadline for production in nearby Endicott. The play Gardner wrote with Liz wasn't accepted by the company there, but that hardly slowed him down. In the winter, a production of his *Rumpelstiltskin* was mounted again in Philadelphia, and the next April, another new play, *Helen at Home,* which imagines Helen of Troy as a bored housewife twenty years after the Trojan War, was performed at Colby College in Maine, as well as at Laurel Street.

As he did in Carbondale, where he led the formation of Boskeydell Artists as a corporation to support and encourage art in the whole community and provide a legal structure for his friends (an imprint under which he also published some of his work), he saw the theater in Susquehanna as a vehicle that could involve everyone in the area who was seriously interested. John himself took on many tasks. Besides working on costume and set design, he had the idea of displaying the work of local artists and helped hang it up around the theater. He played his French horn for other productions; he worked to repair the building itself and labored in the basement with the sump pump; he went to the roof to brush on tar for waterproofing; he designed a trap door for the stage. For a play that Quakenbush wrote in 1980, he constructed a large sign with letters he cut on his band saw, painted, and screwed on to pine backing, which he then helped hang on the front of the building.

The half dozen or so who made up the core of the theater group drew closer together as John spearheaded original productions, and the theater's reputation grew. Jeanette Robertson, originally from Philadelphia, had moved to Susquehanna with her two daughters and with them, had built a house by hand. She remembers meeting John in 1980 at a diner where he had come with a sheaf of papers, carrying his motorcycle helmet and wearing his leather jacket. "He clearly wasn't local," she recalls about that first meeting, but she was curious enough to strike up a conversation, which led to her involvement. "He was so kind and gentle," she says about his work with the others. "And he drew great performances from people who said they couldn't perform."

Jim Rose was another who became a close friend and central

member of the company. Rose was freelancing as an illustrator and graphic designer in Starrucca, another rural town nearby, when Gardner called him and said, "Hi, I'm John Gardner, the famous writer. Do you want to be in this play?"

They got along immediately, regularly visiting at each other's homes, as Gardner relaxed in the comfortable informality. Rose's lower-middle-class Philadelphia background and physical engagement in his country house were personality aspects with which Gardner had always felt an affinity. When they got together, Rose says, Gardner always brought a bottle of whiskey with him "and we'd stay up all night, talking and drinking."

John helped him install a woodstove and, with two or three others, chimney piping, using his chain saw to cut through the roof and floor. He inspired Rose, who'd never had much intellectual interest to become a reader.

As they grew closer, Gardner told him, "You're my best friend"; and when Rose, who was some fifteen years younger, protested, "John, we're friends, but we've only known each other a couple years," Gardner would insist. "I'd just say, okay, fine." Rose says. "He was always a vibrant, strong presence."

At the same time, however, Rose says, "I always got the impression that he was racing against death. . . . Once, in winter, we'd been drinking and were coming out of his house. He slipped and fell and sliced his forehead open and bled on the snow. I saw him a couple days later, he hadn't been to the hospital, there was this open gash, and I said, 'Why don't you go to the hospital and get that fixed.' He said, 'Well, you have to wear your history.'"

Despite the theater company's success, however, not everyone was happy with John's influence. The Susquehanna Choral Society, had, since its formation in 1967, always been a community outlet for traditional fare. It had presented *My Fair Lady, Oklahoma, Ahmal and the Night Visitors,* and the like; it sponsored dance recitals, painting and glassblowing classes, and a teen center. John's vision of the theater as a breeding dish for new art, and his energy to do whatever he could to enable it, pushed the organization beyond the realm of any usual community theater. His literary reputation did much to heighten the company's visibility, and more and more people attended from throughout the area. But he was notoriously disorganized. Details necessary for the smooth running of the project were left to others—usually Liz, who came to assume more and more of the day-to-day responsibilities for productions.

And despite the kindness and support many felt, John was definite and unwavering in his ideas. One board member who had been involved for several years before him, remembers that he misrepresented her stance to a local newspaper reporter, and when she challenged him his response was, in her words, downright "cruel." But for him the theater was a chance to develop and present new art—the most serious business there was—and for the most part, the energy and conviction he brought overcame all the reticence of others. It was the same drive that powered all his work, from his well-received fiction to the storm set off by *On Moral Fiction.* Though the controversy surrounding *On Moral Fiction* wasn't over, the noise had abated, at least for the time being, and John's life continued to stabilize.

The divorce from Joan was finalized the last week of January

1980, and three weeks later, on Valentine's Day, John and Liz were married in a tiny church in a valley outside Susquehanna by a minister they found who would conduct a ceremony that bridged their religion differences. She was liberal enough to officiate, and Liz remembers throwing her the bridal bouquet, even though she was already married, and pregnant. At least in retrospect, the events of the day seemed portentous (if not positively dramatic). Liz recalls the wedding day "was so cold that when we tried to wash the car, all the windows and doors froze shut. . . . as we descended into the valley, the sky suddenly turned very strange—very dark gray, stormy, gorgeous and end-of-the-worldish."

Not that their marriage was at all stormy—at least not in the way John and Joan's had been. But they were both energetic and inventive, and sensitive to "cosmic" notice suggesting the extraordinary in their combination. And all of it was fed as well by the "other world" texture that seemed to go with John.

Neither of their parents came to the small ceremony, and only a handful of friends from the area, most of them colleagues from Binghamton, attended. Poet Milton Kessler recited a poem he had written for the occasion; John himself wore a suit. Liz wore a dress that John had given her as a wedding gift, specially made by a woman he had met at a reading in Kansas City. Liz had sent her measurements with "a plea to make the dress as easy-fitting and fluid as possible, since, I explained, I am a fairly casual and clumsy person." But the woman had other ideas, apparently trying to design something that would be a unique and memorable piece of art. For Liz, however, the result was appalling. "I got Cleopatra's shroud," she says.

At the least, it was unusual, adding to the flavor of the whole event. The hand-woven, floor-length dress was cream colored, with some ocher, gray stripes, and "huge flaps hanging down to the floor from the sleeves." Instead of being tailored, "it had been cut and sewn in a boxy unsophisticated T shape." It was made from wool—to which Liz was allergic—and wearing it, she could only walk "in tiny mincing steps." Ultimately, she and John used it as a wall hanging, and for that, she says, "It was lovely. As a wedding dress it was a disaster."

Neither the dress, nor Liz's dismay at it, did anything to mar the event, however. During the weekend, she and John hosted a larger party at home, to which Priscilla and John Sr. came, along with other friends and family. John's younger brother Jimmy's wife, Wanda, made an elaborate layered wedding cake. Though Liz's parents didn't want to come back north from their winter home in Florida, they sent champagne, and one of her sisters, Ellen, came. Despite whatever ominous portents the cold winter day may have held, the marriage was happily launched. And for John, anyway, it was a seal on what amounted to a major step back into the world of respected, civilized practice from which he'd felt estranged since he'd left Bennington.

The wedding couple's party was at the new house they had bought that fall outside Susquehanna. It had become clear that the Lanesboro house cost way too much just to keep heated, so they had found a farmhouse with thirty acres (though Liz had liked the big Lanesboro house better), a stream running through it, an old rhubarb patch, a sour cherry tree, rosebushes, straw-berries, and a fenced garden that kept out the deer. Oddly enough, the two-story house also had LIZ inscribed on the doorstep, as if to confirm their move. No one knew where it came from, but it remained as almost mystical confirmation.

Liz installed a spinning wheel she planned to use in the large downstairs room, as she tried to fit in as a "country girl," and John set up his office in a smaller room upstairs. The downstairs also had a mudroom, which they turned into a dining room (unheated), and in winter they set up an old-fashioned suit of armor Charles Johnson had given them; it loomed over the dining room table.

Their honeymoon was a trip to Virginia, where John had been invited to read at the University of Richmond. They were met at the plane by poet Elizabeth Seydel Morgan with a bouquet of pink tulips, and at Liz's suggestion they went to the Jefferson Hotel to see its historical staircase. John Barth was there at the same time, and Seydel remembers being told to keep Gardner away from him, as their conflict had become known and officials at the university were anxious to avoid any scene. Barth, though, passed along a wish for a life without "mortal friction"—an obvious play on the title of John's book—and at least for the moment the differences between the novelists were set aside.

By the time *Freddy* came out in March 1980, John was hard at work on a new novel. Once again, he'd created characters patterned after himself and people he knew. In this case, a divorced professor involved with a younger woman lives by himself in a huge old house near Susquehanna. The house, which the professor is working on, turns out to be haunted.

John was also preoccupied with a story that spoke directly to ideas he'd been expounding about the source and meaning of art. Another sort of fairy tale, *Vlemk the Box-Painter* wouldn't be published until the next year, by which time it had grown to the length of *The King's Indian*. But in a later conversation, he said that despite its length he wrote the whole thing in two all-day, all-night sessions.

Its central character, Vlemk, is an artist who makes small boxes (one is reminded of Joseph Cornell's constructions). When the kingdom's princess comes by in her carriage, he boldly proposes marriage to her, and despite their seemingly insurmountable differences, he presses his case. Taken by his artistry, she finally, after much resistance, agrees to the marriage—but only if he can make one of his box paintings alive enough to speak, a condition that seems safely impossible. When he does craft such a box, however, she denies its identity at first, and much ensues before his creation is acknowledged. In the end, as with most fairy tales, all ends happily.

"I had seen a painting in a secondhand bookstore that gave me the idea for the story," Gardner said, and only noticed later that the painting was indeed by an artist named Vlemk.

When the tale was ready, John sent it to a specialty publisher he had come to know who agreed to give it the kind of attention no magazine or usual venue could manage. John had met Herb Yellin, who was a book collector, on a reading trip to southern California in 1978. Yellin had decided to publish limited edition, fine art books and had begun his press by listing authors he wanted to publish. He noticed that most of them were named John and so called his enterprise "Lord John Press." He'd published an edition of John Updike's *Hub Fans Bid Kid Adieu* in 1977. Then he approached Gardner.

After letters and conversations begun when Gardner had been sent west on reading trips, they came to like each other well. Yellin remembers that whenever they got together, the first night they'd always "get roaring drunk." "He didn't like authority," Yellin notes, as many had. He remembers John telling him that at Binghamton "he drove his motorcycle on campus . . . [and would] collect his traffic tickets, and dump [them] on the provost's desk."

Whenever John visited, Yellin recalls, he was always working. "And one of his favorite words [which Rose also recalled] was wonderful," which he'd use to describe students and work he liked. Yellin published a handmade broadside of John's memorial poem to Vergette in 1978 at the same time he published a collection of thirty-seven of John's poems in a limited edition of three hundred. Two years later, they agreed that *Vlemk* would also be a good project for the press. Yellin brought it out in 1981 in an edition of only one thousand, with three hundred numbered and signed, and one hundred leather-bound, with drawings by John.

He seemed to be settling into both personal and literary success. Liz charmed nearly everyone she met, her interest and intelligence making her a perfect companion, the twenty-two-year age difference notwithstanding. But John had been who he was for many years—he certainly wasn't going to change—and the cultural and personal differences were sharp. A popular figure nearly everywhere he went, his continual enthusiasm and energy drew people like a magnet. Though Liz was young and energetic, no one, it seemed, could keep up with him.

"John was driven like no one I have ever known," she wrote

later in a memoir. "I went to sleep to the sound of John's typing —like rain on a metal roof—and woke to the same sound, winter or summer, year in and year out, for most of seven years. He wrote six, eight, sometimes fourteen hours a day."

When he wasn't writing, he was bathed in the attention he attracted at readings and conferences, which by now took him to universities and arts centers around the country. Such attention is a powerful drug, of course, and the attention of young women, as always, was particularly attractive.

In the summer of 1980, he went to Bread Loaf again, holding court late into most nights, long after Liz had gone to bed. He arrived a week late to the two-week conference. "He's a good actor; he likes to make an entrance," Stanley Elkin said sardonically. And so he did.

Remembers Ambrose Clancy, whose first novel was due to come out that summer:

At the beginning of the second week, I was standing in the kitchen, mobbed with people with smiles on their faces shouting at each other. Suddenly the noise level went to a low buzz. Gardner was making his way slowly through the crowd, people stopping him on his procession for a hug, a quick word, a laugh. . . . I was struck by his appearance— the long, life-of-its-own hair, paper white. The eyes of an eager, brilliant, cocky boy that could at times change to a man watching demons at the bottom of a well. The paler-than-pale skin . . . He was dressed in blue jeans that looked as if he'd slept in them, a faded red shirt and shabby jacket. . . . as with everything about him, his work, his conversation, his musical and mischievous voice, every-thing in fact, that made up his presence had to do with a feeling of benign sorcery in the air. It's not too strong a word. To call him charming doesn't begin to describe him.

The social exuberance John brought fit perfectly with the charged atmosphere at the conference where he had become a fixture.

"To understand Bread Loaf in the early 1980s," wrote Susan Thornton, a student in those years, "imagine a remote summer camp of keyed-up adolescents with adult wants and add a patina of liquor. Breathe over it all the aphrodisiac of fame and the throat-closing desire for success, a dash or two of one-upmanship, the sense that 'this is the chance of a lifetime,' and you won't be far wrong."

It was an atmosphere John's presence each August helped in no small part to create. Many nights around eleven o'clock, he would come to Treman House, where faculty writers, fellows, and selected students gathered in the evenings, and stay talking and drinking until dawn. Novelist Ron Hansen was his staff as-sistant in 1980 and recalls waking him late many mornings, to re-mind him that he had to meet a class at one in the afternoon. Often enough John sent Hansen to begin the classes without him while he roused himself and got some coffee. Once he got to class, he'd direct comments toward Hansen, inviting his partic-ipation. John brought his IBM Selectric typewriter and worked when he could find time, which others rarely did. Though teach-ers were only expected to read fifty pages of whatever fiction stu-dents brought, Gardner often read a student's whole novel and

wrote detailed comments, which he went over during conferences. That first year Hansen was John's assistant, and in addition to reading students' fiction John also read four hundred
pages of Hansen's manuscript for the new novel on Jesse James
that Hansen was writing.

Thornton had first come in 1979 as a "contributor," the second
lowest level in the Bread Loaf hierarchy. Her former professor,
poet and conference director Robert Pack, had invited her to
Treman House. She was delighted to have gained admittance to
the august literary company, and she was entranced by her prox-
imity to Gardner, the charismatic star. In 1980, she came as a staff
worker, submitting her fiction manuscript for Gardner's review.
Though he was known for dispensing encouragement generously, he was particularly effusive toward her, and she was taken
by the famous writer's attentions.

"You're the most capable of real art of anyone I've seen here,"
he told her at their first conference. "Your imagination is wonderful. You're a natural."

Thornton may not have lost her balance on the spot, but such
praise was more than enough to turn any aspirant giddy. John
encouraged her to join the writing program at Binghamton, to
learn details of structure and composition he told her she needed
to bring her fiction up to the high standard that he knew she
could reach. Whether it was legitimate enthusiasm for her writing,
recruitment for the program at Binghamton, or just personal
attraction to her—or some combination of all of these—the invitation was persuasive, to say the least.

Thornton wasn't inclined to drop everything and follow his
call, however, despite its appeal. For one thing, she was involved

in a serious romance in Boston. And she had solid connections with people and professional journalism outlets there. As the two-week conference went on, though, the two spent more and more time together. He even met her parents when they stayed over for a brief visit. It was not simply a case of hero worship on her part; the growing flirtation was clearly reciprocal. Though he had been married to Liz for only six months, they had been together four years, long enough for the novelty to have worn off. And late one night, he made his interest in Susan clear. Thornton wrote, "We sat by the edge of the pond for quite a while. At last he importuned me to lie down. He asked if I would make love with him."

She declined, but at the end of the conference she agreed to keep in touch, taking advantage of his offer to critique her stories. And in early October, she made the nine-hour trip from Cambridge up to Binghamton to see him. She knew he was married to Liz; her idea was to take advantage of a private tutorial with a genuine star. But the electricity she had felt between them was unmistakable. Still, she didn't really think there would be any more to it.

The day she arrived, Liz cooked dinner at home for the three of them after John and Susan had conferred about her story in his office at school. Then his parents and aunt Lucy also arrived, as planned, to attend together the premier of a stage version of *The Sunlight Dialogues* to be presented at the university. Susan hadn't been told about this, and John enthusiastically invited her to come along. She declined to join the party, however, agreeing instead to return the following month with the story she was working on.

That visit turned out to be disappointing. John had forgotten the date, and he was embroiled in other plans. Thus, after the long trip and a quick visit, Susan wound up staying with a friend a little way from Susquehanna and driving back to Cambridge the next day. But it seemed clear to her that relations between John and Liz had cooled and that his attraction to her was still simmering.

That summer of 1980 John had read a story at Bread Loaf that he'd had brewing for a while and had finished that spring. "Come On Back" was a kind of tribute to his mother's family and the Welsh settlers who'd come to upstate New York, and his own heritage. Its title was the common good-bye that John remembered people of the area always calling to each other when they left the "songfests" at which they gathered regularly. Almost as if he were coming full circle himself, writing the story was a way of engaging his own beginnings and the elements from which he had come.

Says Clancy, who heard John's reading there, "Wales and the Welsh were important to him. Being around him for any period of time was to see the description of the Celt animated. John was musical, intuitive, impulsive, mystic, melancholy, and had the gifts of humor and, of course, language."

Bread Loaf, almost a second home for John, was a perfect place to present the story. "He was such a star at Bread Loaf," Hansen says, "that he just basked in the glow of people's praise."

But the very homeyness of the place also made it a target for the rancor Joan still felt nearly four years after they separated and seven months after the divorce was final. Though she was happy living with Gene, John's failure to send the alimony and

support money their settlement had called for more than rankled. Despite the success his novels had brought, none had
approached the popularity—and financial payoff—of *The Sunlight Dialogues*. John was driving a used Honda and living in a
modest house of which Liz was half owner. And now, the bank
was foreclosing on the house in Bennington because Joan couldn't
afford the mortgage and John refused to pay. Anxious and out of
patience, Joan schemed to embarrass him and pressure him into
complying with the agreement.

She had hundreds of leaflets printed and hired a private plane
whose pilot she instructed to drop the leaflets on the Bread Loaf
campus. "Wanted," they said, "for Fraud, Falsehood, Violation
of Court Orders, Passing Bad Checks, etc. etc. . . . John Gardner,
author of such frauds as *On Moral Fiction*." It went on to detail
his refusal to honor the terms of the divorce settlement, despite
his 1978 income of nearly ninety thousand dollars.

"Avoid the Subject at any Cost!" the leaflet concluded.

The pilot missed the Bread Loaf campus, however, and dropped
them instead on adjacent land. Nancy Willard's son, and Stanley
Elkin's son and daughter, were the ones who first spotted them,
and they immediately reported this to Robert Pack. He had the
children quickly collect the leaflets and give them to other staff
members to burn. Thus, neither John nor most others even
heard about the incident while at the conference, and so all were
spared embarrassment. Eventually, it leaked out, of course, after
the fact, and most everyone who did come to hear the story
found the whole thing terrifically funny.

It wasn't funny for Joan or John, whose divorce settlement
had come undone. Bill Gardner referred the case to another

attorney, and an appeal was filed to revise the settlement according to John's lesser income. In December John went up to Bennington to appear in court, and his monthly payments were cut by more than half, to just one thousand dollars, though he still owed nearly twenty thousand dollars in back alimony, child support, medical expenses, and attorneys' fees. The debts to the IRS hung over him as well, though he was busy doing the writing that he hoped would pay them off. As 1980 drew to a close, John was driven to complete a new novel.

He had sent a draft of *Mickelsson's Ghosts* to Robert Gottlieb in August. Gottlieb had written back wanting substantial cuts and revisions, and John had gone to work on it. When he had finished by the beginning of November, Gottlieb was pleased.

"I'm happier than I can tell you with the revision of *M's G*," he wrote. "I really like the book *tremendously* now."

Still, there were further revisions Gottlieb felt it needed. Mainly, they were modifications in what Gottlieb felt were unjustified extremes of some situations and characters' behavior.

"Isn't the wife's crazed, ruthless, unreasoning greed a little stretched?" Gottlieb asked about the hero's wife. And observing that the character has a good job and no apparent causes for dire financial circumstances, he further commented that "his situation with bills and money seems a little exaggerated. Over and over you talk about the mountain of bills . . . a useful device, but overdone because not believable."

The references clearly reflected John's extreme frustration with Joan and his own financial trouble, though in answer to questions after the book came out, he emphasized that Mickelsson was definitely not patterned after him. Instead, he said, the character was based on James Dickey. Still, the autobiographical similarities were unmistakable, and in a later interview, he did admit, "I am Mickelsson . . . although I don't think I'm that crazy."

John went back to work then, and another of his students at the time, Sheila Schwartz, who spent Christmas Eve with him and Liz at their house in Susquehanna, vividly remembers his dedication:

> We had a huge Christmas dinner, then sat around the living room washing down dinner with fruitcake and more talk. Around eleven or so, John slipped away to do some writing, a revision of part of *Mickelsson's Ghosts* that Liz had just read and made comments on. It was a terribly cold night, snow-encrusted, windy, and the thought of leaving the fire and our conversation for my frozen car and the long drive back to Binghamton, was not that enticing. Around 1 A.M. John suddenly popped back into the living room and exclaimed, "Look! You don't want to go out there — it's twenty-eight below and if anything happens to your car . . ."
>
> Then he went back to work. I stayed in their guest-room . . . [and] in the morning what woke me was the sound of John coming upstairs to bed, his work completed.

For that night.

14

The Oldest Story

> But the Akkadian artists are dead, praise God, and no
> grand vile hicks can poke their bellies with the pointed
> stick of brainless criticism!
>
> —*The Sunlight Dialogues*

O N A VISIT TO the Brockport Writers Forum near
Rochester in 1976, John had met another English
professor interested in ancient literature. John
Maier had begun looking at old Sumerian, Akkadian, and
Babylonian texts in 1972 and had spent eighteen months between 1974 and 1976 studying the *Gilgamesh* epic. The oldest ex-
tant literary text known in the West—its earliest part traced
back to 2600 B.C.—it comprises several stories, in Sumerian, As-
syrian, and Babylonian languages. No definitive text on which
scholars all agreed existed, however, and Maier and Gardner
thought to compose a version using the latest scholarship,
which, like John's translation of the *Gawain* poet and his biography of Chaucer, would make the work accessible for the non-
scholar. He'd used the epic story and its ideas in *The Sunlight*

Dialogues, and the idea of a complete version for a general audience was a logical extension. He teamed up with Maier, who enlisted the help of Richard Henshaw, an Assyriologist at Colgate, in upstate Hamilton, New York, and the three of them went to work on the project. Maier worked with Henshaw to derive a literal English translation from photos of the original cuneiform texts. John's task was to turn it into poetry.

In the story, Gilgamesh is a king who has constructed the great walls of the city. His subjects cry to the gods for relief from the oppressive rule he imposed for the sake of the construction, and hearing the cry, the gods create Enkidu, a double, or brother, who has been raised in the wild and so embodies the unrealized part of Gilgamesh. The two bond to defeat Humbaba, the monster of the cedar wood, after which the goddess Ishtar offers herself to Gilgamesh as a reward. But he spurns her, and the gods punish him by killing Enkidu. Bereft, Gilgamesh searches for the meaning of his brother's death, finally coming to the supreme deity, Utnapishtim, who tells him that there is no meaning. Death is inevitable; the only meaning of life is the living of it.

The story is not a parallel to John's life, or to anyone's he knew, but as the classic epics do, it creates characters and circumstances that touch powerful human experiences, calling up primary ideas and emotions. Here, Gilbert's accident and fundamental questions about the meaning of death were raised for John once again. And his commitment to rendering the ancient story for a larger audience seemed a logical extension of his early interest.

That spring of 1981, *The Art of Living* had come out, a collection of ten stories he had previously published, going back to

Carbondale, and including the lengthy *Vlemk the Box-Painter*. As one of the reviews noted, the collection "encompasses just about all of Gardner's themes: love and vengeance, fantasy, fear, madness, even occasional tenderness." In fact, the stories touch the central concerns that had fed his writing from the beginning and further coalesced in the last years—from his Welsh heritage, to his brother's death and the redemptive power of art, to the psychological complications of his relationship with Joan.

"These are miracles of stories," Anne Tyler wrote, "fully-realized, far-reaching, greater than the sum of their parts."

The praise was repeated in reviews from several major outlets, though some criticized what they saw as excessive verbal discussion and preachiness—criticisms that had been leveled at Gardner before. But as far as he was concerned, what reviewers wrote was already in the past, and he forged ahead with *Mickelsson's Ghosts*. For one thing, he really needed the money, and this new novel, he thought, could be as popular as *The Sunlight Dialogues*.

Meantime, there was Susan. He hadn't seen her, nor had they had any communication since the foreshortened trip she had made to Binghamton the previous November. But in August, they met again at Bread Loaf. Immediately, the sparks reignited.

Liz stayed in Susquehanna the first week to work on the Laurel Street production of *Meet Me in St. Louis,* which was opening the first weekend after the conference began. She hadn't planned to be left with all that, but this was one of those traditional community theater works John wasn't interested in, and he hadn't arranged for the music the play needed, as he'd said he would. This was, in fact, how she had assumed so much of the day-to-day responsibility of productions: John would agree to do things and then go off for readings and other engagements.

As Susan describes their reunion at Bread Loaf, he'd had his hair trimmed short for his role in the upcoming show and "lost weight and looked trim and attractive, wearing casual slacks, tassel loafers, and a corduroy sport coat in a kind of golden yellow color." He saw her at a party the first night, and she recounts, "[He] darted forward and kissed me on the throat. His mouth was hot and wet. There was a moment of shocked silence."

They became lovers, and by the end of the conference John was trying to convince Susan of his commitment to her. He never told her he would desert Liz but instead urged Susan to come to Binghamton for the graduate writing program where they could work together. In one of his letters to her soon after the conference, he wrote, "Why don't you and me—and Liz— have a really brilliant short life?"

The letters between them were constant and as heated as their affair. He convinced Susan that he loved her, but she had serious reservations. Regardless of his assertions about the incompatibilities and distance that had grown between him and Liz, Susan didn't want to be any kind of homewrecker. She knew well that the married man's girlfriend is invariably the one left alone with the damage.

But John's appeal was magnetic. Susan applied to the graduate writing program at Binghamton, and in October met him at Bread Loaf for a reunion weekend that the conference had organized. Their romance continued, and in November 1981 she drove up to Binghamton again. This time, he was waiting for her. He took her straight to the Holiday Inn where he'd made reservations for her, made love with her, and then took her back to his office at school and gave the story she was working on the attention she hoped for.

Afterward, they met Liz for dinner at a local restaurant and went to see a performance of *Damn Yankees* by a group at the university. Susan felt uncomfortable balancing the affair in Liz's presence and was glad to drive back to Cambridge the next day. But the romance continued in their letters. Though Liz didn't know John and Susan were more than friends, the problems in their marriage had grown, and she had spoken before of moving out of their house and into her own apartment in Binghamton.

Between Christmas and New Year's that year, John went to New York where the controversy raised by *On Moral Fiction* was the subject of a panel at the Modern Language Association's annual conference. To him, the issues were old news, which he would have preferred to avoid, but the panel also offered another chance to clarify his position before a serious audience of academics, whose respect was important to him. He showed up partway through the session and heard some of the papers that were presented, as well as a brief lecture from a minister who was an ex-president of the New York State branch of the Moral Majority, a conservative Christian political organization active at the time. John came dressed more conventionally than had been his wont, wearing a black wool overcoat, suit, tie, and dress shoes. And despite his combative reputation, says critic Leonard Butts, "He avoided a direct confrontation with the Moral Majority speaker by showing tolerance and pity for the rigidity of such thinking, without really condemning it. For his own part, he lamented that 'moral fiction' had become an 'albatross' around his neck that would color all of his work."

Not that he was ducking any challenges, but he seemed more interested in finding middle ground than in stirring up conflicts. Susan met him there along with Ed Epstein, Harold Brodkey and his wife, and his sister, Sandy, and all of them went to lunch together afterward. In January, Susan moved up to begin the program at Binghamton. The romance with John continued, and on Washington's Birthday, he finally told Liz that he and Susan had become lovers. Liz moved out immediately; the same day, Susan moved in.

The split with Liz did not induce any of the fireworks or animosity that his breakup with Joan had, but John's desire to be fully involved with both Liz and Susan, and have them be friends with each other, made things complicated to say the least. After six years, his and Liz's lives were closely intertwined professionally as well as personally. She was the first reader of everything he wrote, his coeditor at the revived *MSS*, which he'd started up again two years before, and he placed great store in her literary judgment. She had come to know many of his friends, who liked her and were comfortable with the arrangement. He didn't want to give up any of that and was determined to keep the triangle working.

Susan kept her apartment in Binghamton. Meantime, Liz moved in with David Bosnick, an old friend from Long Island who had long pursued her and had also moved up to Binghamton to study fiction in the graduate program. Liz kept many of her things at the farmhouse, and over the rest of the winter and spring, she moved back in briefly several times, and Susan returned to Binghamton, while Liz and John tried to work out their relationship.

In March, he had to choose twenty stories for the next year's edition of *The Best American Short Stories*, of which he had been selected guest editor. He had forgotten the deadline, and his selections and introduction were past due when editor Shannon Ravenel called to remind him. Since 1977, she had been the general editor of the series that had begun in 1915 and had worked easily with previous guest editors including Joyce Carol Oates and Stanley Elkin. John felt he certainly belonged in that pantheon, to be "part of the great conversation," as he'd said in Stephen Singular's article, and so he was pleased to be asked.

Ravenel assured him that the encroaching deadline wouldn't be a problem. As she did each year, she had cut the list of stories to 120 recommendations from the 250 magazine subscriptions she received, to send to the guest editor. The hundred he didn't choose would be listed as "Other Distinguished Short Stories."

But he insisted he didn't like any of her choices. He had always been a booster of the lesser-known, "little" literary magazines that published literature outside the mainstream. Though Ravenel had read hundreds of stories from just such literary magazines in the United States and Canada to make her list, John was determined to discover for himself the "best" selections for the volume with his name. He called Robie McCauley, the Houghton Mifflin editor who had chosen John as that year's guest editor, and told him that he didn't like anything Ravenel had sent.

"He hated them all," Ravenel says. "He said that there was not one of the 120 that he would even consider."

Ravenel was understandably miffed at such a blanket rejection, but ultimately, she says, "It made me respect him. . . . He really took it seriously."

Some two thousand stories were published in North American periodicals in 1981, and John wanted to read as many as he could. Ravenel packed up all the literary magazines she had and sent them. He also planned to scour the library and to write to friends and acquaintances to get any other stories he should read. He wanted to read and concentrate around the clock. And he wanted Liz to help.

Susan had always felt sensitive about her position as a "second," since the beginning of their affair. He made no bones about his regard for Liz intellectually, and even since Susan had moved in with him, he hadn't always readily introduced her as his primary partner. Though he always professed his love for her—to her at least—her secondary position in his professional life shaded the personal as well. She had never had any hesitation about deferring to whatever his work required, but she was pained again by his insistence on having Liz move back to work on the project.

In that month, he and Liz read hundreds of the short stories that had been published that year. And despite his protestations, the final selections they mailed back at the end of March included ten of Ravenel's. In his introduction, he carefully credits her taste, as well as Liz's, saying that as a result of their three-way collaboration, the volume "is fairer to elegant writing than it might otherwise have been," as "my highest admiration goes to ferociously and uncivilly powerful fiction." But in the end, he says, their joint effort "enabled me to see things I might otherwise have missed."

Some of the selections chosen were from writers he had long promoted and who had since built substantial reputations—Ray Carver and Joyce Carol Oates, for instance—though Charles Johnson (who was lesser known at the time) and some *MSS* authors were also included in the volume. But, ultimately, none of Gardner's choices strayed far from the usual taste in the literary fiction of the time; the stories were selected from well-established magazines that had existed for several years prior and continue to exist some twenty years later.

After he and Liz finished their selections, Susan moved back into the house, but her unhappiness with their living arrangement increased when John's old student and friend Ray Carver came to visit with his wife, Tess Gallagher, at the end of the month. "John announced that he wasn't ready to have these old friends know he and Liz had separated," Susan says, "so I was to go back to Binghamton and Liz would move out from David's and live in the farmhouse while Ray and Tess were visiting."

The idea was to "keep up appearances." But Susan was outraged. Still, she kept quiet about her hurt, until they went to John Maier's in Brockport the next week. There she confronted John with his treatment of her as adjunct and he apologized profusely. Just after they got back to Susquehanna, in front of Jan Quakenbush who was there after dinner, he asked her to marry him. She was thrilled, and although John and Liz were not yet divorced he and Susan set their own wedding date for that September.

But the complications John invited with his warmth and intensity continued to ferment, while the primal forces that fed them drew closer. As his work took even more the ancient, archetypal directions to which he had always been drawn, the life and death issues of all the classics were becoming more immediate. Besides the *Gilgamesh* translation, the previous fall he'd undertaken to teach *The Iliad,* which he had last done at Carbondale. And that fall, his father had suffered a stroke that left his right side completely paralyzed.

Unable to do the physical work of tending the farm, his father had to sell the cows. But perhaps even more troubling for him, he lost the ability to speak, which made his life suddenly much smaller and more difficult. John had made regular visits to Batavia most every year, but the next spring he and Susan began making the two-hundred-mile trip from Binghamton nearly every weekend to help out with his father's physical therapy and care, and with chores around the farm. John built a wheelchair ramp to the front door of the house for his father and planted a large garden. Often he read aloud to him, as he had to his grandmother when she had lived with them forty years before. An interviewer who came to meet him there on a misty June day in 1982 found him out in the fields in his tasseled loafers, planting potatoes and beans. He did it all without complaint, and his parents were happy to have him around more often. The strain of such a regimen must have exacted a toll, though none of it seemed to slow him.

In May 1982, John had gone to San Diego to deliver the commencement address at San Diego State University. He wasn't the usual sort of graduation speaker, and he made his uncommonness evident from the beginning. He was met at the airport by Leslie Reynolds, the university official who had invited him. After picking him up, she expected to drop him off at his hotel. But

John never liked being alone, even for a short time, and so he went with his hostess to her house where she invited some people for an impromptu dinner party. After a long day and a good deal to drink, he told a dinner guest he was talking with to "hold that thought," and he stepped to the edge of the outdoor deck on which they were sitting. In the middle of the urban neighborhood, surrounded by other houses and backyards, he urinated into the shrubbery.

Reynolds and her husband were amused, though they told him later that their other guests, the university vice president and his wife, "didn't like it so well."

Though it may have been within a range of behavior familiar to those who knew him, even for John, the act was more outrageous than usual. And, in some ways, it set the tone for his commencement speech, which was a chance for him to voice some long-held views to a broader audience than the usual literary-minded ones he'd addressed in the past.

Students were "drones," he said, taught to support the consumer culture, to conform and to please the established order. Graduation was certification of that position. But it was also a chance to begin to work against that, to "quit" and "make something of a nuisance of yourself"—which he advised them to do.

The sentiments weren't necessarily new for students to hear or unusual for John to express. But the message was not at all what a graduation speaker usually offers. And with his new novel due out the next month, the chance to be heard by a larger forum was something John relished. With the novel he hoped to recapture the notice attracted by *Sunlight* and to finally silence the critics that had targeted him in the last few years. The graduation speech was the sound of John Gardner, contrarian, revving his motor.

When *Mickelsson's Ghosts* came out in June and several boxes of it arrived at their house, the day "was like Christmas," Susan wrote. "There it was, a big thick book, the high-quality paper crammed with tiny print, and a photo of John, looking pleased, impish, in his hat and dark coat."

It was his biggest book since *The Sunlight Dialogues,* and reviewers took notice. Anatole Broyard of the *New York Times* said, "It seemed to be doing just about everything a novel can do . . . as if the world had suddenly become unbearably vivid again, after all our disillusionment and irony." *Wall Street Journal* reviewer Edmund Fuller credited John's "most ambitious work since *The Sunlight Dialogues,*" for a "bold attempt," though he didn't think it entirely successful, and in the *Chicago Tribune,* Larry Woiwode called it "the most substantial of Gardner's achievements."

Other reviews, however, were tepid, if not harsh. In the *Saturday Review,* Robert Harris said the novel was "dreadfully long and padded, and it often degenerates into drivel," concluding that "*Mickelsson's Ghosts* is a sham."

All his novels had drawn their share of negative reviews, and John certainly didn't hang his head. But he had had higher expectations for this one, and it would have been hard for anyone to shrug it off. Says Susan, "He kept his distress to himself and focused on the work he still had to do. But his disappointment ran deep and ate away at him."

Still, the difficulties of his personal life that had dogged him the last years seemed to have smoothed as he and Susan began planning their wedding. And now she was pregnant. Originally, she hadn't been at all enthusiastic about being a mother. An active, physical woman, she wasn't interested in the long, consuming commitment a baby required. At thirty-two, however, it certainly seemed time if she were ever to have a child, and she certainly loved him. Early on, she had serious misgivings about John as a husband and father, but by March he had allayed her discomfort about the secondary role he had originally made her play. So there was a baby due in the fall, not long after the wedding.

Whether it was disappointment over the novel's reception or some other gathering cloud, by summer John seemed to be drinking noticeably more than ever. It was beginning to bother Susan. She also liked to drink; it was a pleasant vice they shared. For the sake of her pregnancy, however, she had given it up, and his excesses were becoming a real problem for her.

In late June, when two friends involved with Laurel Street were over for dinner, John had seemed to go truly overboard. That night Laurel Street had done a performance of *Lizzie Borden at Fall River*, another of the typical community theater productions John wanted to replace with original scripts. There had always been a faction of the theater board that favored such traditional work, which consistently brought in larger audiences and the money they needed, and so they managed to persuade the group over John's objections. This time he had come to the performance but sat in the back by himself; then he went outside to ignore the rest of it. When it was over, instead of talking to the cast and others afterward, he hurriedly left with Susan. At home, with their guests Joanna Higgins and Jeff Ford, he headed straight for the liquor cabinet and began what Higgins later described as "fierce, awesome drinking."

Remembers Susan, "John sat in his odd, almost medieval chair with its unnaturally high arms and nodded forward over his pipe. When he got up to go to the kitchen for more ice, he stumbled and nearly fell. He brought out the gin bottle, now almost empty, and left it by his chair. . . . At one point John went upstairs; we heard him fall down in the bedroom."

He came back and Susan went to bed soon after, whereupon John retired to the study with Jeff and a bottle of Jameson. When Jeff finally got in his car to go, he backed it into a ditch along the drive. John went to the garage for a chain to wrap around Ford's car and his own to pull it out, but he slipped on the snow and fell on an iron pipe jutting from the floor. He cut the side of his nose. "He was standing [with] blood smeared over his forehead and across his hair," Susan recalls. He swayed back and forth with the chain in his hand. . . . He headed toward our car, leaning forward as if walking in a heavy wind, now and then stumbling to the side but catching himself. He was determined to attach the chain to the rear axle and . . . [tow] Jeff's car."

When Susan tried to stop him, he punched her in the arm. She took Jeff home, leaving him to get his car another day. When she returned the next day, she heard from their neighbors, who had been out trying to help them, that John had continued his drunken ranting before finally stumbling home to sleep.

A few days later they went to New York for publicity appearances for *Mickelsson's Ghosts* that Knopf had arranged. One was an interview with writer Curt Suplee of the *Washington Post*, whom they met in the lobby of the Plaza Hotel where they were staying. They went to a bar nearby, and by now Susan was truly worried about the drinking, which like so many aspects of his life seemed excessive if not out of control. In his profile, Suplee wrote, "The martini count approaches double-digits, the pronunciation turns muddy, and the pipe drops occasionally from his mouth."

"John talked, smoked, ordered so many martinis," Susan wrote, "that at last the worried-looking waiter chose not to listen, pretending he didn't hear the order."

During the New York trip, they also had lunch at a Chinese restaurant with composer Robert Blue, with whom John was working on an opera of *Grendel.* As in his collaborations with Joe Baber, Blue was composing the music and John was writing the libretto. After many drinks at lunchtime, Blue said to Susan at the cashier's, "You've got to do something about John. Does he always drink like this?"

The answer had for many years been yes, though it seemed to have become more extreme. And the anxieties that fed John's troubles were exacerbated when Susan went to the hospital a week later for a routine examination. She went by herself, and as she lay on the examining table the doctor slowly went over her abdomen with the ultrasound sensor. She watched, not understanding what he was looking for, then got dressed and waited.

He came back quickly and said, "You've got nothing alive in there."

The fetus was dead. She could only go home and wait until she felt cramps and then go to the hospital while her body expelled it.

Having gone through several miscarriages with Joan, the sad

news wasn't an unprecedented shock for John. It was one more thing to get through, though. A few days later they went to the Laurel Street Theater's rehearsal of *You're a Good Man, Charlie Brown*, which was to open in two weeks, and the cramping began. He took her to the hospital, and when she was admitted and as comfortable as she could be he went over to Liz's. Afterward, Liz came to the hospital to see Susan and told her that when John had come over, he told her how Susan had carefully sewn an emblem she bought on his motorcycle jacket and how he had cried as he told this story of her devotion.

When he called Susan's parents with the news, her mother said later, "He was crying so hard I couldn't understand him at first. He kept saying, *She was so brave, she was so brave.*"

Though he had gone through miscarriages before, the disappointment for him was profound. In a letter Susan came across later to old friends, he had written twice, "Why couldn't this little one have survived?"

"That we lost the baby seemed to plunge John into an abyss of gloom," Susan wrote.

He went back to work, shadowed by another tragedy, and poured himself into it. He was working hardest now on translation of the *Gilgamesh* epic, which he planned to teach in the fall. In between work sessions, he and Susan made the four-hour drive to Rochester to work with Maier and Henshaw. At the same time, pressure from members of the theater board to further accommodate popular taste and make needed money irritated John more. They did finally agree on a compromise, though from John's point of view it was entirely the wrong thing to do. Still, on another side, he found some relief in his personal affairs as he made final arrangements with the IRS to settle those obligations. Though financial concerns had always been at the bottom of the pile of things he attended to, the relief was welcome.

It was clear at this point that *Mickelsson's Ghosts* would not earn the money he had hoped for, and he would have to make it up somehow. Part would come from the contract he signed with Knopf for the instruction books, on which he was finishing the final revisions, and for *Shadows*, the detective novel he had been working on. To cover the rest, he arranged to sell his papers to the Rush Rhees Library at the University of Rochester. Peter Dzwonkoski of the library came to Susquehanna in late July to inventory the materials, and the final arrangements were a relief to both John and Susan, as the financial weight finally felt lifted. Thus, with the wedding plans set, they left for a weeklong trip to California, where John was scheduled to read.

In San Diego they stayed with Kapiloffs, with whom John had formed a friendship during his trip the year before. There to give a speech before the San Diego City Club, he also met Los Angeles mayor Tom Bradley, whom he liked immediately. They talked about Susan and his moving to San Diego and his writing speeches for Bradley. Before, he'd never much liked what he knew of California, but clearly he wanted a new start. He had turned forty-nine July 21, and in September he would be part of a new family. He was serious about turning a page.

Back home in Binghamton, that sense of a new start continued. When he and Susan were packing to leave for Bread Loaf in the middle of August, he said, "Maybe this will be my last Bread Loaf conference." It seemed the sort of idle musing many might voice. But once he was there, it seemed to many who knew him that John was indeed at some sort of turning point.

He spent as much time at Treman as ever, talking and drinking. Susan, however, found herself in something akin to what Liz's position had been, and it wasn't comfortable. One night, John's flirtation with a young woman led to his falling asleep on the Treman floor with his arm around her. Susan had left to go to bed earlier, and when she woke alone later she went looking for him. When she saw him on the floor with the other woman, the sight was wrenching. In the end, she suspected that John may well have succumbed to an affair.

That summer, the powerful presences of poet Carolyn Forche and essayist Terrence Des Pres strongly influenced the gathering. Both of them addressed their work to the political issues seething in Latin America, and their ideas about the unacknowledged political dimensions of all writing came to the fore. John, looking for a new direction, was listening. At the same time, however, his resolve seemed to lead to a disconnection that concerned several there who knew him well. Says Robert Pack:

> The last summer he set out to do what he'd done many times in the past, which was to get to the podium and improvise a lecture. And he had always been able to bring that off and do it brilliantly. But this particular summer, I think it was early in the morning, he went to give his lecture, and he just couldn't bring it off. He couldn't develop an argument, organize his materials there on the spot. I remember it was a very distressing performance, and many of us were aware that there was something wrong, that we had seen a

kind of breakdown there. There was a kind of feeling of shock in the community, that something had short circuited in John.

Word had circulated that he would say something very different in his lecture, and when he got to the podium that morning the little theater was full.

"I'm not going to do a lecture about literature," he began, "because I'm not that interested in literature anymore. I'm not really interested in writing anymore. I'm sort of interested in politics now. I think that's what all of us writers should be interested in now." He went on to give a few examples of social injustices, concluding, "If you're not writing politically, you're not writing."

After little more than fifteen minutes—of what was usually an hour lecture—he was done. He went on during the rest of the conference to talk when he could about the government's role in world hunger and political circumstances generally. It was a subject he'd never much engaged, but his charismatic style always drew adherents, and listeners surrounded him. That he was looking for a new direction was clear.

Like some others, writer David Bain thought his glumness had a lot to do with the mixed reception of his novel. Says Bain, "For some reason when *Mickelsson's Ghosts* came out he thought it would be his breakthrough commercial book. Which it wasn't. And he was very disappointed."

Not that he had turned entirely dark and pessimistic. Ron Hansen, who worked as his assistant again that summer, went to dinner with him, and Hansen remembers his being as cheerful and energetic as ever. Hansen knew that others saw a darker side, but when he and his wife went out with John, "He kept emphasizing how much he was in love with Susan. He was ebullient, and we promised we would come to the wedding. So everything seemed jim-dandy as far as we could see."

Hansen explained the darker mood that others noted. "People must have thought he was depressed, because he was kind of tired of teaching fiction writing and didn't want to do the same kind of workshops he'd done before which people were demanding of him because he was so good at it." But to Hansen, it only seemed that "he was kind of passing the baton to others to do that sort of thing."

When he and Susan got back to Susquehanna, they finished setting the plans for their marriage. Susan had left most of the details to her mother in Rochester, where the wedding would be, at an Episcopal church. They invited some 150 friends and relatives, and though they hadn't planned a real honeymoon they would make a four-day visit to Carbondale where John had agreed to read and talk to students and visit old friends.

He had to finish the *Gilgamesh* translation in time to use it in the class on epics he was scheduled to teach with a colleague in the fall semester. With time running out, he set to work with his usual single-minded focus. Susan remembers that he worked for six straight nights, from somewhere around eleven till seven or eight in the morning. She remembers distinctly one night, however, he did come to sleep just after midnight, early for him, then woke up around three and got dressed.

"Time to do God's work," he said, and headed back downstairs to his study.

Another warm night that week when he was taking a break from the translation, he was outside with Susan, and she remembers his standing with his pipe and gazing off into the darkness.

"I've got it," he said. "I've figured it out."

This time he was talking about *Shadows*. More than seven years since he'd first begun it, he'd been at it almost as long as he'd worked on *The Sunlight Dialogues*. Now, he was convinced he finally knew how to finish it. But *Gilgamesh* was first.

15

The Last Trip

The motorcycle hummed under him and roared when he
accelerated and popped and crackled when he cut back
the spark for a sharp curve or the crest of a hill.

—*The Sunlight Dialogues*

ON THE SATURDAY two weeks before their wedding, John found Susan still awake and up late in the warm September night when he came out of his study. He told her to come with him to their friend Jeanette Robertson's, one of their Laurel Street Theater cohorts, who lived nearby. After being there for some time, Susan went to sleep on a couch while John and Jeanette took a rowboat out to the middle of the small lake very near the house. There, John poured out the despair he'd fought against as long as he could remember and that seemed to Robertson to have been shadowing him even more closely, despite his happiness with Susan and their impending marriage.

"He was so sad," Robertson said later. "I rowed out to the center of the pond and then kept the boat still. He talked about death, about Gilbert, about a young man he had seen killed in a motorcycle race when he was young. He told me he was afraid he was going to die."

The despair that regularly beset him—severely at times— was usually overshadowed by his many commitments, and as the wedding approached, there were plenty. On Wednesday, September 8, ten days before the ceremony, papers finalizing the divorce from Liz arrived, giving both John and Susan a burst of euphoria. Now, nothing was in the way of their marriage. Still, John had been clear from the beginning that these legal arrangements didn't mean anything in his ongoing relationship with Liz. Though it may have long ceased being romantic, intellectually, she was still his primary partner, as he was hers. And he saw no reason that shouldn't continue.

Susan remained uncomfortable about the closeness between them, but the bond she felt with John made her overlook any apparent obstacle. Just the week before the wedding, he had awakened her near dawn, gleefully announcing that Liz had "freed" them. He'd written Liz that even at this point, he'd leave Susan for her if she felt irreparably heartbroken, but Liz had written a letter asserting her disinterest. Susan admits having been aghast that he would write such a proposal. And even as the marriage approached, John kept Liz involved in all its details, much to Susan's discomfort, though she continued to adjust to the awkward situation John had insisted on from the beginning.

On Thursday night, he finally finished the translation of *Gilgamesh*. Friday, he had a full day of teaching and meetings, so he took the poem up to campus with him to be photocopied. On the verge of their wedding, everything seemed to be falling into place.

On Saturday, he and Susan went to Manhattan with two crates of *MSS* to deliver to the Strand, one of the major literary bookstores. John's ongoing effort to publicize important new writers never diminished. It was a fine clear day for the drive on his motorcycle. They got a late start for the three-hour trip, though, and Susan knew by the way her feet wouldn't stay on the footrests that they were going over ninety-five miles an hour. She didn't like the speed, but she also knew there was no point in trying to say anything. He would go as fast as he wanted.

When they got to the store in the Village, the clerk was locking the door to close. Wearing ragged jeans and carrying his motorcycle helmet, with Susan next to him in her summer dress and sandals, John was met with skepticism when he tried to explain his errand. The clerk had them wait while he fetched the manager, and when he came, John persuaded him that he was indeed the famous author, that these were copies of the literary magazines he directed, and that the Strand must certainly want to carry them if it was a leading literary bookstore. The covers were discolored by the vibration of the motorcycle, which rubbed them together and made the fresh ink run, but the manager agreed to take them at a discounted price.

Liz and David had come in for the weekend, and after dropping off the books John and Susan met them for dinner. After the meal, John and Susan headed straight back to Susquehanna. It was late by now, and Susan felt John falling asleep on the way, so partway back they stopped at a motel.

John had another full day of teaching at Binghamton on Monday. On Tuesday, there was a meeting for *Marvin's on the Distant Shore*, the musical that was scheduled to run in November. It was about a group putting together a radio soap opera, *On the Distant Shore*, which Marvin, the playwright character, had quit. John had concocted the story, along with some of the music and lyrics, with the help of a few of the others, and the lyrics he had written for the lead song played off the title. They were intended as an affirmation of faith in "the distant shore" where the world of eternal life exists.

The meeting was to assign parts and draw up a rehearsal schedule. More people had come wanting to be involved than there were parts for. John had structured the play as a revue, though, and he agreed to write additional roles to accommodate everyone who was interested.

The meeting began at the auditorium-gymnasium of the old grammar school that served as the theater, and after the business had been settled, a half-dozen or so of the core group moved on to Coleridge Road. Most would be at the wedding on Saturday, and there was much talk about it and admiration for the artistic, oversized wedding-announcement card Jeanette Robertson had made. Susan particularly remembers Jim Rose, who was to be John's best man, being "in rare form, leaning forward over his glass, telling improbable, obscene and funny stories until my face hurt [from laughing]."

After midnight, another acquaintance showed up, drunk, with a woman they didn't know and who was not his wife. Susan told John he'd have to send these people home; it was late, she had to teach her class the next day, and she wasn't going to host this guy's affair at all hours. John had business the next day too, but with his usual social embrace he protested that the party was just beginning. Susan stalked off angrily to sleep in the spare room upstairs, leaving their bedroom empty for him whenever he decided to use it.

"Not even married yet, and already in trouble," Rose chided him after Susan left.

John retorted, "I've been working really hard. I deserve to have a little fun."

Then after everyone had left, in the dark, early morning hours, he called Liz. "I love you terribly," he told her. She could tell he was drunk, or nearly so, but she knew as well that he meant it.

They talked for a while, and after the call he found Susan asleep in the spare room upstairs. He lay down on the floor next to the bed, and she heard him and stirred, reached down to touch his shoulder, inviting him to join her. He crawled up into the bed with her and fell asleep.

She woke around eight thirty and got ready to teach her eleven-twenty class. It was her first creative writing class ever, and though she was as well prepared as she knew how to be, she was still a little nervous. She left food for Teddy, the friendly and completely undisciplined German shepherd both she and John loved, and started up their old 1975 Honda sedan for the forty-five minute drive. It was a clear warm day and John would want to take his Harley anyway.

When he got up, he made a chocolate milkshake for breakfast, then went upstairs to his desk where he worked until the phone rang. He made a two o'clock appointment at his SUNY office with Edward Hower, a young novelist who lived in the area. John had met Hower and his wife, novelist Allison Lurie, several times. They had been to John and Liz's wedding and they'd had John and Liz to dinner at their home when John had given a reading in Ithaca. Hower remembers talking that night about their mutual enthusiasm for opera and horses, and their taking a walk out back to look at the horses he and Lurie kept.

John thought Hower's first novel, *The New Life Hotel,* was terrific, and he'd written a glowing promotional blurb for its dust jacket. But like many first novels, it hadn't sold particularly well, and Hower wasn't able to get the kind of teaching job he wanted. Recently, he'd called to talk about his job situation, and John suggested he come and discuss his prospects and the program at Bennington.

Now Hower was wondering about their appointment. It was after two and someone in the English Department office suggested that he call John at home, which he did. John quickly apologized, admitting he'd forgotten, and suggested they meet at a restaurant in Windsor, a town near Binghamton. He washed the dishes, gathered up the student papers, and went out to rev up the Harley.

Susan's first class, meantime, had gone on without incident, and she was ready to go home shortly after one. Some people she'd met on the faculty, though, had carried on about Philadelphia Sales, a great outlet store in Johnson City, near Binghamton, and this seemed a fine time to see it. Though Binghamton is hardly a big city—its population a little under sixty-five thousand—it's big enough to be a little confusing to a stranger, and Susan wound up losing her way. After twenty minutes or so of wrong turns and unfamiliar roads, she'd had enough. She'd find it another time.

John headed north on the two-lane, tree-lined highway along

the Susquehanna. The river was some fifty or so feet wide there, flashing sporadically through the trees, and on such a blue day the stretch of road was nothing less than breathtaking. Riding about fifty miles an hour, he came to an easy left curve a few miles up the highway from their house. It was one of several, and less than ninety degrees. The highway is flat there, though for about twenty yards, the trees he was rounding shielded his view of anything coming.

He passed by the white frame house sunk half below the roadway at the end of the curve, where the road dips gently downward as it opens into a flat straightaway. The gritty dirt shoulder, level with the road, extends four to six feet to the low guardrail. He headed on toward a house trailer, another twenty yards on, where a dog lived. The big dog loved to race motorcycles and bark like mad—though John couldn't have heard it if it did come out.

On the straightaway, the bike edged onto the shoulder, tipped off balance, and spilled. John was thrown onto the road, scattering student stories and notes from his saddlebags up and down the roadway. A handlebar jabbed his abdomen where the cancer operation had left a scar, and ruptured his spleen. The wound underneath the skin opened and bled.

Millie Woods, who lived in the white house on the curve, had often heard John's motorcycle go by. With the river right behind, the house was tucked in a beautiful spot, though traffic got a little worse every year and seemed pretty constant now, at least during the day. But the steady traffic also meant that more people might see the AMMO sign her husband, James, had posted, advertising for hunters. Her windows were wide open on such a warm day, and right after John's bike passed she heard the crash. When she ran outside to see what happened, a green flatbed truck towing a trailer was heading toward her. It stopped to meet her at the end of her driveway, and the driver asked if she had called an ambulance. A man was lying on the road. She ran back into her house to make the call, and when she got back the truck was gone.

Minutes later, the ambulance arrived with its siren screaming. Two paramedics got out, quickly examined John's unconscious figure, and eased him onto their stretcher. They loaded it into the ambulance and raced off for the ten-minute drive to Barnes-Kasson Hospital.

Susan got off the expressway at exit 171 and headed for Teddy's, a local store in Susquehanna. She wanted to stop and pick up some of the special homemade cottage cheese that they made and sold in wax paper. It was the kind of rural treat that made people, especially newcomers, love the country despite inconveniences. When she came out of the store, she heard a siren—not a common sound in the country, but not something to take particular note of either.

A few minutes later she pulled into the driveway. She entered the house, dumped off her things, and put the cottage cheese in the refrigerator. John's old dishwater was left in the sink, so she pulled the drain to finish the cleanup. The water was still warm; she hadn't missed him by much. Then she started to fix a snack for lunch.

The clock said two forty-five when the phone rang. What sounded like an East Indian voice asked for Mrs. Gardner. When Susan responded, the voice told her that her husband had been in a serious accident. She asked if she should come right to the hospital, and the voice said, "Yes, I wish you would."

Teddy jumped into the car with her and wouldn't leave. On the short drive, Susan worried what the nurse meant by "serious" and figured that they would have to put off the wedding. Susquehanna has only a few streets, but when she got to town she couldn't find the hospital and had to stop and ask directions. It was just up a hill a few blocks from where she'd stopped to ask, and when she got there she hurried in to ask where John Gardner was. A nurse appeared who told her that a doctor wanted to see her. She was led to a small room where a doctor came in and stood with his hands in the pockets of his white smock as he talked. The only thing Susan remembers his saying is the phrase "No vital signs."

Unable to believe it, she demanded to see him, but the nurse was reluctant, telling her that there were head injuries. Susan insisted and was led to a small room where John lay on a gurney. He was wearing his motorcycle helmet, his blue work shirt, his khaki pants. The ambulance crew had torn the shirt open, and a small plastic tube stuck out from his mouth. His left shoulder was scraped, but there were no other visible marks. The nurse's warning about "head injuries" had apparently only been to discourage Susan. She cradled his head, felt his still warm chest, and couldn't believe it. She opened his left eye.

"When I saw the dirt in the lower lid," she wrote, "I knew this was real."

The nurse led her away.

ON THE SIX O'CLOCK news that night, Dan Rather reported Gardner's death in a few sentences. As word spread, the

Bread Loaf switchboard was flooded by more than two hundred calls.

The following Sunday, the Batavia Presbyterian Church was overflowing, with people spilling out the door and standing on the steps outside. The local paper estimated there were six hundred at the funeral. Many were students and friends from the last few years, though others had known John much longer. It was the Jewish New Year, the first of the High Holy Days, which kept some away, and Batavia was too distant and remote for others. But many had traveled a long way to be there. It was the day after John and Susan were to have married.

In the second row, wearing a simple cotton skirt and blouse, Susan was seated next to Priscilla's sister, Lucy. In the first row, Joan sat with Joel and the younger Lucy. Across the aisle Liz sat with David Bosnick. Next to them were Priscilla and John Sr. In front of the altar steps was the coffin. The service itself began with a tape of John and Joel's French horn rendition of "Amazing Grace." But Susan couldn't stand it. Moments after it began, she ran out of the church.

Many years later, she said that on that day a friend had been awakened by the crash of a vase that had been sitting in the center of a table; that a single rose bloomed in a friend's daughter's garden; that three other friends on the way home from the funeral saw a shooting star across the sky. And eighteen years afterward, a poppy plant that John gave a friend near Susquehanna still blooms each year.

Blue Argo, one of Gardner's Bread Loaf students that last August, visited the accident site just off the western bank of the

Susquehanna in 1998. Stunned by its beauty, she was surprised that no one had mentioned it in accounts she had read.

"In the mythology of death," she wrote, "one must cross the river; and there it was. All he had to do was get up, brush the grit off his trousers and step across."

SELECTED BIBLIOGRAPHY

I N ADDITION TO the sources cited below, some background information and many quotations that appear
in this book come from personal interviews con-
ducted by the author between 1989 and 2003 with friends, family, and acquaintances of John Gardner.

Works by John Gardner

NOVELS

Freddy's Book. New York: Knopf, 1980.
Grendel. New York: Knopf, 1971.
Mickelsson's Ghosts. New York: Knopf, 1982.
Nickel Mountain: A Pastoral Novel. New York: Knopf, 1973.
October Light. New York: Knopf, 1976.
The Resurrection. New York: New American Library, 1966.
Stillness; and Shadows. Edited by Nicholas Delbanco. New York: Knopf, 1986.
The Sunlight Dialogues. New York: Knopf, 1972.
Vlemk the Box-Painter. Northridge, Calif.: Lord John Press, 1979.
The Wreckage of Agathon. New York: Harper and Row, 1970.

STORIES

The Art of Living and Other Stories. New York: Knopf, 1981.
"A Little Night Music." *Northwest Review* vol 4., no. 2 (spring 1961): 30–40.

POETRY AND TRANSLATION

The Alliterative Morte Arthure, The Owl and the Nightingale, and Five Other English Poems in a Modernized Version with Comments on the Poems and Notes. Carbondale: Southern Illinois University Press, 1971.

A Child's Bestiary. New York: Knopf, 1977 (includes poems by Lucy Gardner and Gene Rudzewicz and drawings by Lucy Gardner, Joel Gardner, and Joan Gardner).

The Complete Works of the Gawain-Poet with a Critical Introduction by John Gardner. Chicago: University of Chicago Press, 1965.

Gilgamesh, with John Maier. New York: Knopf, 1984.

Jason and Medeia. New York, Knopf, 1973.

"Nicholas Vergette: 1923–1974." *Craft Horizons* 34 (April 1974): 7.

Poems. Northridge, Calif.: Lord John Press, 1978.

Tengu Child: Stories by Kikuo Haya, with Nobuko Tsukui. Carbondale: Southern Illinois University Press, 1983.

NONFICTION AND CRITICISM

The Art of Fiction: Notes on Craft for Young Writers. New York: Knopf, 1984.

" 'Bartleby': Art and Social Commitment." *Philosophical Quarterly* 43 (January 1964): 87–98.

The Construction of Christian Poetry in Old English. Carbondale: Southern Illinois University Press, 1975.

The Construction of the Wakefield Cycle. Carbondale: University of Illinois Press, 1974.

"Death by Art; or, 'Some Men Kill You with a Six-Gun, Some Men with a Pen.' " *Critical Inquiry* 3 (summer 1977): 741–77.

The Forms of Fiction. Edited with commentaries by John Gardner and Lennis Dunlap. New York: Random House, 1962.

"An Invective against Mere Fiction." In *On Writers and Writing,* edited by Stewart O'Nan, 13–34. Reading, Mass.: Addison-Wesley, 1994.

Lies! Lies! Lies!: A College Journal of John Gardner, with an introduction by Thomas Gavin. Rochester, N.Y.: University of Rochester Libraries, 1999.

The Life and Times of Chaucer. New York: Knopf, 1977.

On Becoming a Novelist. New York: Harper and Row, 1983.

On Moral Fiction. New York: Basic Books, 1978.

On Writers and Writing, with an introduction by Charles Johnson. Edited by Stewart O'Nan. Reading, Mass.: Addison-Wesley, 1994.

The Poetry of Chaucer. Carbondale: Southern Illinois University Press, 1977.

"Saint Walt." In *On Writers and Writing*, edited by Stewart O'Nan. 78–85. Reading, Mass.: Addison-Wesley, 1994.

"The Way We Write Now." In *On Writers and Writing*, edited by Stewart O'Nan, 70–77. Reading, Mass.: Addison-Wesley, 1994.

"We Teach and Study and Raise All the Hell We Can." Illustrated by Herb Fink. *Change* 5 (June 1975): 42–47.

CHILDREN'S AND YOUNG ADULT STORIES

Dragon, Dragon and Other Tales. New York: Knopf, 1975.

Gudgekin the Thistle Girl and Other Tales. New York: Knopf, 1976.

In the Suicide Mountains. New York: Knopf, 1977.

The King of the Hummingbirds and Other Tales. New York: Knopf, 1977.

OPERA LIBRETTOS

Frankenstein. Dallas, Tex.: New London Press, 1979.

Rumpelstiltskin. Dallas, Tex.: New London Press, 1978.

William Wilson. Dallas, Tex.: New London Press, 1979.

MISCELLANEOUS

Bread Loaf lecture. Bread Loaf Writers' Conference, Middlebury, Vt., August 1982.

"Freshman." *Boulder* (DePauw University, Greencastle, Ind.), 15 February, 1952.

"Help Stamp Out Superiority." Commencement speech. San Diego, State University, San Diego, Calif., June 8, 1982.

Letter to college president Glenn Kendall. Chico State College, Chico, Calif., May 26, 1961.

Letter to Joel Gardner. 1979.

"That Face! . . ." Cartoon. *Seventeen* (July 1947): 82.

"The Old Men." Ph.D. dissertation. Ann Arbor, Mich.: University Microfilms, 1959.

RELATED SOURCES

Artman, Marion J., comp. *Gardiners of Narragansett: A History of the Descendants of George Gardiner, Colonist.* Providence, R.I., 1919.

Baber, Joseph. "John Gardner, Librettist." In *John Gardner: Critical Perspectives,* edited by Robert A. Morace and Kathryn VanSpanckeren, 97–105. Carbondale: Southern Illinois Press, 1982.

Bain, David Haward, and Mary Smyth Duffy. *Whose Woods These Are: A History of the Bread Loaf Writers' Conference from 1926–1992.* New York: Ecco Press, 1993.

Batavia Daily News. Various issues, 1893–1985.

Beers, F. W., ed. *Gazetteer and Biographical Record of Genesee County, N.Y., 1780–1890.* Syracuse, N.Y.: J. W. Vose, 1890.

Broyard, Anatole. "A Scrabbling in the Soul." *New York Times,* 12 June 1982, 19.

Butts, Leonard. "John Gardner: A True Artist." *MSS* (State University of New York, Binghamton) 4, no. 1–2 (1984): 282–87.

Carver, Raymond. *Fires.* Santa Barbara, Calif.: Capra Press, 1983.

Chavkin, Allan, ed. *Conversations with John Gardner.* Jackson: University Press of Mississippi, 1990.

Choice 3 (June 1966): 306.

Choice 4 (May 1967): 288.

Christian, Ed. "An Interview with John Gardner." In *Conversations with John Gardner,* edited by Allan Chavkin. 183–203. Jackson: University Press of Mississippi, 1990.

Clancy, Ambrose. "John Gardner: The Art of Living." Unpublished.

Cochrane, Diane. "John Napper: The Return of the Illustrated Novel." *American Artist* 37 (July 1973): 26–31, 65, 70.

Des Pres, Terrence. "Accident and Its Scent: Reflections on the Death of John Gardner." *Yale Review* 73 (1993): 145–60.

Dryden, John, trans. *Plutarch's Lives of the Ancient Grecians and Romans.* New York: Modern Library, n.d.

Edwards, Thomas. "Academic Vaudeville." *New York Review of Books* (February 20, 1975): 34–36.

English Department of Pan American University. "Interview with John

Gardner." In *Conversations with John Gardner,* edited by Allan Chavkin, 252–70. Jackson: University Press of Mississippi, 1990.

Ferguson, Paul F., with John R. Maier, Frank McConnell, and Sara Matthiessen. "John Gardner: The Art of Fiction LXXIII." In *Conversations with John Gardner,* edited by Allan Chavkin, 143–71. Jackson: University Press of Mississippi, 1990.

Ferris, Sumner. Review of *The Life and Times of Chaucer,* by John Gardner. *Speculum* 52 (October 1977): 970–74.

Freedman, Ralph. Academic recommendation. State University of Iowa, Iowa City, 1958.

Freemont-Smith, Elliot. Review of *October Light,* by John Gardner. *Village Voice,* 17 January 1977, 77.

Friedman, Alan. "A John Gardner Spectrum." *New York Times Book Review,* 15 December 1974, 1–2.

Fuller, Edmund. Review of *Mickelsson's Ghosts,* by John Gardner. *Wall Street Journal,* 14 June 1982, 20.

Gardner, John, and Shannon Ravenel, eds. *The Best American Short Stories 1982.* Boston: Houghton Mifflin. 1982.

Gardner, Priscilla. "A Conversation with Priscilla Gardner." *MSS* (State University of New York, Binghamton) 4, no. 1–2 (1984): 233–49.

Gottlieb, Robert. Gottlieb archive. Columbia Unversity, New York.

Harris, Robert. "What's So Moral about John Gardner's Fiction?" *Saturday Review* (June 1982): 71.

Henderson, Jeff, ed. *Thor's Hammer: Essays on John Gardner.* Conway: University of Central Arkansas Press, 1985.

Hicks, Granville. "Strange Games and Sea Changes." *Saturday Review* 49 (July 16, 1966): 25–26.

Howell, John. *A Bibliographic Profile.* Carbondale: Southern Illinois University Press, 1980.

John C. Gardner Appreciation Page. http://sunygenesee.cc.ny.us/gardner

Johnson, Charles. "John Gardner as Mentor." *African-American Review* 30, no. 4 (1996): 619–24.

Kendall, Glenn. Memo to Ben Franklin. Chico State College, Chico, Calif., June 8, 1961.

Kennedy, William. Review of *The King's Indian: Stories and Tales,* by John Gardner. *New Republic* 171 (December 7, 1974): 19–20.

LeClair, Thomas. "William Gass and John Gardner: A Debate on Fiction." In *Conversations with John Gardner,* edited by Allan Chavkin, 172–82. Jackson: University Press of Mississippi, 1990.

Lehmann-Haupt, Christopher. "John Gardner down to Earth." *New York Times,* 20 December 1973.

Levine, George. "The Name of the Game." *Partisan Review* 42 (1975): 291–97.

"Li'l Ole Pussycat." *Baltimore Sun,* 6 May 1978, B6.

Lillibridge, G. D., chairman. "Report of the Committee to Investigate Whether Policies and Procedures Had Been Faithfully Carried Out in the Consideration for Promotion of Dr. Warren Olson and Dr. John Gardner," Chico State College, Chico, Calif., May 23, 1961, Appendix B, pp. 2, 5.

Locke, Richard. "'Grendel' Is a Beauty of a Beast." *New York Times,* 4 September 1971, 19.

Lumiansky, R. M. "The Old Made New." *New York Times Book Review,* 28 November 1965, 28.

Maddocks, Melvin. "Making Ends Meet." *Time* 108 (December 20, 1976): 74.

Mano, Keith. "Grendel." *New York Times Book Review,* 18 September 1971, 6, 12, 18.

Marshall, Harvey L. "Where Philosophy and Fiction Meet: An Interview with John Gardner," in *Conversations with John Gardner,* edited by Allan Chavkin, 84–98. Jackson: University Press of Mississippi, 1990.

McCulley, Mary, ed. *History of Genesee County, New York, 1890–1982.* Interlaken, N.Y.: Heart of the Lakes, 1985.

McEvoy, Ruth. *A History of the City of Batavia.* Batavia, N.Y.: Hodgkins Printing, 1993.

Mitcham, Judson, and William Richard. "An Interview with John Gardner." In *Conversations with John Gardner,* edited by Allan Chavkin, 235–51. Jackson: University Press of Mississippi, 1990.

Morace, Robert A. "New Fiction, Popular Fiction." In *John Gardner: Critical Perspectives,* edited by Robert A. Morace and Kathryn VanSpanckeren, 130–45. Carbondale: Southern Illinois University Press, 1982.

Morace, Robert A., and Kathryn VanSpanckeren, eds. *John Gardner: Critical Perspectives.* Carbondale: Southern Illinois University Press, 1982.

Morris, Gregory L. "Interview with John Gardner." In *Conversations with John Gardner*, edited by Allan Chavkin, 204–11. Jackson: University Press of Mississippi, 1990.

————. "The Matter of John Gardner's Sources." In *Thor's Hammer: Essays on John Gardner*, edited by Jeff Henderson, 33–44. Conway: University of Central Arkansas Press, 1985.

————. *A World of Order and Light: The Fiction of John Gardner*. Athens: University of Georgia, 1984.

New Century Atlas of Genesee County, N.Y. Philadelphia: Century Map, 1906.

Nugent, Ted. "Pair of Literary Lions Tangle." *Baltimore Sun*, 16 May 1978, A11.

Our County and Its People, Genesee County, New York. Boston: The Boston History Company, 1899.

PBS. *Dick Cavett Show*, 16 May 1978.

Prescott, Peter. "Modest Monster." *Newsweek* (September 13, 1971): 102.

————. "Theft or Paraphrase?" *Newsweek* (April 10, 1978): 94.

Quackenbush, Jan. "Moon to Shore: John Gardner and the Laurel Street Theater." *New Myths/MSS* (State University of New York, Binghamton) 2, no. 2, 3, no. 1 (1995): 349–58.

Reilly, Charlie. "A Conversation with John Gardner." In *Conversations with John Gardner*, edited by Allan Chavkin, 50–83. Jackson: University of Mississippi Press, 1990.

Riley, Craig. Review of *The Art of Fiction*, by John Gardner. *Best Sellers* 44, no. 1 (April 1984): 2.

Schwartz, Sheila. "A Student's Memoir." *MSS* (State University of New York, Binghamton) 4, no. 1–2 (1984): 253–60.

Singular, Stephen. "The Sound and Fury over Fiction." In *Conversations with John Gardner*, edited by Allan Chavkin, 220–34. Jackson: University Press of Mississippi, 1990.

Suplee, Curt. "John Gardner, Flat Out." In *Conversations with John Gardner*, edited by Allan Chavkin, 282–90. Jackson: University Press of Mississippi, 1990.

Thornton, Susan. *On Broken Glass: Loving and Losing John Gardner*. New York: Carroll and Graf, 2000.

Woiwode, Larry. "Gardner's Ghost Story a Philosophical Spellbinder." *Chicago Tribune*, 13 June 1982.

INDEX

Accent, 59, 82, 83–84
Advertisements for Myself (Mailer), 254
African Americans, 23
Albee, Edward, 90, 140
Alexander Central School, 31, 32
Algonquin Hotel, 227
Algren, Nelson, 209
Alice in Wonderland (Carroll), 192
"A Little Night Music," 85–86, 146
Alliterative Morte Arthure, The (Gardner), 106, 107, 184
"Amarand," 272
American Association of University Professors, 161
American Nazi Party, 256
American Originals, 207–8
Ancient Mesopotamia: Portrait of a Dead Civilization (Oppenheim), 146
Anna Karenina (Tolstoy), 74, 110
Antioch College, 160
anti-Semitism, 155
Apollonius Rhodius, 109, 187
Argo, Blue, 327–28
Argonautica (Apollonius), 109, 124, 186, 187
Art of Fiction, The (Gardner), xiii, 268
described, xiv
working title, 249, 259
Art of Living, The (Gardner), 298–99

Asahi Journal, 220
Atlantic Monthly, The, 221, 260, 272
Auden, Wystan Hugh, 208
Audience, 177, 221

Baber, Joe, 131–35, 143, 159, 264–65, 311
on Gardner, 131–34, 139, 140–41
Babylonia, 146–48
Baltimore Sun, 257
Barnes-Kasson Hospital, 325
Barth, John, 207
on Gardner, 270
Gardner's criticism of, 234, 256–57, 258, 286
Barthelme, Donald, 219–20
Gardner's criticism of, 234, 255, 278
"Bartleby," 107–9
Basic Books, 243
Batavia Civic Orchestra, 35, 36
Batavia Presbyterian Church, 327
Beckett, Samuel, 97, 122
Being and Nothingness (Sartre), 149–50, 165
Bellit, Ben, 231
Bellow, Saul, 209, 220
Gardner's criticism of, 234, 255, 278
Benet, Stephen Vincent, 209
"Benito Cereno," 88

Bennington College, 212–17, 221–38, 240, 323
  Delbanco and, 212–17
  Gardner leaves, 235–38
  interest in teaching at, 214–15
  introduction to, 212–14
  novels and stories written at, 223–29
  social activities at, 222
  Southern Illinois connection and, 216
Beowulf, 58, 120, 164, 165
Berg, Herman, 39
Berkeley Free Speech movement, 104
Berquist, Lars Goren, 273, 275
Berry, John, 38, 39
Berryman, John, 56
Best American Short Stories, The, 260
  Gardner as guest editor, 303–5
Best Sellers, xiv
"bicentennial novel," 224–26
Bidwell, John, 78
Big Tree Treaty, 9–10
Binghampton, New York, 263, 323
"black book," 249, 259, 268
Blake, William, 278
Blue, Robert, 311
Bly, Robert, 56
Bolsheviks, 34
Book-of-the-Month Club, 226
Borchardt, Georges, 192
Boskeydell farm:
  activities at, 125–31, 156
  additions to, 198–99
  described, 124–25
  guests at, 128, 139–44, 178–79, 194–95, 197, 199, 205

  music at, 135
  sale of, 266
  Vietnam War protests and, 158–59
Bosnick, David, 302, 305, 320, 327
Boulder, 42
Bourjaily, Vance, 56
Bradley, Tom, 313
Bread Loaf Writers' Conference, 209–11, 240, 289, 327
  atmosphere at, 290
  Clancy on, 289–90, 293
  divorce leaflets at, 294
  fame at, 293
  Hansen on, 290–91, 293
  last visit to, 313–16
  notables at, 209
  teaching at, 290–92
  Thornton at, 290, 291–93, 299–300
  tribute to mother's family at, 293
Brockport Writers Forum, 297, 305
Brodkey, Harold, 302
Browne, Sir Thomas, 273
Brown University, 253
Broyard, Anatole, 308
Burlingame, Edward, 114
Burns, Bill, 156–57
Butts, Leonard, 301–2

Calabro, Lou, 264
Calcagno, Anne, 238–39
Canterbury Tales (Chaucer), 58, 63
Carleton College, 202
Carroll, Lewis, 48, 192
Carson, Josephine, 213
Carver, Raymond, 80–81, 305
Cassill, R. V., 56, 60
Caucus Race, The (Gardner), 48

Index

Change, 205
Charley's Pad, 196
Chaucer, Geoffrey, 58, 76, 163
  biography of, 106–7, 122, 162, 221,
    261–63
Cheever, John, 185
Cheuse, Alan, xiii, xiv, 239
  at Bennington, 212–15, 231–32
Chicago Tribune, 308
Chico State University, 78–97, 110,
    120
  anthology at, 87–90
  Creative Writing Program at, 79,
    81–82
  denied promotion at, 94–97
  history of, 93–96
  literary magazine at, 82–85, 95
  theater production at, 90–91
Choice, 114, 115
Civil Rights movement, 94, 103, 152,
    153, 154
Civil War, 69
Clancy, Ambrose, 289–90
Clark, Clifford, 75
CliffsNotes, 127, 162–63
Cohn, Ruby, 97, 105
Colby College, 280
Colgate University, 298
"Come on Back," 293
*Complete Works of the Gawain-Poet,
  The* (Gardner), 115
*Construction of Christian Poetry in
  Old English, The* (Gardner), 221
*Construction of the Wakefield Cycle in
  Old English* (Gardner), 221
Coover, Robert, 181, 182, 274
Cornell, Joseph, 287

Couples (Updike), 150, 185–86
Cowley, David, 160
Crane, Stephen, 99
Creeley, Robert, 261
Crime and Punishment
    (Dostoyevsky), 255, 256

Dana, Robert, 56
Dante, 192
Day, Dick, 57, 64
Day, Fannie, 11
Day, Harris, 11
Day, William Harris, 11
Days of Vengeance (Gardner), 280
Dayton, Warren, 30–31, 38, 40
"Death by Art; or 'Some Men Will
    Kill You with a Six-Gun, Some
    Men with a Pen'," 32–34
"Death of Mrs. Sheer, The," 85
Defoe, Daniel, 45–46
Delbanco, Elena, 227, 250
Delbanco, Nicholas, 225, 227
  breakup of Gardner's marriage
    and, 235, 236
  described, 212
  Gardner at Bennington and,
    212–17, 222
  Gardner's cancer and, 249–50
  Rosenberg and, 229–31
Deliverance (Dickey), 250
Demski, Stanley, 3
Dennis, Carl, 100–1, 236
De Pauw University, 36–50, 52, 72
  chemistry at, 40
  decision to attend, 36–38
  described, 38, 39
  homesickness at, 42

De Pauw University *(continued)*
  journal kept at, 42–48, 82
  literature at, 40–42
  Monon, 47–48
  music at, 39–40, 47–48
Derge, David, 204–5
Des Pres, Terrence, 314
Devon Stock Farm, 18, 25
Dharma Bums, The (Kerouac), 230
Dick Cavett Show, xvi, 253–55
Dickens, Charles, 41
Dickey, James, 253, 296
  described, 250–52
Dickey, William, 56, 106
Dimisura, 220
Disney, Walt, 32, 41, 53, 113, 147, 165,
  221
Dore, Gustave, 192
Dostoyevsky, Feodor, xiv, 88, 254
"Dragon, Dragon," 93, 223
Dragon, Dragon and Other Tales
  (Gardner), 223
Dunlap, Lennis, 79, 81, 85, 87–88,
  92–93, 96, 139, 221
Dzwonkoski, Peter, 313

Eastman School of Music, 33–36, 39
East Tennessee University, 253
Eden's Rock (Quakenbush), 280
"Edge of the Woods, The," 110
Edwards, Thomas, 222
Eisenhower, Dwight D., 247
Eliot, T. S., 52
Elkin, Joan, 181–84, 211–12
Elkin, Stanley, 84, 181–84, 211–12,
  289, 294, 303
  Gardner admits mistakes on, 258

Elliot, George P., 56, 83
Ellison, Ralph, 209
England, 181–92
Engle, Paul, 51–52, 56, 58
"Epic Conversation, The," 124
  basis of, 109, 186
Epstein, Eddie, 135, 148, 162, 181, 302
  described, 119–20
  on Gardner, 119, 131, 153, 155, 159,
  199
Epstein, Tegwin, 181
Esquire, 180, 221
Euripides, 187
"Evaluations: Quick and Expensive
  Comments on Talent in the
  Room," 254
Existentialism, 164
experimental theater, 90–91

Faith and the Good Thing (Johnson),
  197
Falcolne, Stephen, 121–22, 136
Falwell, Jerry, 256
Faner, Robert, 116, 122
Fantastic Science Fiction and Fantasy,
  221
Farrar, John, 209
Farrar, Straus and Giroux, 148
Faulkner, William, 88, 95
Ferris, Sumner, 261–62
Fiedler, Leslie, 170
Fielding, Henry, 43, 45, 47
Finkel, Donald, 56, 59–60, 83, 106
Finnegan's Wake (Joyce), 154
Fitzgerald, Zelda and Scott, 183
Fizette, Ken, 172, 173, 174
Forche, Carolyn, 314

Ford, Jeff, 309, 310
Forms of Fiction, The (Gardner and
  Dunlap), 87–90, 109, 221
Frankenstein (Gardner), 132–33, 134,
  264
Freddy's Book (Gardner), 272, 286
  Gardner on, 277–78
  plot of, 275–76
  reviews of, 276–77
Freedman, Ralph, 67, 68
"Freshman," 42
Friedman, Alan, 222
Frost, Robert, 47, 82, 209
Fuller, Buckminster, 212
Fuller, Edmund, 308
"Furious Seasons, The," 81

Gallagher, Tess, 305
Gardiner, George, 8–9
Gardiner, Sir Thomas, 8
Gardner, Alice Day (grandmother),
  10–11, 12, 13, 18, 25, 27
Gardner, Arthur (uncle), 13, 36, 38
Gardner, Audrey Jean (cousin), 26
Gardner, Bill (cousin), 2, 14, 25
  John Gardner and, 25–27, 204,
  267–68, 294
Gardner, Cora (great aunt), 12–13
Gardner, Fred (grandfather), 10, 11,
  12, 13, 26, 27
Gardner, Gilbert (Gib) (brother), 23
  accidental death of, 1–5, 28–29,
  33, 105, 200, 259–60, 298
Gardner, Grant (uncle), 13
Gardner, Greg (cousin), 21, 141–43
Gardner, Harris (uncle), 11, 13–14,
  17, 26, 28

Gardner, Howard (uncle), 13
Gardner, Jimmy (brother), 127, 285
  birth of, 29
Gardner, Joan Patterson (first wife),
  327
  in Carbondale, 139–44, 214
  contributions to John Gardner's
  novels, 167, 224–25
  described, 24, 38, 49–51, 76–77,
  97, 100, 163, 184, 209, 213
  deteriorated marriage, 228–29,
  235–36, 260, 267
  in Detroit, 171–74
  divorce, 266, 268, 283, 294–96
  domestic life, 61, 77, 91–92, 99,
  100, 183
  husband's cancer and, 246, 248
  ill health, 142–43, 190, 200, 205
  infidelities, 104–5, 151–52, 200
  in John Gardner's fiction, 152,
  228–29
  in London, 183, 184, 190
  marital violence, 105, 140, 235, 267
  marriage, 48–51
  miscarriages of, 236
  music and, 35–36, 38–39, 55, 91
  1960s and, 103–4, 115
  relationship with John Gardner,
  29, 35–36, 38–39, 101–5, 116–17,
  126, 139–43, 178, 200, 203
  Rudzewicz and, 172–73, 183, 200,
  229, 267
  sale of Boskeydell and, 266
  taxes and, 267–68
  as teacher, 55, 56, 61, 99
  Vietnam protest meeting and,
  159

Gardner, Joel (son), 54, 130, 151,
  155–56, 178, 248, 327
  accidental fall, 92
  birth of, 91
  in Detroit, 168, 174
  in London, 181, 182
  parents' marital difficulties and,
    143, 144
Gardner, John (ancestor), 9–10
Gardner, John Champlin, Jr. (Bud):
  accidental death of brother, 1–5,
    28–29, 105, 200, 298
    story about, 4–5, 33, 259–60
  agent of, 114
  ancestors of, 7–18
  in Austria, 239
  birth of, 18
  at Bread Loaf, *see* Bread Loaf
    Writers' Conference
  breakdown of, 314–16
  in Cambridge, New York, 236–39
  cars of, 199, 210, 240–41, 245, 294,
    322
  as cartoonist, 32–33, 41, 47, 53
  childhood, 19–37
    athletics, 30
    cartoons, 32–33
    cousin Bill, 25–27
    cousin Joan, 23, 29, 35–36
    fighting, 25
    first publication, 32–33
    music, 33–36
    schooling, 24, 30–32
    Boy Scouts, 28
    writing, 27
  children's stories, 93, 223
  in college, 36–68
    De Pauw, *see* De Pauw University

Iowa, *see* University of Iowa
  Washington University, 50–55
  colon cancer, 244–53, 264
    health insurance and, 246
    operations on, 247–49, 252
    volunteers for experiments, 248
  commencement address at San
    Diego State, 306–8
  as critic, 75
    of Chaucer, 106–7
    of contemporary writers,
      232–34, 243–44, 254–58
    of Gass, 84
    of Melville, 107–9
    softening of opinions, 278
    of Solomon, 99–100
    of Tolstoy, 110–12
    of Updike, 185–86
    of Young, 63
  death of, 322–28
    accident site, 324, 327–28
    funeral, 327
    premonition of, 318–19
  described, xii–xvii, 98
    by Baber, 131–34, 139, 140–41
    by Bain, 315
    by Barth, 257, 270
    by brother, 127
    by Burns, 156–57
    by Butts, 301–2
    by Calcagno, 238–39
    by Carver, 80–81
    by Cheuse, xiii, xiv, 213, 214, 231
    by Clancy, 289–90, 293
    by Clark, 75
    by Cohn, 105
    by cousin Bill, 204
    by daughter, 173, 217, 218–19

by Day, 57, 64
by Delbanco, 213, 227
by Dennis, 100–1, 104
by Dunlop, 79, 87, 92–93
by Edwards, 222
by Elkins, 182, 183, 184, 211–12,
   289
by Epstein, 119, 131, 153, 155, 159,
   199
by Falcolne, 121–22, 136
by Faner, 122
by Finkel, 59–60, 106
by Freedman, 67, 68
by Friedman, 222
by Gass, 84, 271
by Gavin, 46–47
by Gottlieb, 192, 193
by Granzel, 72–78
by Gray, 120–21, 126, 127,
   136–38, 140
by Griffith, 63
by Handler, 203–4
by Hansen, 293, 315–16
by Heller, 271
by Howell, 199, 225
by Johnson, xiv, 194–97, 201–2
by Justice, 60–61
by Kelley, 242–47
by Kennedy, 222
by Malamud, 270
by McGalliard, 58
by Merrill, 210–11
by Morace, 274–75
by Murray, 59
by Oates, 50, 85
by Osbourne, 125–26, 127, 159
by Pack, 314–15
by Parini, xii–xiv, 210

by Petersons, 73, 74, 76–77
by Pigott, 170, 171, 172
by Porter, 171, 173, 174
by Quackenbush, 280
by Ray, 102–3
by Rileys, xiv, 123, 124, 126–27,
   144
by Robertson, 281–82, 318–19
by Rose, 282–83
by Rosenberg, xv, xvi, 231,
   250–51, 252
by Rosenthal, 73
by Sanders, 123, 126, 127, 154–55
by Schwartz, 296
by Segal, 178–79
self-, 50, 53–54, 57, 62, 104, 219
by Singular, 270
by Solomon, 99–100, 105, 203
by Soule, 71–74, 202–3
by Thornton, 310, 312
by Thurston, 52
by Towers, 270
by Wolitzer, 210
on the *Dick Cavett Show,* xvi,
   253–55
as editor, 83, 84, 122, 127, 303–5
editors of, *see* Gottlieb, Robert;
   Segal, David
as essayist, 107–9, 185–86, 220,
   232–34
family characteristics:
   community service and, 12, 17
   determined, single-minded
      women, 9, 10–12, 14
   education and, 14
   emotions and sentiment, 25,
      26–27
   industriousness, 28

family characteristics *(continued)*
  mental illness and, 12–13
  populist politics and, 12, 22–23
finances, 61, 97, 163, 167, 184–85,
  190, 198–99, 202
  divorce and, 294–96
  reduced, 240–41, 260, 266, 299,
    313
  sale of private papers and, 313
foreign languages, 218–19
Gass and, 258
guilt, 5, 93, 141, 144, 150, 165, 166,
  200, 237, 259–60
Illinois String Quartet, 159–62
illustrated novels, 190–92, 206
injuries, 92–93, 141, 166–67,
  177–78, 182, 245, 282–83, 310
in Japan, 217–19
in Lanesboro, Pennsylvania, 269,
  285
line between academic writing
  and a larger audience, 115
in London, 181–92
  modernizing medieval classics,
    184–85
  visitors to, 181–84
  writing his own epic, 186–92
lost interest in literature, 315
marriages:
  first, *see* Gardner, Joan
    Patterson
  second, *see* Gardner, Liz
    Rosenberg
  see also Thornton, Susan
as metafictionist, 207–8, 220, 226,
  274–75
misjudgments, 220, 278

motorcycles and, 48, 245, 269, 279
  fatal accident on, 322–28
  traffic tickets on, 288
  trip to New York City on, 320
music and, 202
  banjo, 110
  at Boskeydell, 135
  in childhood, 33–36
  in college, 39–40, 47–48, 51
  medieval ballads, 123, 163
  opera, 131–35, 264–65, 311
parody and, 274–75
personal characteristics, 59–60
  air of crisis, 91–93, 213
  alcohol, 100, 105, 125–28, 136,
    139, 199–200, 201, 209–10,
    213, 217, 239, 282, 288, 307,
    309–11, 322
  aloneness, 227–28
  antiauthority temperament, 31,
    60, 91, 96, 153, 204
  changes in, due to fame of,
    202–4, 211–12
  clothing, 80–81, 212, 213, 227,
    231, 241, 289, 300, 301
  conversation, 101, 184, 210, 255
  daemonic compulsiveness, 259,
    260
  despair, 316–19
  diet, 202
  elaborate tastes, 199, 208
  energy, 79, 86–91, 93, 99, 105–7,
    110, 139, 162–63, 174, 278–83,
    288–89
  hair, 98, 119, 120–21, 178, 212,
    231, 239, 270, 280, 289
  horses and, 128, 130, 166, 177, 324

household responsibilities,
101–3, 183, 200
image, 119, 187, 209, 210, 227–28
inconsistencies and contradictions, 154, 219–20
infidelities, 104–5, 140, 151–52,
200–1, 229–32
late-night writing, 41, 75, 179,
289, 316
philosophy and, 54–55, 190
physical recklessness, 218, 245
polymath, 196
pontification, 202–4, 299
populist sympathies, 154–57,
256
rural intellectual outsider, 125,
256
self-invention, 56–57, 62
self-perception, 61, 125
smoking, 57, 81, 95, 98, 119,
213–14
tardiness, 96–97
voice, 231
watching TV, 249
plagiarism, 148–49, 261–63, 265
plans for a new start, 313–15
as poet, 52, 186–89
memorial to Vergette, 207–8,
288
politics and, 104, 153–62, 175, 219,
224, 256, 313, 314–15
on "primary" and "secondary"
fiction, 257
"psychohistory" and, 275–76
publications of, *see specific titles*
recurring themes:
ancient stories and ideas, 9, 16,

57–58, 66, 71, 93, 105–7, 109,
122–24, 146–49, 223, 297–98,
305–6
autobiographical characters, 49,
147, 151–52, 205, 228–29,
259–60, 286–87
collapsing of time and speculation, 149
conflict, 65, 107–9, 147, 150, 190,
224, 225–26
failure of all systems, 176
faith and the search for it, 65
ghosts, 64–65
grotesque characters, 113, 274
morality, 89, 108–9, 111, 255–56,
259, 276
no choice but to continue,
176–77
philosophical novelist, 112–13,
195
primary qualities for successful
stories, 88–89, 277–78
religion, 108–9, 111
significance of art in culture,
206–7, 219, 254, 255
true artist, 189, 211, 291
vivid and continuous dream,
265–66, 277
returning to upstate New York,
260–64
as school board candidate,
155–57
secretary of, 198, 200–1, 202
in Stockholm, 272–73
success and fame of, 197–98,
201–4, 209, 214, 220–21, 228,
258–59, 268–69, 289

in Susquehanna, Pennsylvania,
285–86, 296, 316–17
tax problems, 267–68, 272, 295
resolving of, 313
as teacher, 47, 52
at Bennington, *see* Bennington
College
at Bread Loaf, *see* Bread Loaf
Writers' Conference
at Chico State, *see* Chico State
University
classroom style, 74
at George Mason, 240, 250, 253
grading student papers, 72
in high school, 55
at Northwestern, 197
at Oberlin, 68–78, 120, 129
popularity, 72–74, 78, 101,
120–22, 124, 128, 170–71, 210,
231
prodigious workload, 86–91,
93, 105–7, 110
at San Francisco State, *see* San
Francisco State College
at Southern Illinois, *see* Southern Illinois University
at SUNY Binghampton, *see*
SUNY Binghampton
teacherly discouragement, 80,
169–70, 196
teaching assistant, 60, 63
at the University of Detroit,
see University of Detroit
at Williams, 238–39
writing and, 75, 79, 169–70
television documentaries on,
208–9, 243

theater productions:
conflicts over, 283, 299, 309, 312
at De Pauw, 47–48
Liz and, 283, 299–300
Quackenbush and, 278–81
Robertson and, 281–82
Rose and, 282–83
at Southern Illinois, 135–39
at Susquehanna, 278–83, 320–21
as translator:
of ancient classics, 297–98, 312,
316–17, 319
at Chico State, 87
in college, 52, 67–68
of medieval classics, 184–85, 221
at Oberlin, 74, 75–76
at San Francisco State, 105–7,
109
at Southern Illinois, 135–38
university histories:
Chico State, 93–96
Southern Illinois, 204–5
Vietnam War, 157–59
Welsh culture, 33, 293
Gardner, John Champlin, Sr.
(father), 236, 260, 285, 292, 327
accidental death of son (Gib), 1–5,
28–29
book dedicated to, 224
described, 1, 7–8, 19–23
home life, 19–37
home of, 20–21
infidelities of, 5
John Gardner's marriage and, 49
motorcycles and, 20
stroke victim, 306
wife and, 5, 7–8, 14–18

Index

Gardner, John Champlin II (great-grandfather), 10, 11
Gardner, Liz Rosenberg (second wife), xv, xvi, 229–32, 260, 269
  Best American Short Stories and, 303–5
  cancer of John Gardner and, 245–53
  described, 230, 236, 288
  on Dickey, 250–51
  differences between John Gardner and, 288–89, 292, 293, 300, 301
  end of marriage, 302–3, 319, 322
  finance of John Gardner and, 241
  in graduate school, 240, 243, 257
  honeymoon, 286
  interest in work of, 234–35
  John Gardner's fiction and, 276, 295, 302, 304, 319
  meets John Gardner, 229–31
  moves in with John Gardner, 235–39
  openness of relationship, 236
  parents of, 236, 245–46, 249
  on *Singular*, 270
  at SUNY Binghampton, 264
  in Sweden, 273
  theater productions and, 283, 299–300
  Thornton and, 300–5, 312, 319, 320
  wedding, 284–85
Gardner, Lucy (daughter), 151, 155–56, 173, 178, 248, 327
  birth of, 92
  in Detroit, 168–69, 174
  ill health, 237

  in Japan, 217, 218–19
  in London, 181
  music and, 135, 202
  parents' marital difficulties and, 143–44, 268
Gardner, Mildred Stamp (Millie) (aunt), 13–14, 26, 28, 141
Gardner, Priscilla (Sandy) (sister), 2, 3, 21, 151, 302
  at Boskeydell, 141, 143
Gardner, Priscilla Jones (mother), 42, 49, 236, 260, 285, 292, 327
  accidental death of son Gib and, 2–5, 28–29
  described, 21, 22
  home life, 19–37
  husband and, 5, 7–8, 14–18
  in theater production, 280
Gardner, Sarah (ancestor), 11, 13
Gardner, Wanda (sister-in-law), 285
Gass, William, 52, 83–84, 163, 170, 181
  friendship with Gardner, 84, 258, 265
  on Gardner, 271
  Gardner editing, 84
Gavin, Thomas, 46–47
George Mason University, 240, 250, 251, 253
Gilgamesh (Gardner and Maier), 297–98, 306, 312, 316–17, 319
Gilgamesh epic, 124, 147–48
  translation of, 297–98, 306, 312, 316–17, 319
Ginsberg, Allen, 103, 230
Gottlieb, Robert, 192
  conflict of interest over *On Moral Fiction*, 243–44

Gottlieb, Robert *(continued)*
 editing Gardner, 193, 295–96
 Gardner's tax problems and, 268
Granzel, Dewey, 72–78
Gray, Pat, 120–21, 126, 127, 136–38,
 140, 200
Great Depression, 18, 24, 26
Greco, Mary, 32
Grendel (Gardner), xii–xiiii, 7, 47,
 177, 208–9, 274
 described, 165–66
 fame due to publication of, 185,
  190, 192, 195
 Gardner on, 220
 ideas for, 76–77, 164–65
 illustrations for, 191
 Joan's contribution to, 167
 opera of, 311
 reviews of, 180–81, 183–84
Griffith, Clark, 63, 67
Guggenheim grant, 198
Gulliver's Travels (Swift), 47
Guthrie, Sir Tyrone, 168

Hadley fellowship, 215
hallucinogenic drugs, 103
Handler, Jerry, 119, 129, 203–4
Hansen, Ron, 290–91, 293, 315–16
Harnack, Curtis, 63
Harper & Row, 152, 163, 177
Harris, Robert, 308
Hartman, Jeffrey, 59
Hawkes, John, 83, 258
Hazo, Samuel, 168
Helen at Home (Gardner), 280
Heller, Joseph, 220, 270–71
 Gardner admits mistakes on, 278

Henshaw, Richard, 298, 312
Herzog (Bellow), 220
Hicks, Granville, 114
Hicks, Herodias Long, 8–9
Hicks, John, 8
Higgins, Joanna, 309–10
Hinckley, Duncan, 26
Hinckley, Percy, 18, 26
Hinckley, Sarah, 26
Hoefer, Jacqueline, 97
Hoefer, Peter, 97
Homer, 70–71, 109, 186, 187
Houghton Mifflin, 148
Howard, Richard, 272
Howell, John, 120, 181, 195, 216
 at Boskeydell, 126, 135, 266
 on Gardner's showmanship, 199
 on Longwell, 201
 on *October Light,* 225
Howells, William Dean, 274
Hower, Edward, 322–23
"Howl," 230
Hub Fans Bid Kid Adieu (Updike), 287
Hudson Review, 188
Humboldt's Gift (Bellow), 220

Iliad, The (Homer), 70–71, 306
 The Odyssey and, 109, 186
Illinois String Quartet, 159–62
Independent Voters of Illinois, 156
*In the Heart of the Heart of the Coun-
 try* (Gass), 84
Iowa Writers' Workshop, 55–57, 170
 participation in, 56
 as separate from University of
  Iowa, 58–59
Iroquois Confederacy, 9–10

IRS, 267–68, 272, 295
Ivan the Fool (Gardner), 264

Japan, 217–19
Jarrell, Randall, 54
"Jason: An Epic Poem," 187
Jason and Medeia (Gardner), 175, 198
  as epic poem, 186–89
  illustrations in, 190–92
  origin of, 186–87
  plot of, 189
  reviews of, 201–2
Jeffers, Robinson, 54
Johns Hopkins Hospital, 246–52
Johns Hopkins University, 240, 256–57
Johnson, Charles, 205–6, 222, 286, 305
  as cartoonist, 196
  on Gardner, xiv, 194–97, 201–2
  as student, 195, 196–97
Jones, James, 15
Jones, John, 15–16
Jones, Lucy (aunt), 15, 17, 49
Jones, Lucy (grandmother), 15, 16
Joyce, James, 154, 186
Justice, Donald, 56
  on Gardner, 60–61

Kapiloff family, 313
Kartman, Myron, 160–62
Kelley, Michael, 240–47
  on Dickey, 251–52
  Gardner's cancer and, 246–47
  Gardner's help with son, 243
  On Moral Fiction controversies
    and, 243, 244
  motorcycle accident of Gardner
    and, 245

rents room to Gardner, 241–42
  as single parent, 241, 242
Kelley, Owen, 242
  Gardner and, 243
  ill health of, 241
Kendall, Glenn, 93–96
Kennedy, William, 222
Kenyon Review, 188
Kerouac, Jack, 103, 230
Kessler, Milton, 284
Kierkegaard, Søren, 101
King, Martin Luther, 103
"King Gustav, Lars and the Devil,"
  273–74
King's Indian, The: Stories and Tales
  (Gardner), 179, 194, 277
  described, 221
  Gardner on, 207
  as a metafiction, 206–7, 274
  reviews of, 222
  Vergette and, 206
Kinnell, Galway, 278
Kinsella, Thomas, 123, 181
Knopf, 192, 313
  conflict of interest over *On Moral
    Fiction*, 243–44
  Dragon, Dragon and, 223
  Grendel and, 167, 177
  Jason and Medeia and, 190
  Life and Times of Chaucer and,
    221, 261
  Mickelsson's Ghosts and, 310–11
  Nickel Mountain and, 179
  October Light and, 226–27
  Sunlight Dialogues and, 167, 177
  Wreckage of Agathon and, 177
Krantz, Judith, xiv

Lanchester, Duane, 137
"Last Days of the Seer, The," 148
Laurel Street Theater, 280–83,
   299–300, 309, 312, 318
Leary, Timothy, 103
LeClair, Thomas, 276, 277
LeGuin, Ursula, 276
Lehmann-Haupt, Christopher, 163,
   197
Le Morte d'Arthur (Malory), 127, 162
Levine, Philip, 56
Levy, Albert, 54
Lewis, Sinclair, 209
Liberto, Joe, 209
Library Journal, 276
Library of Congress, 240
"Lies! Lies! Lies!," 42–48
Life and Times of Chaucer
   (Gardner), 106–7, 122, 162, 221
plagiarism in, 261–63, 265
Lincoln, Abraham, 113
Lives of the Noble Grecians and
   Romans (Plutarch), 148–49
Locke, Richard, 180
Locust Level farm, 2–5, 10, 13, 18, 24,
   27, 43
Logan, John, 102
Longwell, Nancy, 200–1, 202, 229
Lord John Press, 287
Lowell, Robert, 56
Lurie, Allison, 322, 323

McCauley, Robie, 303
McGalliard, John, 57–58, 75
McIntosh, Mavis, 114
Macleish, Archibald, 209
Macmillan, 148

McVicker, Robert, 161
Mahoney, John, 167, 173–74
Maier, John, 297–98, 305, 312
Mailer, Norman, 254
Making of Ashenden, The (Elkin), 182
Malamud, Bernard, 270
Malory, Sir Thomas, 127, 162
Manhattan group, 90–91
Mano, Keith, 180
Marvin's on the Distant Shore,
   320–21
Mayo, E. L., 85
Mehta, Ved, 238
Melville, Herman, 41, 88, 101
   Gardner's essay on, 107–9
Merrill, Chris, 210–11
Merwin, W. S., 52, 83
metafiction, 207–8, 220, 226, 274–75
Michener, James, 85
Mickelsson's Ghosts (Gardner), 253,
   269
   as autobiographical, 295–96
   hopes for, 299, 307, 308, 309, 313,
   315
   publication of, 308
   publicity appearance, 310–11
   reviews of, 308
   revisions to, 295–96
Middlebury College, 209
"Midwesterner, The," 201
Milwaukee Journal, 226
Miss McIntosh, My Darling (Young),
   63
Moby-Dick (Melville), 101
Modern Language Association, 301
Moll Flanders (Defoe), 45–46
Monroe, Harriet, 209

Index

Morace, Robert, 274–75

"Moral Fiction," 109

Moral Majority, 301

Morris, Gregory, 263

Morrow, Ken, 82

MSS, 82–85, 95, 169, 302, 305, 320

Murray, William Cotter, 56, 59, 62

"Myth, Society, and the Search for Meaning," 202

NAACP, 94

Napper, John, 191–92

Nation, The, 212

National Book Award, 196, 226, 250

National Book Critic's Circle Award for Fiction, 226, 228

National Endowment for the Arts, 190, 243

National Public Radio, 264

New American Library, 114, 145, 148

New Criticism, 88, 90

New Life Hotel, The (Hower), 323

New Republic, 222

Newsweek, 180, 262

New Yorker, 238

New York Review of Books, 222

New York State College for Teachers in Albany, 13, 16, 26

New York Times, xvi, 163, 180, 197, 308

best-seller list, xiii, 197–98, 226

Outstanding Book of the Year, 223

New York Times Book Review, 115, 163–64, 222, 270, 276

Gardner's articles in, 185–86, 220

New York Times Magazine, 269

"Nicholas Vergette: 1923-1974," 208

"Nickel Mountain," 53, 63, 85

Nickel Mountain (Gardner), 53–54, 63, 64, 98, 110, 145, 177

revision of, 114, 179, 198

"Nimram," 272

1960s turmoil, 103–4, 115, 152–62, 175

Nobel Prize, 95

Noonday Press, 119

Norris, Frank, 274

Northwest Review, 85, 110, 146

O. Henry, 9

Oates, Joyce Carol, 169, 181, 303

on Gardner, 50, 85

published in *MSS*, 84–85, 305

Oberlin College, 68–78, 100, 110, 120, 129

O'Connor, Flannery, 52, 56

October Light (Gardner), 216

as autobiographical, 228–29

Joan's contribution to, 224–25

as a metafiction, 226, 274

plot of, 224

pulp novel within, 224–25, 228–29

reviews of, 226

sources of ideas for, 225

success of, 226–27

Odyssey, The (Homer), 124

The Iliad and, 109, 186

Odyssey Press, 90

"Old Men, The," 64–67

Olson, Warren, 94

On Becoming a Novelist (Gardner), 259, 268

One World movement, 22–23

On Moral Fiction (Gardner), 220
controversy surrounding, 254–58,
    265, 269–71, 278, 283, 301–2
critical assessments of his own fic-
    tion and, 276–77
Freddy's Book and, 277–78
Knopf turns down, 243–44
plagiarism in Chaucer biography
    and, 262–63
regrets over mistakes in, 278
TV interview and, 254–55
opera, 131–35, 264–65, 311
as "greatest librettist," 265
Oppenheim, A. Leo, 146
Osbourne, Jerry, 125–26, 127, 131, 159
Owl and the Nightingale, The (trans-
    lation by Gardner), 184

Pack, Robert, 291, 294, 314–15
Palmer Woods, 168, 173
Papers on Language and Literature,
    122
Parini, Jay, xiii–xiv, 210
Paris Review, The, 255
Parker, Gail Thain, 215
Partisan Review, 222
"Pastoral Care," 175–77, 179, 214
Patience (unknown), 105, 106, 115
Patterson, Gilbert, 24
Patterson, Nellie, 54
Paul, Alex, 128–29, 141
PBS, 253–55
Pearl, The (unknown), 105
"Pedersen Kid, The," 84
Pence, Raymond, 41
PEN International Conference,
    272–73

Perspective, 52, 82, 84, 188
Petersen, Harold, 39–41, 42
Peterson, Carl, 71, 73, 74
Peterson, Thalia, 73, 76–77
Phi Beta Kappa, 55
Philadelphia Opera Company, 265
Philadelphia Sales, 323
Phillips Collection, 160
Philosophical Quarterly, The, 109
Pied Piper of Hamelin, The
    (Gardner), 264
Pigott, Margaret, 170, 171, 172
Plutarch, 148–49
Poe, Edgar Allan, 264
"Poetry: Form and Substance," 90
Porter, John, 9
Porter, Tom, 170, 171, 173, 174
Possession (Delbanco), 225
Prescott, Peter, 180–81, 262–63,
    265
Preston, George, 17, 147
Preston, Lucy Jones, 15, 17, 18, 292,
    327
Proust, Marcel, 54
Purity (unknown), 105, 106, 115

Quakenbush, Jan, 278–81, 305
Quarterly Review of Literature, 110

Random House, 90
Ransom, John Crowe, 209
Rather, Dan, 326
"Ravages of Spring, The," 221
Ravenel, Shannon, 303–4
Ray, David, 102–3
realists, 274
Rector Scholarship, 36

"Redemption," 4–5, 33, 259–60
Reed College, 250
Reflections, 51–54
Religio Medici (Browne), 273
Resurrection, The (Gardner), 69,
    112–15, 145, 146, 277
    key elements of, 112–13, 195
    reviews of, 114–15
Resurrection, The (Tolstoy), 110–12
Reynolds, Leslie, 306–7
Rich, Adrienne, 209
Richardson, Samuel, 43
Riley, Brent, 123, 126–27, 144
Riley, Carroll (Cal), 123, 126, 135
Riley, Craig, xiv
Riley, Cynthia, 144
Robertson, Jeanette, 281–82, 318–19,
    321
Romano, John, 276
Rose, Jim, 281–82, 288, 321, 322
Rosenberg, Anton, 230
Rosenberg, Ellen, 285
Rosenthal, Bernard, 73
Roth, Philip, 56
Royal Academy, 183, 191
"Rude Heads That Staresquint,"
    273–74, 275
Rudzewicz, Gene, 172–74, 293
    in London, 183
    as member of Gardner house-
    hold, 172–73, 183, 200, 229,
    267
Rumpelstiltskin (Gardner), 133–34,
    264–65, 280
Rush Rhees Library, 313
Russell, Bob, 151–52
Russell, Leonore, 151–52

St. Louis Philharmonic Orchestra, 51
Samson and the Witch (Gardner),
    134–35
Sanders, Barry, 122–23, 126, 127
    politics and, 154–55
San Diego City Club, 313
San Diego State University, 306–8
San Francisco State College, 97–117
    disaffection with, 115–17
    essay on "Bartleby," 107–9
    hectic life at, 100, 105–7
    housing at, 98, 101–2
    Joan at, 99, 115
    music at, 109–10
    1960s at, 103–4
    novel written at, 110–15
    stormy relationships at, 101–5
Sartre, Jean-Paul, 55, 274
    as inspiration for Gardner,
    149–50, 164–65, 202
Saturday Evening Post, The, 54
Saturday Review, 63, 114, 276, 308
Savio, Mario, 104
Schwartz, Sheila, 296
Second Shepherd's Play (Wakefield
    Master), 138
Segal, David:
    death of, 177–80, 192
    editing style, 193
    publishing Gardner, 163, 164, 167,
    179, 191
Segal, Lore, 178–80, 182, 197, 200,
    222
Selections, 81
Seneca Indians, 9–10
Serpent and the Dove, The, 47–48
Seventeen, 32–33

Sexton, Anne, 209
Seydel Morgan, Elizabeth, 286
Shakespeare, William, 7, 21
Shreve, Susan, 240
Singular, Stephen, 269–71, 303
Sir Erkenwald (unknown), 105
Sir Gawain and the Green Knight
    (unknown), 75–76, 87, 105, 162
six-stress verse, 188
Skidmore College, 238
Smith, Ray, 169, 181
Smith College, 11
"Smugglers of Lost Souls Rock,
    The," 224–25
Snodgrass, W. D., 56
Solomon, Eric, 99–100, 105, 203
Solomon, Irene, 99
Something Happened (Heller), 220
Sotweed Factor (Barth), 207
Soule, George, 70–71, 76
    on Gardner, 71–74, 202–3
southern Illinois, 204–5
Southern Illinois Hunt Club, 199
Southern Illinois Peace Committee,
    154
Southern Illinois University, 116–67,
    194–209, 212
    Bennington College and, 216
    Boskeydell farm at, *see* Boskeydell
    farm
    expansion of, 152–53
    history of, 204–5
    Joan at, 139–44, 214
    job offer at, 116–17
    marital difficulties at, 139–44
    other professors at, 118–20, 123,
    129–32

promotion to full professor, 163
on sabbatical, 181–92
string quartet at, 159–62
turmoil of the 1960s and, 152–62,
    175
Vietnam Study Center at, 158
Southern Illinois University Press,
    54, 184, 185, 221, 240
Southern Review, The, 63, 85, 185, 188
Speculum, 261
"Spotted Horses," 88
"sprung hexameter," 188
Spurbeck, Peter, 160
"Squirrels," 64, 85, 145
Stafford, William, 83
Stegner, Wallace, 209
Stern, Richard, 56
Stevens, Wallace, 54
Stillness; and Shadows (Gardner)
    ("Carbondale novel"), 38, 313
    as biographical, 49, 60, 61
    introduction to, 228
    plot of, 223
    struggle with, 250, 317
Strand bookstore, 320
Sunlight Dialogues, The (Gardner),
    xi, 47, 153, 167, 177, 190, 195
    as autobiographical, 228
    illustrations for, 191
    plot of, x, 145–48, 175, 297
    reviews of, 197, 212
    stage version of, 292
    success of, xii–xiii, 197–98, 202,
    294
SUNY Binghampton, 253, 269, 273,
    278–79, 302
    job offer to Gardner at, 263–64

theater productions while at,
278–83, 320–21
Thornton at, 291–92, 300–2,
321–23
SUNY Buffalo, 170, 261, 263
Suplee, Curt, 310–11
Susann, Jacqueline, xiv
Susquehanna Choral Society,
280–83
Susquehanna River, 324, 327–28
Sweet Enemy, The (Oates), 85
Swift, Jonathan, 47

Taggart, Moses, 10–11
Teddy (dog), 322, 326
"Temptation of St. Ivo, The," 190
Tenniel, John, 192
Thackeray, William Makepeace, 47
Thornton, Susan, 5, 105, 317
    affair with Gardner, 292, 299–304
    at Binghampton, 300–2
    at Bread Loaf, 290, 291–93,
        299–300
    death of Gardner and, 322–27
    Gardner's drinking and, 309–11
    invitation to enroll at Binghamp-
        ton, 291–92, 300
    Liz and, 300–5, 312, 319, 320
    miscarriage of, 311–12
    pregnancy of, 309
    publication of *Mickelsson's Ghost*
        and, 308
    suspects Gardner of an affair, 314
    wedding plans, 305, 308–9, 313,
        316, 319, 321–22
Thurston, Jarvis, 51–59, 100
Time, 164, 222, 226, 276

Tolstoy, Leo, 74, 88, 264
    criticism of, 110–12
    life follows art and, 254
    moral art and, 89, 109, 234
Tom Jones (Fielding), 45, 47
Towers, Robert, 270
Tri-Quarterly, 221
Turner, Janet, 82
Tyler, Anne, 299

United Nations, 22
U.S. Information Agency, 219
University of Chicago Press, 115
University of Detroit, 167–74
    children in school near, 168–69
    described, 169
    environs of, 168
    move made at, 173–74
    social life at, 170–72
University of Indiana, 253
University of Iowa, 52, 55–68, 72, 73
    masters degree, 63
    Ph.D. from, 57, 67–68
University of Kentucky, 132–34,
    264
University of Louisville, 52
University of Oregon, 85
University of Richmond, 286
University of Rochester, 313
University of Texas, 136
Updike, John, 150, 185–86, 278, 287
Urdang, Constance, 56, 61, 83, 106

Van Duyn, Mona, 52
Vendler, Helen, 181
Vergette, Helen, 129, 130, 181, 208
Vergette, Marcus, 130, 144, 208

Vergette, Nicholas, 138, 181, 199
  death of, 205–6
  described, 129–31
  memorial service for, 207–8, 288
"Vergette Makes a Pot," 129–30
Vernon, Ann, 263–64
Vernon, Jack, 263–64
Vietnam War, 147, 152, 153, 155, 175
violent protests, 157–59
Village Voice, The, 226
Virgil, 187
"vivid and continuous dream," 277
  first use of phrase, 265–66
Vlemk the Box-Painter (Gardner),
  286–88, 299
  plot of, 287
  publisher of, 287–88
Vonnegut, Kurt, 255, 278

Wakefield Master, 135–38, 139, 143,
  184–85, 221
Wall Street Journal, 253, 254, 308
Washington Post, 310–11
Washington Post Book World, 276
Washington University, 50–55, 72,
  97, 100
"Way We Write Now, The," 185–86
Webb, Howard, 181–82, 195
Weber, Burton, 54, 55
Welty, Eudora, 220
West, Paul, 163–64
Western Review, 64, 82
What Is Art? (Tolstoy), 89, 234
"When the Jingling Stops," 112

Who's Afraid of Virgnia Woolf?
  (Albee), 140
Willard, Nancy, 294
Willard, Stanley, 294
Willard Hospital, 12–13
Williams, William Carlos, 54
Williams College, 238–39
William Wilson (Gardner), 264
Winnie-the-Pooh (Milne), 27
Wittgenstein, Ludwig, 55
Woiwode, Larry, 308
Wolitzer, Hilma, 210
Woodrow Wilson fellowship, 54, 55
Woods, Millie, 324–25
World's Fair of 1964, 113
Wreckage of Agathon, The (Gardner),
  118, 140, 177
  Gardner's negative assessment of,
    150–51
  models for characters in, 151–52
  plot of, 150, 175
  Plutarch and, 148–49
  reviews of, 163–64
  Sartre and, 149–50

Yale University Press, 162
Yeats, William Butler, 208
Yegudkin, Arcady, 33–35
Yellin, Herb, 287–88
Young, Marguerite, 62–63
You're a Good Man, Charlie Brown,
  312

Zoo Story, The, (Albee), 90

PERMISSIONS